Persia and the Gulf

Persepolis: Stone Relief of Darius the Great

Persia and the Gulf

Retrospect and Prospect

John F. Standish

CURZON

First published in 1998
by Curzon Press
15 The Quadrant, Richmond
Surrey, TW9 1BP

© 1998 Curzon Press

Typeset by LaserScript, Mitcham, Surrey
Printed in Great Britain by
Biddles Ltd, Guildford and King's Lynn

British Library Cataloguing in Publication Data
A catalogue record for this book is available from the British Library

Library of Congress in Publication Data
A catalogue record for this book has been requested

ISBN 0–7007–0341–1 (Hbk)
ISBN 0–7007–0237–7 (Pbk)

Contents

v

List of Figures

Preface

In the East my pleasure lies. O, come, Ventidius!
You must to Parthia.

Shakespeare: Antony and Cleopatra; II, iii

There has, in recent years, been no dearth of books on Persia, nor can the country claim to be unknown to the West, for was it not the Prince of Morocco who declared that

> The Hyrcanian deserts and the vasty wilds
> Of wide Arabia are as thoroughfares now ...?
> *Shakespeare: The Merchant of Venice; II, vii*

Yet in extenuation it is pleaded that this is not a descriptive volume, it is not a record of travels or personal recollections, nor is it an attempt to unfold the history of a country that was old even in Biblical times. Instead, consideration is given to three themes – historical, geographical and cultural – these forming three strands of the one cord that binds the country and its people together into a unitary whole.

'Persia is the greatest empire in the world', observed Sir John Chardin in 1720, 'if you consider it according to the geographical description given by the Persians, because they represent it to the full extent of its ancient boundaries, which are four great seas; the Black Sea, the Red Sea, the Caspian Sea and the Gulph of Persica.'[1] Even in Chardin's day that description was hardly true; today, the only maritime provinces remaining are those bordering the Caspian and the Gulf. Yet a great tract of territory remains, to which consideration will be given.

The first part is devoted to Persia's history from ancient times until recently, and this is necessary in order to establish a sense of perspective. Furthermore, there is an attempt to define the position of the strategic Caspian Gates, drawn mainly from ancient sources. Yet the history of Persia is not complete unless its relationship with the 'Gulph of Persica' is made clear. Thus, three later chapters explore this theme, serving to illustrate the impotency of Persia upon the bosom of those waters, thus creating a vacuum to be filled by Britain in her need to protect the western approaches to the Indian Empire. These narratives are drawn from official sources, and even today they convey a sense of immediacy and awareness in the transactions between the Home and Indian Governments and with the subordinate officers in the field.

The Persian terrain is indeed formidable, yet it too must be understood in order to gain an appreciation of the land and the people, and to provide a geographical background to the country's history. *Persia deserta* forms an immense barrier to movements, with few tracks across the great arid basin, so that roads and settlements are sited mainly on the perimeter. An attempt to describe this vast area of desolation is made in discussing the Lut.

Religion, culture and the transfer of ideas and practices have also been noted in other chapters. In this field of activity, Persia has offered much and Persian influences have greatly enriched the lands of its neighbours.

Spelling, or rather the transliteration of Persian names, presents its usual problems, so a compromise is effected by retaining the familiar, e.g. Meshed instead of Mashhad, likewise Omar for 'Umar, whilst diacritical marks have been reduced to bare necessity. No apology is made for preferring 'Persia' to 'Iran'; it is more euphonious, with a pleasing classical ring, but a further reference deals with this point more fully.[2]

The Notes give, *inter alia*, full details of the sources of the quotations, and so it has not been thought necessary to repeat this information in a separate list of bibliographical references.

Some of the contents of this volume originally appeared as articles in journals, and grateful acknowledgment is made to their publishers for permission to reprint them here, even though they have subsequently been revised for inclusion in this book. In particular, I thank Frank Cass & Co. Ltd., London (*Middle Eastern Studies*, Vol. 3, Nos. 1 and 4); the Clarendon Press, Oxford (*Greece and Rome*, Vol. XVII, No. 1; *The Islamic Quarterly*, Vol. XII, No. 3); the Royal

Society for Asian Affairs (*Journal*, Vol. 51, No. 3); and the East Indian Association (*Asian Review*, Vol. 3, No. 1).

Unless otherwise mentioned, the official documents referred to throughout belong to the India Office Records, and grateful acknowledgment is accorded to the Keeper of the Records for assistance given by his staff during the period of research. Unpublished material from the Records is Crown Copyright, and the extracts transcribed in this volume appear by permission of Her Majesty's Secretary of State for Foreign and Commonwealth Affairs.

Notes

1 The Travels of Sir John Chardin, ed. by N.M. Penzer (London, 1927), 125.
2 See Chapter 1, Note 1, p. 17.

ONE

Time and Place

This world is the journal of kings. If they are good, they are blessed and well remembered; if they are evil, they are cursed and ill remembered.

Nizam al-Mulk: The Siyasat-nama

To travel in Persia is to travel in time, for scattered around are all the vestiges of an ancient civilization. Biblical references abound concerning this great kingdom which in Old Testament times was under the sway of the Achaemenids, whilst Herodotus has given us graphic accounts of the influence and impress Persia exerted upon the Hellenic world; but it was left to Alexander the Great to find out for himself the extent and variety of the empire of Darius III and in so doing to alter the course of history.

It has often been observed that the land of old Iran and newer Persia[1] has been the great crossroads of peoples, bridging the East and the West, and thereby extending its own cultural influence whilst at the same time absorbing some of the qualities of those who tarried and those others who passed by. Although in present-day Persia, whose confines are somewhat less than those of Eranshahr, the great heartland of the Sasanids, there are different ethnic and linguistic groups – Kurds, Turks, Arabs, Afghans, Armenians, Baluchis, and so on – it is nevertheless true to say that there is a fairly clearly definable Iranian type commonly encountered which forms the stock of the population and whose language is Persian. Indeed one recognizes amongst the mass of the citizenry today the facial types and characteristics of those early profiles depicted on ancient coins and bas-reliefs.

First then, what is the nature of the country which has cradled these people and given birth to a distinct and continuous civilization, and to what extent has it moulded its children? Long ago, Strabo had noted that

> Persia is of a threefold character, as we regard its natural condition and the quality of the air. First, the coast, extending for about 4,400 or 4,300 stadia, is burnt up with heat; it is sandy, producing little except palm trees and terminates at the greatest river in those parts, the name of which is Oroatis. Secondly, the country above the coast produces everything, and is a plain; it is excellently adapted for the rearing of cattle, and abounds with rivers and lakes. The third portion lies towards the north and is bleak and mountainous. On its borders live the camel breeders. (xv, iii, i)

Whilst this early description is by no means inexact it requires amplification.

A glance at the map shows that Persia is ringed by mountains with maritime frontiers to the north and south, and these natural characteristics are not without significance since they form the defences, the ramparts which invaders must assault and penetrate and in so doing expose themselves to the possibility of becoming drawn into a conquered realm which can stealthily become their own conqueror. Like Ireland of old, Persia has captivated her captors, rendering them susceptible to her own influences so that in time they lose their old identity in assuming the new, and then for good measure they sometimes go on further, as for instance the Turkmans did, to assail other nations and establish themselves abroad in Asia Minor, yet carrying with them in the course of their transit some of those refining and improving susceptibilities which in time softened the wild horsemen from the steppe into the more sophisticated progenitors of the Ottoman empire.

Despite some desultory attacks upon their coastline in the Gulf, notably on two occasions during the nineteenth century when Britain brought pressure to bear upon a Persia intent on seeking aggrandisement in Afghanistan, and an incursion during the Second World War, Persia has never been invaded by sea. The inhospitable northern shores of the Persian Gulf are backed by the mighty Zagros range which runs parallel to the coastline, and with its lofty eminences, deep valleys and ravines it forms a natural barrier to any force attempting to cross its grain; so together the forbidding terrain and the uninviting coastal climate have ensured that that part of the country has remained almost inviolate. Indeed, there has been a reciprocity of influences at work here, for those two same considerations have tended to shut Persia in both mentally and physically from the sea, so that despite the presence of over a thousand miles of southern coastline, Persia has never been a maritime power nor possessed a nautical tradition. Her great poet Hafiz unconsciously demonstrated the Persian dread of the sea, 'a disposition of the Persians', observed Malcolm, 'of whom all classes have an unconquerable antipathy to that element', for having been invited to visit the court of the King of the Deccan during the thirteenth century he fell so ill of seasickness when embarking on board ship at Hormuz that he promptly repaired ashore again and then proceeded to make the arduous return land journey to his native Shiraz rather than face the unspeakable terrors of the passage across the Arabian Sea. Thus it was that since Sassanid times the seapower in the Gulf was, until the coming of the Portuguese, in the hands of the Arab maritime tribes of the opposite littoral.[2]

Likewise the Caspian has played but a minor role in Persian history. Few invaders have crossed the waters of that inland sea and indeed they had little inducement since the marauding hordes from Central Asia or the Caucasus region were land peoples with their own latent dread or suspicion of the mighty waters upon whose bosom they so rarely consigned themselves. So it was that Persia's contacts with neighbouring countries were mainly by land, and even if at a much later date her predominant European visitors – Portuguese, English, Dutch and French – made their entry into the Shah's domains by way of the Persian Gulf, such incursions were usually trading expeditions making little impact if any beyond the establishment of factories at useful points.

Landward the story is different. The easiest point of entry into Persia is from the north-east where the mountains, instead of forming a barrier, provide a corridor and have thereby invited the unwelcome intruder from those regions beyond; the early Aryans, from which name Iran is derived, had long ago tested that approach. A glance at the map shows how easy it has been for invaders to enter from that quarter and possibly the earliest wave of forcible immigrants in historical times were those peoples subsequently called the Medes who entered Turkestan about the eight century B.C., in due course settling in the north-west of the country with their capital at Ecbatana, the earth-covered mounds of which lie outside the present city of Hamadan. Not much of this early settlement is known to us, though the immutability of 'the law of the Medes and Persians, which altereth not' is recorded, whilst in later times classical writers made

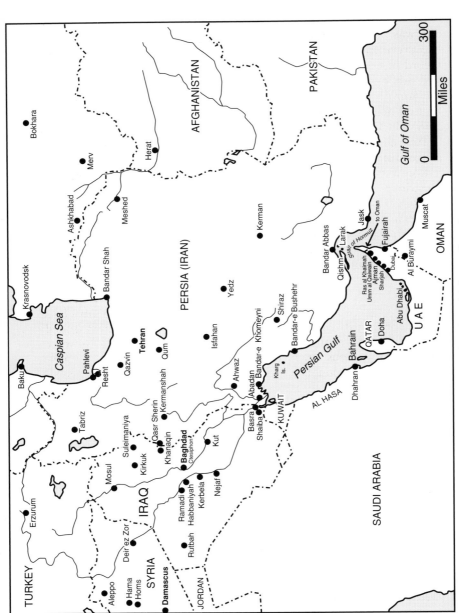

Figure 1 Map of Persia and Adjacent Countries

extensive references to this people. Media[3] extended her territories and was herself later subjected to the sway of the Achaemenids who had previously been tributary chiefs, and of that great dynasty some record has been preserved in script whilst vestiges of their buildings and other edifices remain. These Achaemenids in many respects are the prime dynastic house and founders of the Persian nation, for their Central Asian forbears had settled in that south-western part of Persia from which the whole country derives its name.

Achaemenes is a Greek name for Hakhamanish, and he was the progenitor of that renowned family which moulded Persia into a nation and then an empire. The earliest record we possess of this illustrious house comes from the king Ariaramnes, brother of Cyrus I, whose gold tablet exists today bearing this inscription: 'This land of the Persians which I possess, provided with fine horses and good men: it is the great god Ahuramazda who has given it to me. I am the king of this land.' Yet it was Cyrus II who by defeating Astyages the Mede in the sixth century B.C. united Parsa and Media into one great state, for it was this Cyrus too who, confronted by Croesus the Lydian king of fabled opulence, defeated him in 516 B.C., whereby the Persian empire now extended to the Aegean itself. Croesus, as Herodotus tells us, had previously consulted the Delphic oracle on his recommended course of action against the growing power of Cyrus and the reply came that if Croesus attacked the Persians he would destroy a mighty empire. Acting upon this presumably impeccable advice Croesus advanced, to be beaten decisively and taken captive by the Persian king; thus too did he fulfil the prophecy that he would destroy a mighty empire – his own.

Cyrus, Darius, Xerxes and Artaxerxes, these are the names pre-eminent amongst those of the Achaemenid kings during whose rule the Persian empire stretched westward to embrace Egypt; truly could the great Achaemenid boast in that famous rock inscription at Bisitun (Behistun) near Hamadan:

> I am Darius the great King, the King of kings . . . the Achaemenian . . . These are the countries which have fallen into my hands; by the grace of Ormazd I have become king of them: Persia, Susiana, Babylonia, Assyria, Arabia, Egypt . . . Sparta and Ionia, Armenia, Cappadocia, Parthia, Zarangia, Aria, Chorasmia, Bactria, Sogdiana, Gandaria, the Sacae, the Sattagydes, Arachotia, and the Mecians; the total amount being twenty-one countries.

Figure 2 Stone Slab with Figure of a Sphinx
(from the Palace of Darius at Persepolis, late 6th century B.C.)

Such is Rawlinson's famous decipherment which, reduced to its essentials, proclaims the rule of Darius embracing all the lands between the Nile and the Indus, a proud claim never before realized in the history of empires. He it was who further disposed the empire into satrapies[4] or provinces, an arrangement continued by Alexander after his conquest of Persia; Darius built roads and imperial highways, reformed taxation, systematized the coinage and endowed the empire with its greatest degree of political organization.

Probably during the seventh century B.C., though the date is obscure, there lived Zoroaster, or Zarathustra, the prophet and founder of the creed sometimes known as the Religion of the Good Life, a cult which bears his name and which was to be elevated to an established status within the state. Whether this was at the instigation of Darius, whose inscriptions bear the statement: 'By the favour of Ahuramazda I am king, Ahuramazda bestowed the kingdom upon me', is a matter which scholars have not finally resolved, and it has been noted that such a claim was earlier made by Ariaramnes; yet the frequent repetition in the inscriptions of the Great King's acknowledgment of Ahuramazda above all other gods is not without its significance.

It is sufficient here to say that Zoroastrianism postulated an age-old struggle between the forces of good and evil, Ahuramazda being the spirit of Good or Light, and Ahriman the principle of Evil or Darkness, between whom Man must make his choice; both deities however remaining subordinate to the One Creator God whose role is ill defined. Zoroastrianism is therefore a theology based upon dualism, that struggle within man's heart and mind which has been waged incessantly ever since religious speculation had its beginnings. As Ahuramazda or Ormazd was the positive spirit venerated by the followers of Zoroaster it was natural that, since the spirit was represented by the sun or by fire, they should be regarded as fire-worshippers and although that appellation is not strictly correct the old fire altars and modern fire temples lend some substance to the charge. Their priests, probably precursors of Zoroaster, were called Mobed or Magi from whom derives our present 'magician'[5] and later, by repute, they included in their numbers the Three Wise Men who visited the Christ child at his birth; they were also the custodians of the sacred writings, the Avesta, in which the divine precepts were recorded. Their dead could be neither buried nor burned (though this was perhaps a later development) since this would result in defilement of the sacred earth and the sacred fire, so their bodies were exposed in order to be devoured by carrion birds in special buildings, the towers of silence or *dakhma*, and this funeral rite survives to this present day. Certain it is that this religion was a unifying principle in shaping and preserving ancient Persian civilization for over a thousand years until it fell before the vigorous onslaught of the victorious Muslims, but its essence remains to endow that spirit of proud nationalism and self-assertion which is characteristic there today.[6]

The empire of the Achaemenids came to an end when the third Darius was defeated by Alexander and slain by one of his own entourage, Bessus the satrap of Bactria, but of Alexander in Persia little can here be said since his untimely death in Babylon in 323 B.C. allowed him no time wherein to consolidate his hold upon a Persia in which his sojourn had been devoted to battles, marches and an unfortunate episode at Persepolis. His epic march homewards across the desert wastes of Persia, reinforced by the arms of his general Krateros and the aid of his admiral Nearchus still excite admiration in the minds of geographers and others who are conscious of the immense hazards of this forbidding route, whilst his attempt to fuse the civilizations of East and West thereby summoning into being the *oikoumene*, the concept of the one inhabited world, may at best be considered as premature.

Alexander's successors, the Seleucids, took their name from the satrap Seleucus, one of Alexander's generals, but incompetence, a persistency in remaining obstinately Greek amongst Persians and a series of disastrous wars caused the Persian domains to fall to the Parthians. The fundamental weakness in the House of Seleucus was that, in turning its back upon Alexander's ambition to unite East and West on terms of equality, it also alienated the loyalties of its Persian subjects and thus created fatal stresses within. To his seventy-two satrapies Seleucus appointed either Macedonians or Greeks, and not one Persian was admitted to the administration other than at low or menial levels, whilst his Asiatic army was officered entirely by Europeans; when to these slights were added both arrogance and injustice together with a resultant rift between the ruling Greeks and the native landed gentry it was not surprising that little national resistance was offered to a vigorous usurper. Furthermore, the Seleucids were incapable of maintaining the artistic and architectural traditions of the Achaemenids, thus a debased style incorporating Hellenistic intrusions characterised their period.

The Parthians,[7] a militant and invading people came, as has been so often the case in Persian history, from Transoxiana and, settling down in north-eastern Persia, had revolted against the Seleucids in the third century B.C. Their great king Mithridates of the Arsacid dynasty consolidated the kingdom which extended over what is now northern Persia and Afghanistan and later extended the western frontiers to include Armenia and Mesopotamia. These Parthians effected a break with the Hellenistic influences of the Seleucids, reverting in architecture and sculpture to an orientalized Iranian mode, though little exists today beyond fragmentary remains. Perhaps their most apparent legacy is the long vaulted hall, tunnel shaped, as exemplified at the great palace of Ctesiphon, an edifice of the Sassanid period though deriving its inspiration from the Parthians. Tolerant in religious matters but deficient of a literature or an indigenous culture and thereby unrespected by their more gifted native Persian subjects, they too fell prey to internal disorders and dynastic anarchy which was viewed with indifference by the bulk of the nation. To them we are indebted for *Pahlavi*, a Middle Persian language with an ideographic script, a word which much later lent itself to the name of a peaked cap and to a dynasty inaugurated by the late Reza Shah.

Throughout the whole of the period from Cyrus the Great in 559 B.C. to the collapse of Parthia in A.D. 226 the Persians had been preoccupied with the West. Cyrus had fought and won campaigns which had made him master of Asia Minor, Darius had invaded Greece only to meet disaster at Marathon whilst Xerxes, who succeeded him, witnessed the destruction of his navy at Salamis. No doubt these reverses abroad caused the Greek historian Polybius to observe that 'the Persians for a certain period possessed a great rule and dominion, but so often as they ventured to overstep the boundaries of Asia they imperilled not only the security of their empire, but their own existence', the truth of which remains undiminished. During the reign of Artaxerxes occurred the memorable retreat of the Ten Thousand, the Greek *Anabasis* or Journey Up Country, the record of which rings down the corridors of history in Xenophon's imperishable narrative. Alexander brought his Hellenes with him, the Parthians and the Romans were continually at loggerheads, whilst Greek was a language currently and officially employed in the Parthian kingdom (the peach was known to the Greeks as the 'Persian apple'), and during this time esoteric and exotic religious influences penetrated Persia: religious tolerance early permitted the establishment of Christian dioceses within the bounds of the empire.

A vassal of the Parthian King Artobanus, in the third century A.D., was a certain Artaxerxes or Ardashir, as he is usually styled. Ardashir claimed to be the descendant of Sassan, an elusive and somewhat legendary figure of whose origin much remains in doubt, though it was most likely that he was an hereditary satrap of the Parthian monarch and therefore in a position to influence a revolt. A more important claim was that Ardashir, through Sassan, was a descendant of the Achaemenid line, whereby an aura of legitimacy surrounded his name and this desire to be recognized as being in the right line of succession has ever played a prominent part in Persian dynastic history, as will be noticed later. In A.D. 212 Ardashir rebelled and established himself in south-western Persia; fourteen years later he became master of all Persia and the empire, transferred his capital to Ctesiphon and proclaimed the Sassanid dynasty. He re-established Zoroastrianism as the national religion, this having been disestablished during the Parthian rule, and then set about consolidating his reign. During the time of the later Sassanid king Shapur I, in the latter part of the third century A.D., there arose a new prophet, Mani, the founder of the religion of the Manichees, who preached a radically reformed version of Zoroastrianism wherein its dualism resolved itself into relating matter to evil and spirit to good, but the entrenched and conservative Magi were too strong for him and his downfall occurred in A.D. 276. After being flayed alive his skin, stuffed with straw, was suspended over one of the gates of the city of Shapur; but despite this warning Manichaeism spread far afield leaving its mark beyond the confines of Parthia, and even St. Augustine of Hippo dallied with it.[8] The Sassanids, who lasted for four centuries, may rightly claim to be the last of the great national dynasties of Persia until the coming of the Safavids in the sixteenth century, and though peace was not ensured the period was one of prosperity and orderly government.

At that time Armenia was the cockpit between East and West, and over that vexed country more battles were fought and more treasure expended between Persia and Rome than the forbidding terrain would seem to have warranted, so that both sides succeeded in exhausting themselves without material advantage. One Roman emperor, Valerian, attacked Persia only to be defeated by his adversary Shapur I, Ardashir's son, and contemporary rock carvings depicting the submission of the Roman to the Persian are to be seen in parts of Persia, the one most commonly encountered being at Naqsh-i-Rustam near Persepolis. The consequence of these wars of attrition was to be as profound as it was unforeseen.

Towards the end of the fifth century A.D. Persia was confronted with two heresies: Mazdakism and Nestorianism. Of the former it may be said that Mazdak, the chief Magus, preached a form of communism the principal aspect of which, the redistribution of wealth and wives, did not commend itself to those who enjoyed power and privilege, and so we are told that Mazdak's disciples, having been invited to a royal banquet, were dispatched by armed guards and buried upside down so that only their feet projected above the ground. Mazdak was later invited to take a turn in the garden where he was dismayed to see this pedestrian form of floral display, but his emotion was of short duration since he too was speedily disposed of and with him went the last of that strange and austere creed. The Nestorians, however, were a different consideration, for their heresy was not a revolt against the established religion in Persia but an aberration of a foreign cult, Christianity, whose principal seat was then at Byzantium. Their doctrines and their fortunes, which waxed only in due course to wane, are now of small account, and today there is a vestigial community of Nestorians residing around the shores of Lake Urmia in north-west Persia.

Persia and Byzantium had for so long assaulted each other to no lasting advantage that both great empires were reduced to a state of exhaustion and their peoples largely to a condition of deprivation and despair. Perhaps a stalemate would have occurred whereby each antagonist might have achieved a respite so that the vast region from the Bosphorus to the Oxus could have attained tranquillity and prosperity but fate, in the guise of Islam, intervened with incalculable consequences. The belligerent and crusading followers of the prophet Muhammad, imbued with religious zeal and proselytizing fervour, ventured from their holy cities of Medina and Mecca to find little effective opposition to their assaults upon neighbouring countries; thus in A.D. 641 the last of the Sassanids, Yazdigird III, was defeated at Nihavand. With the fall of Yazdigird comes the close of the ancient world of the Orient and the dawn of the Middle Ages; a millennium of history, philosophy, religion and culture, epitomized in the long and continuous civilization of the Plateau since the time of the first of the Achaemenids, had come to an end and a new era, building anew upon the foundations of the old, was to begin.

This Arab conquest was quite unlike all other conquests of Persia whereby in former times organized armies had advanced under their generals from the West, or great nomadic hordes had occupied the country from the East. The Arabs were neither a disciplined army nor a vast horde, but they were favoured by two particular considerations: an impelling rallying cry in the name of Allah, and the almost complete destitution of the two great empires upon whom their assaults were launched. Their total victory over the Persians had one other unprecedented effect: the imposition of a new and alien religion upon the people which was to change the habits and temper of the Persians with even greater consequence than the earlier advent of the Achaemenids. The Muslim impact upon Persian architecture was considerable and in the ecclesiastical field even revolutionary. A religion basically fundamentalist, initially devoid of a sense of mystery and proclaiming the brotherhood of the faithful and the oneness of God favoured, in place of the old temple, the new mosque where the interior was expansive and open to view: a prayer and preaching chamber where a sense of community had displaced the esoteric mysteries of the Magi.

The original line of Caliphs, the Omayyids, were established at Damascus, but they were dispossessed in A.D. 750 by a new dynastic caliphate, the Abbasids, who with Persian assistance assumed the Prophet's mantle and transferred their capital to Baghdad three years later; thus, on a site close to historic Ctesiphon and even older Babylon, the caliphate was established within the bounds of greater Persia. This inevitably meant, as it always has signified to the invaders of that country, whether peaceful or bellicose, the pervasion of Persian influences in the caliph's court, and thus Persian ideas and customs travelled far within the Muslim world, even to the shores of the Atlantic in Spain and Morocco. The Abbasids, however, were not endowed with qualities requisite for a dominant and enduring dynasty, and they degenerated into the role of puppets of various potentates whilst Persia herself again became torn between rival dynasties. The Abbasids in their decline were followed by the Samanids from Khurasan, who inaugurated a brief Persian renaissance, themselves to be succeeded by the Ghaznavids, whilst in Central Persia arose the cultivated Buwayhid (Buyid) dynasty, amongst whom were worthy builders, some of whose work remains in the Masjid-i-Jameh at Isfahan, though their sway was of barely a century's duration. There followed, however, a virile power from the north-east, the Seljuks, who entered Khurasan from Turkestan and proceeded to establish their capital at Rayy near modern Tehran. These Turkish Seljuks were perceptive enough to adopt Persian manners and culture and to employ Persians in the high offices of government so that their reign of about one hundred years is notable for the fostering of art and literature, their architectural remains reveal a blending of sensitivity and power, whilst in the great *vizier* Nizam al-Mulk is seen the epitome of the mediaeval Muslim administrator and counsellor of kings.

The death of Malik Shah in 1092 marked the beginning of the decline of Seljuk power and the consequent fragmentation of an empire extending from the Levant to Transoxiana, though an interesting by-product of this fissiparous process was the establishment of the Sultanate of Rum, the precursor of the Ottoman empire, whilst in the Elburz range Hasan-i-Sabah founded an order of Assassins and a new theological imperium which lasted until their power was destroyed by the Mongols in the late thirteenth century.

The century of disorder following the disruption of Seljuk rule, during which time eastern Persia fell under the sway of the Khwarizm chiefs from Khiva, was followed by that great cataclysm which was to have far reaching geographical and historical effects: the Mongol invasion and conquest of western Asia. Other invaders had been successfully absorbed into the Persian setting, yet the Mongols came not to admire but to destroy, not merely obliterating much of the traditional framework of politics and national identities but also substituting Mongolic influences both of people and ideas. Thus, instead of containing the eastern marches of an empire whose centre had been in Mesopotamia, Persia found herself a western dependency of an oriental despotism stretching from distant Cathay.

Jenghiz Khan in 1220 defeated his Khwarizm adversary because he was ably supported by his *urdu* (mounted 'hordes', properly 'military encampments'). They were no respecters of foreign cultures, and their trail of despoliation is recorded by the earth mounds which mark the sites of once flourishing cities, whilst the culmination of their victorious advance was the sacking of Baghdad under Hulugu, grandson of Jenghiz, and the extinction of the caliphate in 1258. Two years previously Hulugu had conquered and destroyed the citadel of the Assassins at Alamut, thereby occasioning the dispersion of that Isma'ili order.

Civilization in Persia was not, however, completely destroyed since successive Mongol rulers were obliged to apply themselves to an orderly administration which is incumbent upon all nomadic peoples when they are forced by circumstances to adopt a more sedentary form of existence. Their paganism predisposed them to Christians as readily as to Muslims whilst they willingly received emissaries from the West who brought into the realms of the Great Khan new ideas and the missionary zeal of the Church of the late Middle Ages. Marco Polo is perhaps the best known of all those travellers in the lands of the Mongols during the latter part of the thirteenth century, whilst another though less-known figure was Geoffrey de Langley who visited the Mongol court as ambassador of Edward I of England. Arghun Khan (1284–1294) was favourably inclined towards a Mongol-Christian alliance to drive the Muslims from the Holy Land but his successor Ghazan became a Muslim convert and, as is so often the case in newly-found religious fervour, he persecuted his Christian subjects harshly.

These later Mongols were known as Il Khans and they denote a break with the primitive ferocity of their conquering forbears in that they were disposed towards a patronage of the arts. Ghazan indeed carried this commendable activity a stage further in overhauling taxation and the postal services and in endowing schools, libraries and hospitals, so it was truly a flowering of Persian culture enlivened by marked Chinese influences which culminated their dynastic rule.

Nevertheless, an inability to maintain that rule unbroken over the extent of their dominions and the almost inevitable tendency towards dissolution weakened their position; thus, after a period of enfeeblement the way was paved for Timur the Lame, Tamerlane, Conqueror of the World.

Timur headed a second invasion from the Mongolian hinterland and was so successful that by 1393 his rule extended over Persia and Mesopotamia and at the time of his death in 1405 he had penetrated Asia Minor, Russia and India. Unfortunately, and as might be expected, such forceful generalship did not go hand-in-hand with a sensitive appreciation of the countries he had conquered, so destruction rather than consolidation followed in his train, and though Shah Rukh, his son, and successive Timurid princes laboured to repair the damage, they too were powerless to maintain the unity of their dominions. Thus once more was demonstrated the truth that only under a firm, central and enduring rule could the arts and good order prosper in the principalities and kingdoms of the Eastern world.

The fleeting successors of the Timurids were now confronted with a fresh threat from a hitherto unsuspected quarter, for the new conqueror of Persia was not to come, like his predecessors, from the lands beyond the Oxus but from those sheltering in the southern slopes of the Caucasus. In the town of Ardabil had died in the fourteenth century a venerable Sufi mystic, Safi-ud-Din, who claimed direct descent from the Shi'a Imam Musa al-Khadim, seventh in line of succession from the Prophet's cousin and son-in-law 'Ali. From this Safi descended still further one Isma'il who, with the aid of the Qizilbash tribes[9] and by superior generalship, succeeded in defeating his quarrelling adversaries of the so-called White Sheep clan of Turkmans; Isma'il then proceeded to have himself proclaimed Shah at Tabriz in the year 1500. Here at first seemed yet another minor revolt with possibly the usual short-lived consequences, but in fact by this act the most outstanding dynasty of Persia since the Sassanids was born, and Persia commenced to move on to the stage of modern history.

Taking his dynastic name from that of his saintly forbear, Isma'il inaugurated the Safavid era (of which great monuments stand today), and once more called into being Persia as a coherent national state and established enduring relations with not only immediate neighbours but also the powers of Western Europe. But even more importantly, Isma'il was a devout Shi'a, of that sect of Islam then so greatly at variance with the Sunni that each held the other in mutual detestation, with profound results which transcended the bounds of theology and were to leave an indelible mark upon international politics.[10] Of Shi'ism more will be said later and it is here sufficient to observe its implications in the political sphere. Between her Sunni neighbours to both east and west Persia interposed a wedge of Shi'ism which split the unity of Islam, and that theological division remains even today though in a less exacerbated form that hitherto. More than that, the elevation of Shi'ism as the established religion consolidated Persian national unity in the face of hostility from western Ottomans and eastern Uzbeks, giving the new state that cause for a deeper loyalty which had been conspicuously lacking since the overthrow of Zoroastrianism nine centuries earlier; hence religious differences, whilst tending to alienate Persia from her neighbouring Islamic states, helped to afford her that solid base upon which to build the national structure which we now witness. Yet another consequence was the proprietary interest Persia was to take in her co-religionists in Mesopotamia, later to be styled Iraq, where are to be found some of the most holy and ancient Shi'a places of pilgrimage, of which Karbala, Samarra and Najaf are perhaps most notable, so that these Ottoman lands were to be a further cause of dispute between the Sublime Porte and the Great Sophy.

The significance of Isma'il's reign which lasted until 1524 can only be appreciated when viewed in its religious setting. He was founding a theocratic state, in the face of the fact that purely national feeling had been overwhelmed by the successive waves from east and west, all alien to Persian consciousness and sentiment. Isma'il's court language was Turkish, his supporting tribes were Turkman and even the Persian people at that time numbered many Sunnis. When Isma'il set about elevating the Shi'a on his accession he was warned that no less than two-thirds of the population of Tabriz were Sunnis whereupon, it is reported, he swore that if one word of protest against their conversion were made not one would be left alive. The thoroughness of the new Shah's application to this task is evident today where, in a predominantly Shi'a population, other religious attitudes can be regarded as almost inconceivable. Thus did Isma'il lay and then consolidate the foundation of the new monarchy, the restoration of an old empire, his divine descent from the illustrious 'Ali bearing witness to his unimpeachable claim to reign and rule.

The three consecutive successors to Isma'il, namely Tahmasp, Isma'il II and Khudabandeh, left nothing remarkable other than a series of exhausting wars with the Ottoman Turks and a prudent removal of the capital from Tabriz to Qazvin, though during Tahmasp's reign there was a minor flowering of the arts. It is not until the succession of Shah Abbas I, the Great, in 1587 that attention should be directed to the cultural and political achievements of the Safavids, which are all the more remarkable since the dynasty had been gravely weakened by the state of near anarchy which the preceding reigns had permitted. Unquestionably Abbas conferred upon Persia the most brilliant regime of modern times, and his achievements were manifold. Initially, he saw what was needed to ensure order and prosperity, and these two desiderata he safeguarded first of all by a reorganization of the army, supplemented by the introduction of artillery under the supervision of those two extraordinary Shirley brothers, Sir Robert and Sir Anthony, by which means he was enabled to press the Turks back within their own frontiers and also to advance into Afghanistan to recover Kandahar, that cockpit of Central Asia. Abbas encouraged building construction and other engineering works whereby caravansarais, roads and bridges were undertaken so that the safety and speed of travellers were assisted. His reign is outstanding especially for the superb design and embellishment of mosques, public buildings, palaces, parks and other adornments of cities, whilst in transferring his capital to Isfahan he presented the opportunity of its becoming so bedecked as to rival Meshed in being the glory of the Shi'a world. Not, however, that he neglected that holy city, for he signalled its importance as a pilgrim centre by undertaking the whole distance thence from Isfahan, some 800 weary miles, on foot, whilst to protect that venerable shrine of the eighth Imam and as a defence of the vulnerable north-east against Uzbek invaders he transferred from Kurdistan to the Atrek valley a number of Kurdish tribesmen whose descendants live there today.

To Isfahan he made another transfer of peoples, that of the Armenians from Julfa on the Aras at the foothills of the Caucasus, in order to enhance the trade of his new capital; he entered into negotiations with the Christian powers of the West against his mortal enemies the Turks; he conspired with the English to oust the Portuguese in the Persian Gulf; he encouraged commerce and agriculture; he was well disposed towards religious tolerance, and, in short, left nothing undone to secure the country from menaces within and against threats from without.

The extraordinary thing is that the Safavid dynasty did not collapse when Abbas died in 1629, for his successors were not of his stamina and remind us of the Mughals in India after Jahangir's death. His genius for creation and his capacity to make use of all available resources left a legacy which not even the incompetence and bigotry of the four following Shahs could dissipate, and so it was left to the Afghans under Mahmud to bring down the regime by superior force of arms at the capitulation of Isfahan in 1722. Mahmud's position, however, was never secure, for apart from the legitimist claims of the Pretender, Tahmasp II and of his infant son who were the last surviving Safavids, he had to meet the more formidable claims of Nadir Quli who, as a soldier in Mahmud's service, eventually arose to defeat his master and to assume the crown of Persia.

Nadir Quli Shah was a brilliant soldier who defeated the Turks, once more recovered Kandahar, marched to Delhi to sack that city and to seize the Peacock Throne of the Mughals, and next advanced into the Central Asian khanates to subdue the Uzbek rulers. He abjured the Shi'a doctrine in favour of a modified Sunni concept, though this concession failed to commend him to the Turks. He then essayed to build up a fleet in the Persian Gulf, hauling from the forests of the Caspian provinces across the wastes of the central plateau timber for ship construction at Bushire on the Gulf, but he chose as director of construction an unfortunate Fleming who had no knowledge of shipbuilding and died of anxiety. His internal administration was firm, built upon the ruthless elimination of all opposition combined with an absence of justice, but it was without sure foundation and death at an assassin's hand overtook him in 1747.

The Zend dynasty, of Kurdish stock, succeeded Nadir Shah for a brief if brilliant interregnum, and their most illustrious member, Karim Khan, did much to beautify Shiraz during his twenty years' sway. The Zends, however, were ill equipped to withstand the assaults of the Qajars from the north-west (see note 9) who, coming to ascendance, eliminated their opponents in a most bloodthirsty manner and thus Agha Muhammad Khan, a Qajar noble, assumed the title of Shah and so established a ruling house which lasted until 1925.

The Qajar period is full of incident, largely of an international character. Broadly, the situation was one of continued reverses, the Russians and Turks inflicting defeats and consequently depriving Persia of her border provinces. Two disastrous attempts to secure Herat and then Kandahar, which had mesmerized Persian rulers throughout Islamic times, were repulsed by British intervention in the Gulf, since Britain was unwilling to see Persia standing at the threshold of the Indian empire and thereby affording a weak buffer between Britain and Russia in the East. Noteworthy, however, was Nasir-ud-Din, the first Persian monarch to travel abroad to Europe since Xerxes, who has left us some engaging diaries of his experiences during the years 1873 to 1889. Nasir-ud-Din was unable, nevertheless, to transmit his personality and vigour to the remaining Qajars so that the dynasty strongly resembled that of the Ottomans, and together these two oriental monarchies creaked their way along the downward path of incompetence and intrigue, exposed to the cold winds from greater powers which finally blew them off their rickety thrones in the years following the First World War.

An officer of the Cossack Brigade, Reza Khan, seized power in 1921 as chief minister and four years later deposed Ahmad Shah, the last of the Qajars, ascending the throne in his stead. Reza's accession inaugurated the new Pahlavi royal house, the name recalling pre-Islamic greatness, though his subsequent abdication in 1941 was the result of Allied war-time pressure; with the rule of his son and successor Muhammad Reza Shah, later succeeded by the Ayatollah Khomeini, we arrive within the context of our own times.

Notes

1 The word *Iran* is derived from the Middle-Persian *Eran* which in turn stems from *Ariana*, the country of the Aryans. Eratosthenes, according to Strabo (xv, 723), stated that 'Ariana is bounded on the east by the Indus, on the south by the Great Sea, on the north by the Paropamisus and the succeeding chain of mountains as far as the Caspian Gates, on the west by the same limits by which the territory of the Parthians is separated from Media, and Carmania from Paraetacene and Persia.' On the other hand, Pliny (*N.H.* vi, 93) confuses Ariana with Aria, the region in which Herat is situated (Old Persian *Haraiva*), whilst Herodotus (vii, 62) states that ancient peoples knew the Medes as Aryans. During the Sassanid period the term *Eranshahr* was employed to denote the region also known as Greater Iran comprising Persia, Afghanistan, part of Baluchistan and also Mesopotamia in which the Sassanid capital, Ctesiphon, was situated. Today Persians refer to their country as Iran and to themselves as Iranians.

Persia, on the other hand, derives from Pars (arabicized as Fars) which in turn comes from Parsa, known to the Greeks as Persis. This originally referred to the province now known as Fars whence sprang the Achaemenid dynasty and which name was extended to cover the whole country and also its people. Today, the language of Persia (Persian) is known colloquially as *Farsi* and it is held that the purest form of that tongue is still to be encountered in Fars province. The modern Parsis, followers of the ancient Zoroastrian religion and a great many of whom now live in India, retain in their name the old Persian spelling.

2 A contrary argument has been advanced by Hadi Hasan (*History of Persian Navigation*, London, 1928), but in the main Persia has throughout history remained a continental nation with no maritime tradition. Perhaps the stay-at-home Hafiz bore in mind the Persian proverb, *Az safar saqar* (travel is travail).

3 Polybius (c, 44), writing in the second century B.C., states that 'Media is the most powerful of all the kingdoms of Asia, whether we consider the extent of the country, or the numbers and goodness of the men, and also of the horses which are there produced', whilst two centuries later Strabo (xi, 523), writing of Media under the Parthian occupation, says that the country 'is divided into two parts, one of which is called Greater Media. Its capital is Ecbatana, a large city containing the royal seat of the Median empire. This palace the Parthians continue to occupy even at this time . . . The only other division is Atropatian Media . . . [which] borders upon Armenia and Matiane towards the east, towards the west on Greater Media, and on both towards the north.' Herodotus (i, 74), who wrote during the fifth century B.C., informs us that the Medes, under Cyaxares, warred with the Lydians for over five years until an eclipse of the sun when 'day was turned into night', and peace was thereupon concluded; this occurrence together with a dynastic marriage secured the borders of Media and accorded the country a definite geographical expression.

4 The Greek word *satrapes* or governor is derived from the Median *kshathrapa* or *khshatrapavan*, though this appears to have been borrowed from the *pakhatu* of the Assyrians; thus the term has a respectable and ancient lineage. Herodotus (i, 192) considered this form of government to be by far the best, observing also that Darius the Great had set up twenty local governments under this title, 'assigning to each its governor, and fixing the tribute which was to be paid to him by the several nations. And generally he joined together in one satrapy the nations that were neighbours, but sometimes he passed over the nearer tribes, and put in their stead those which were more remote.' (iii, 89). It should be noted, however, that Persia came directly under the rule of the royal house, satrapies being reserved for the remoter parts of the empire. The inscription at Bisitun lists the twenty satrapies which together with Persia account for the twenty-one countries then under Achaemenid rule. They formed autonomous governments raising their own tributes for the imperial exchequer, and usually this was paid by the gold *daric*, a coin named after the august ruler and a monetary innovation which tended to bind the empire in matters of finance and trade. This system of government prevailed until the time of Seleucus who substituted for the civil satrap a military *strategos* or general whose presence will later be noted, but by that much later time the almost perfect system of imperial administration under Darius, with its integrated forms of trade, customs, taxation and communications, had degenerated into less efficient military governates.

5 The Magi were undoubtedly an ascendant caste of the Median people and their privileged position in the structure of Aryan Persia was, like that of the Brahmins in India, based upon religious and supernatural dominance. Their association with the wise men from the east (Matthew ii, 1) was much later echoed in Milton's 'the star-led wizards haste with odours

sweet', and thus also they appear to have been in the vanguard of religious speculation.

The magical art (*ars magica*) comes to us etymologically from the religious sciences of the Magi, and since in ancient times and in various lands it was difficult if not wholly impossible to separate religion from superstition, it followed that necromancy played an important part in Magian lore. Herodotus (i, 107) tells us that the Magi had the gift of interpreting dreams, whilst their supernatural powers were such that 'by offering victims to the winds, and charming them with the help of conjurors . . . [the Magians] succeeded in laying the storm four days after it first begun . . .' This must be the first recorded attempt to control the elements, whilst much later Ovid (*Metamorph.* vii, 195) refers to *cantus artesque magarum*, implying that the incantations and spells of witches were still among their priestly attributes.

To sustain the craft of magic by the use of drugs has been a common practice at all times and in diverse places whatever the ascendant religious doctrine might be, and at this the Magi appeared to be adept. That magic originated in medicine, Pliny avers, 'no one entertains a doubt, or that, under the plausible guise of promoting health, it insinuated itself among mankind, as a higher and more holy branch of the medical art.' (xxx, 1). Pliny has little respect for such medical practitioners who, in his opinion, are mere witch doctors and he specifically mentions the Magi who, by means of the plant *aglaophotis*, 'can summon the deities into their presence when they please.' (xxiv, 102).

The strictures of these earlier writers may be unnecessarily severe, for it is customary to impute the malefic practices of the few to those of the many of the same profession; if the Magi included sorcerers they also certainly included the learned and the wise, and it was their fate as well as their misfortune to influence political and social life at all levels. Such influence had of necessity at times to be sustained by dubious means.

6 In Sassanid times, Yazd was one of the principal cities of Zoroastrian worship, and the relicts of that great national religion remain there in the persons of the Guebres whose name is possibly derived from the Arabic *kafr* denoting an infidel as seen through Muslim eyes. They number today less than 10,000 in Yazd and its environs, emigration and their disposition towards consanguinous marriage tending to impose a limitation upon appreciable increase. Their modern fire-temple at Yazd is not without architectural interest. Therein the *mobeds* chant their age-old litanies, their mouths veiled to prevent their breath from contaminating the sacred fire around which they dispose themselves as they have done through time immemorial, recalling to mind perhaps the words of Shelley's Prometheus:

> Ere Babylon was dust,
> The Magus Zoroaster, my dead child,
> Met his own image walking in the garden.
> That apparition, sole of men, he saw.
> For know there are two worlds of life and death
> One of which thou beholdest; but the other
> Is underneath the grave . . .

A common link in early Indo-Iranian mythology is the worship of Mithras or Mithra who in Avestan time became the most popular of the *yazata* or angels in the Zoroastriam hierarchy. We read in those early scriptures of invocations to this 'swift-horsed sun immortal' to whom is due all honour and propitiation by the highest ordinance since 'Ahura Mazda spoke unto Spitama Zarathustra, saying, "Verily, when I created Mithra, the lord of wide pastures, O Spitama!, I created him as worthy of sacrifice, as worthy of prayer as myself, Ahura Mazda"' (Mihir Yasht, x. I. i). It would appear, however, that in pre-Zoroastrianism Mithra had been accorded divine status although his origin remains obscure, but he was always associated with the shining sun which signified not merely the visible light but also the inner light of truth which triumphs over the powers of darkness or falsehood. It follows that his accommodation in Zoroastrianism was the consequence of an easy migration since the clash between light and darkness, good and evil, is a cardinal point in Zoroastrian theology. Strabo (xv, iii, 13) explicitly identifies Mithra as the sun-god.

Mithra was for long held in high esteem in Persia, as is evidenced by the many princes and potentates who bore names compounded of his and of which Mithridates is best known.

Xenophon (Cyr. vii, 5, 53) has Cyrus the Younger swear by Mithra, and his perennial youth and invincible heroism commended him to the martial mind. Thus the Mithraic cult spread westwards with Persian conquests so that the god was firmly established as a patron of the Roman legions until his final vanquishment towards the end of the fourth century A.D. by a triumphant Christianity.

7 The Parthians, a nomadic people and supposedly of Scythian origin, took their name from the former Achaemenid province of Parthava which corresponded roughly with present-day Khurasan. To what extent their name is etymologically associated with Parsa and Pathan is a point still under debate by competent scholars and cannot be resolved here, and the situation is further complicated by the fusion of the Parthians with the more settled Parni people of the same region, members of the Hyrcanian Dahae.

8 *Itaque indici in homines superbe delirantes, carnales nimis et loquaces* (*Confessionum*, iii, 6). Much of St. Augustine's Confessions are devoted to a retrospective wrestling with the Manichees who had corrupted him in his early life and on whose 'glorious phantasies . . . I fell to and fed.'

9 *Qizilbash* is a Turkish name given to the seven Turkoman tribes settled in Azerbaijan who adhered to the Shi'a shaikhs of Ardebil and who conferred that support upon Isma'il when he claimed the Persian throne. This nickname, 'Redheads', derives from the red turban worn as their distinctive head-dress. One of these seven tribes was that of the Qajars who will again be noticed below (page 17).

10 *Sunni* take their name from *sunna* which, in this context, means the custom of the Islamic community, following the usage established by the Prophet himself. It therefore implies consensus of theological opinion and thence a form of religious discipline and standard of conduct. *Ahl as-sunna wa'l jama'a*, the people of the *sunna* and of the community, those

who from the corpus of 'catholic' and conformist Muslims, are thus designated Sunni or Sunnites.

Shiʿa, on the other hand, derive their name from *shiʿat ʿAli*, the party of 'Ali, and thus they are sometimes referred to as 'partisans'. Shiʿism began with a political bias among the Arabs who looked to ʿAli, the cousin and son-in-law of Muhammad, and to his descendants for leadership. Gradually, this political aspiration created for itself a doctrinal basis of which the most important element is the doctrine of the Imamate, whereby the sinless Imam is a divinely appointed ruler and teacher of the faithful, heir and successor to the Prophet himself, a belief exalted into an additional 'pillar of Islam'. This goes far beyond the Sunni concept of the Caliph as head of the community, elective, and without claim to spiritual absolutism.

This theme is more fully developed in Chapter 4.

TWO

The Caspian Gates

His women and covered wagons and such other gear as he still had with him he sent to the pass known as the Caspian Gates.

Arrian: Life of Alexander the Great, III, 19

The exact situation of this historic opening within the compass of the Elburz mountains has long been in dispute among travellers and scholars, so a fresh review of the evidence is not untimely.

The Greeks, as usual, had a word for it and it was long ago latinized in various ways. Strabo, amongst other ancient writers, refers frequently in his *Geography* to the Caspian Gates as the datum point for establishing distances throughout the Persian Empire, and two of his references are interesting if by no means conclusive. 'The distance from the Caspian Gates to Rhagae [Rayy]', he states, 'is five hundred stadia, as Apollodorus says, and to Hecatompylus, the royal seat of the Parthians, one thousand two hundred and sixty' (xi, 9, i). Next, he observes, quoting Eratosthenes, that 'as far as Alexandreia in the country of the Arii [i.e. the people of the Herat district] from the Caspian Gates through the country of the Parthians, there is one and the same road' (xv, 2, 8). A further reference is made to the coldness of the mountains about Rhagae and the Gates but, he adds, 'the region below the Caspian Gates, consisting of low-lying hands and hollows, is very fertile and productive of everything but the olive' (xi, 13, 7).

Pliny, in his *Natural History*, is perhaps the most explicit of the ancients in his description of this mountain pass which, as in the case of similar passes in Asia, at a narrow and strategic point had gates, with iron-covered beams, placed so as to command the defile. 'The reason for the name "Gates" is the same as that stated above.' He further writes: 'The range is here pierced by a narrow pass eight miles long, scarcely broad enough for a single line of wagon traffic, the whole of it a work of engineering. It is overhung on either side by crags that look as if they had been exposed to the action of fire, the country over a range of twenty-eight miles being entirely waterless' (vi, 17, 43). He alludes also to liquid salt oozing from the rocks and to the multitude of serpents infesting the pass (ibid.). Continuing, he says: 'Running up to these [Gates] are the Parthian deserts and the Citheni range; and then comes the very agreeable locality, also belonging to Parthia, called Choara. Here are the two Parthian towns, formerly serving for protection against the Medes; Calliope and, on another rock, Issatis; but the actual capital of Parthia, Hecatompylos, is 133 miles from the Gates – so effectively is the Parthian kingdom also shut off by passes. Going out of the Gates one comes at once to the Caspian nation, which extends down to the coast; it is from this people that the pass and the sea obtain their name. On the left there is a mountainous district' (vi, 17, 44). Pliny requires to be quoted at length, since he has frequently been cited in support of conflicting arguments.

Polybius, on the contrary, in his *Histories* is less explicit. 'For outside its [Media's] eastern border', he observes, 'it has the desert plain that separates Persia from Parthia; it overlooks and commands the so-called Caspian Gates, and reaches as far as the mountains of the Tapyri, which are not far distant from the Hyrcanian sea' (v, 44, 5), whilst Ptolemy is no more helpful in stating that 'Areia lies under the same parallel as the Caspian Gates' (*Geographia* i, 12). Diodorus Siculus alludes to 'Persis and Susiana and Caspiana, as it is called, which is entered by exceedingly narrow passes, known for that reason as the Caspian Gates' (ii, 2, 3); Isidorus of Charax makes a fleeting reference to the Caspian mountains and gates,[1] whilst tantalizingly Dionysius Periegetes wrote in Greek hexameters of the Caspian Gates, where the way extends to the north and springs from the south (*Geographia* xxvii, 875–9).

We must turn then to Arrian for the next major reference in ancient times. In his pursuit of the fugitive Darius, Alexander marched from Ecbatana to Rhagae, but 'so rapid was the march that many of the men, unable to stand the pace, dropped out, and a number of horses were worked to death; but Alexander pressed on regardless of loss, and in eleven days reached Rhagae, a day's march – at this speed – from the Caspian Gates. Darius, however, had already passed through' (*Anabasis* iii, 20, 2). It has been estimated by Tarn[2] that this rate of marching averaged 36 miles a day, the significance of which will be considered later. After a five day's march he halted close to the Caspian Gates; on the second day he passed through, and advanced to the limit of the cultivated land' (*Anab*, iii, 20, 4). Arrian further informs us that on his last spurt to overtake the Achaemenid, Alexander advanced fifty miles without a halt, only to find Darius murdered (*Anab*. iii, 21, 9).

From the earlier accounts it is now appropriate to turn to later travellers and authorities, beginning with Pietro della Valle. This peripatetic Roman was on the scene in 1618, having crossed the *kavir* from the Siah Kuh by Shah Abbas's *sangfarsh*, the stone causeway at that time under construction and overlying an earlier caravan track, stopping at Reskmé [Rishmeh] and thence to Mahallé Bagh [Aradan]. From the latter village he entered the mountains northwards 'by way of a deep and narrow valley . . . and in parts the passage is so narrow where the road winds that one could scarcely get through it with a litter'. A stream running along the track was bitter to the taste, 'which quality, on examination, I discovered to proceed from one of its currents of supply running over a vein of salt as it winded along'.[3] Proceeding further along the incised valley of the Hableh Rud he reached the village of Firuzkuh, and from that point he progressed towards the Caspian shore.

Nine years later, Sir Thomas Herbert traversed that identical route and accorded it his usual entertaining description. The entrance to the valley of the Hableh Rud, quoting ancient sources, he unhesitatingly and at some length identifies with the Caspian Gates and 'this narrow strait is not more than forty yards broad, and eight miles long, but the mountain on either side is precipitous; and so high, as it is much above what an arrow could reach at twice the shooting were it possible to begin the second where the first shot ended'.[4] He too passed on through Firuzkuh on his way to Ashraf on the Caspian. There is indeed a remarkable accord between the descriptions of these two seventeenth-century travellers and that of Pliny, if snakes be excluded.

Two centuries afterwards came Morier who, after drawing the wrong conclusion about the course of the Nim Rud, ventured the opinion that the *Pylae Caspiae* coincided with the Tang-i-Sar-i-Darreh, a narrow defile running roughly east and west between the Kuh-i-Surkh, a rocky southern outcrof of the Elburz, and the main mountain range. His conclusion is based on the fact that the western end is not more than forty miles (a day's march by Macedonian standards) from Rayy, that there is an abundance of salt streams and otherwise general aridity, as mentioned by Pliny, and lastly that it lies on the main highway to Khurasan.[5]

25

A contemporary of Morier was Ouseley, who gave the matter careful consideration in his compendious work on Eastern travel. This scholarly adventurer was of the opinion that the remarkable strait through which both della Valle and Herbert had progressed, that of the Hableh Rud, agrees better with Pliny's account of the Gates than any other defile in the vicinity, and moreover that Alexander's camp was at or near the halting place of these two earlier voyagers before they severally entered the defile, that is, at Mahalleh-i-bagh or Aradan. 'Now I should expect to find', he adds, 'the southern entrance of that strait through which Alexander passed, whether its northern outlet be at Gilard, Serbandan or Firuzkuh; and as Arrian places the Macedonian camp close to the *Pylae Caspiae*, it seems probable that the southern entrance, more particularly, bore this name among the Greeks and Romans, who adopted it as a central point of measurement in their Asiatic itineraries.'[6]

A few years later came Fraser, and he appraised the respective merits of the Hableh Rud valley and the Sar-i-Darreh; whilst he is disposed to favour the latter as more nearly coinciding with Arrian's account, yet he cautiously suggests that the name of the Gates may have lent itself to both passes. 'It is also possible', he argues, 'and the suspicion has more than once occurred to me, that some confusion may have arisen in the historian's mind, where two remarkable defiles, situated so near to each other, were in question.'[7] Next followed Burnes, who concluded that the pass of Guduk above Firuzkuh must have been the site of the Gates, though this lies some ninety miles from Rayy, a full two days' march by even Alexander's best standards.[8]

Ferrier, the itinerant French soldier of fortune, passed through the Sar-i-Darreh in 1845 and concluded that it was none other than the famous Gates, while he offered the interesting observation that Rhagae, in earlier times, extended as far as the present villages of Khatunabad and Hisar Amir, both of which lie some 25 miles in a south-easterly direction from Rayy; if this were so, then Alexander's march to this pass would have been considerably shortened.[9] Subsequently Eastwick appeared on the scene, lending his concurrence[10] to Ferrier, while not long afterwards came Napier, who placed the Gates at the Tang-i-Shamsherbur to the north of Damghan, an erroneous assumption in almost all respects.[11] Finally, there is Curzon, who gave this matter his customary searching review, but even he, the deliverer of sound judgements, temporizes upon this issue, suggesting that there might be more than one claimant to the title and that Pliny's gates may not necessarily have been the same as those through which Darius and Alexander repeatedly passed.[12]

Others have vicariously turned their attention to this matter. Rennell defines the Gates as being 'the Strait or Passage of Khowar' and by implication the Sar-i-Darreh,[13] whilst Wheeler favours 'a strong and narrow strait . . . so called because it led through the Caspian mountains, now called the Elburz, down to the sea',[14] and he finds support for his argument in D'Anville.[15] George Rawlinson opts for the Sar-i-Darreh, stating in agreement with Ferrier that ancient Rhagae must have been considerably to the east of modern Rayy and probably was the present Kaleh Erij near Veramin; in support he calls upon his illustrious brother Henry to comment that 'in Erij we have probably a corruption of Rhag-es'.[16] Stahl, who more recently reviewed the whole question, comes to a conclusion similar to Curzon's in that possibly more than one defile bore the name of the Caspian Gates, yet he holds that the pass referred to by Arrian and through which Alexander travelled was the Sar-i-Darreh or perhaps even its northerly neighbour the Sialek defile.[17]

Obviously some sort of synthesis of ancient and modern should now be attempted. The name itself requires consideration, and Pliny, for instance, states that it was from the Caspian people that the pass and the sea obtain their name; Isidorus of Charax refers to the mountain called Caspius, from which, he says, is derived *Caspiae Portae*, whilst a modern authority on old Iran expresses the opinion that 'Caspian' may preserve the memory of the ancient Kassites, the *Kassaioi* of Strabo.[18] It would appear, then, that the name Caspian refers both to the sea and to the mountains extending along its southern littoral, and in consequence it is to be expected that a pass bearing that name would be directly connected with the hills and the sea of the Caspii.

Then it is important to note that the Gates represented a fixed geographical position from which distances were measured, though Ibn Khaldun, fourteen centuries after Strabo, referred generally to 'the country of the Gates',[19] perhaps in accord with Polybius. There is also the marked concurrence already noted between Strabo and Pliny concerning the distance of the Gates from Hecatompylos (though both may have been relying upon Apollodorus), and if that distance is accepted from Damghan, near the site of the Parthian capital, then it brings us to the point where the Hableh Rud emerges from the mountains on to the plain of Khuar below. From this position to Rayy, passing through the defile of the Sar-i-Darreh north of the Kuh-i-

Surkh near Aivaneki, is approximately 55 miles, corresponding with Strabo's 500 stadia from Rhagae.

The strategic position of these early 'gates' also merits attention, since they were primarily defensive posts commanding routes along which armies and caravans must march. The Sar-i-Darreh is indeed such a defile through which runs a track at the present day, but it by no means commands the highway leading from Rayy to Khurasan, for it is possible to pass under the southern foot of the Kuh-i-Surkh along a narrow strip skirting the edge of the Kavir, a passage which by no means possesses the narrow defensive quality of a defile and along which today run both railway and road to Veramin and Tehran. On the other hand, the valleys of the Hableh and Talar rivers afford a natural and ancient thoroughfare linking the shores of the Caspian with the plains of the plateau and along this course, especially at the point where mountain meets plain, a strong commanding position could be established. This indicates that consideration should be given to whether the Gates did, in fact, command a north-south route, between sea and plain, or an east-west route, between Media and Parthia. Dionysius, as already noted, stresses the former quality, but from other ancient sources deductions must be made; Strabo, for instance, refers to the low-lying terrain below the Caspian Gates, thereby suggesting a pass leading into uplands.

Pliny further has told us that the Gates represent a sudden break in the chain of mountains which implies a northerly course. The narrowness of the pass for a distance of eight miles is in broad agreement with the entrance to the Hableh Rud, though his statement concerning the tract of waterless country requires consideration. Obviously he is not here referring to the pass itself, through which the river courses, so presumably he means the stretch of highway leading from Media to this entrance and this approximates the distance between the Zam Rud and the Hableh Rud. Pliny's later reference to the Gates being bounded at one end by the Parthian deserts and Choara (Khuar) is capable of being interpreted as the land to the south and east of the entrance to the Hableh Rud.

Turning once more to Arrian, we learn that over a period of eleven days Alexander averaged 36 miles, whilst his final dash to the dying Darius covered 50 miles. If an allowance of 40 miles is made for the Macedonian's first stage east of Rayy then that would bring him to the banks of the Zam Rud and a prudent watering place 'close to the Caspian Gates'. On the second day, we are informed, Alexander passed through the Gates and reached the limit of cultivated land,

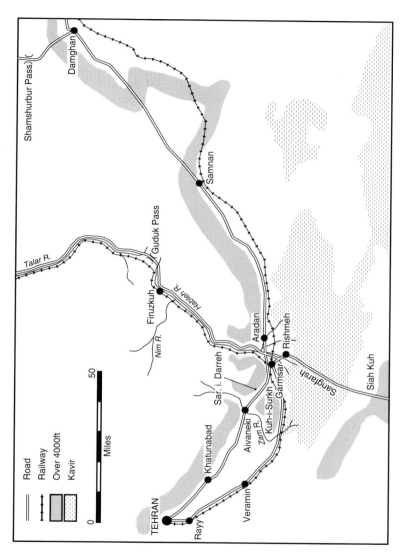

Figure 3 Map of the Caspian Gates

which would have taken him beyond Aradan where the cultivations of the district of Khuar peter out in the face of the desert. There is not the slightest evidence that either Darius or Alexander turned northwards at this stage, an easterly advance towards Hecatompylos being maintained.

Strabo has stated that the way from Rhagae to Hecatompylos and beyond to the land of the Arii was one and the same, whilst Hamd Allah Mustaufi, writing in the early fourteenth century,[20] gives us the itinerary of the 'great eastern highroad' from Rayy to Khurasan, which agrees with the route probably taken by Darius and Alexander, passing through Khuar-i-Rayy, otherwise Mahalleh-i-bagh or Aradan, this district being unquestionably the Choara of Pliny.

It must be allowed that the early evidence is vague, admitting of more than one interpretation. The Sar-i-Darreh lies some twenty miles westwards of the entrance to the valley of the Hableh Rud, and this intervening space within the district of Khuar was of necessity a crossroads for traffic proceeding between Media and Parthia and thus avoiding the desert to the south, and for traffic proceeding northwards to the Caspian or southwards over the less frequented caravan route to distant desert cities. Through this relatively fertile and watered plain travellers must pass to achieve their further object. Whether the Gates which Arrian had in mind conformed precisely with those of Pliny, or whether there was confusion between the two defiles amongst antique minds as well as those of more recent years, is a matter which cannot here be resolved, nor are the limits of early Rhagae capable of precise definition to accommodate the stadia given.

What does seem conclusive, however, is that a point established in the ancient world for measurement of distances should undoubtedly have had a fixed geographical identity, and this would obviously refer to the only effective and consequential crossroads in the dominating position situated near the exit of the Hableh Rud, a point of refreshment as well, if one considers the aridity of the terrain extending in most directions from it.

Notes

1 C. Müller (ed.), *Geographi Graeci Minores* (Paris, 1855–61), ii, 168.
2 W.W. Tarn, *Alexander the Great* (Cambridge, 1948), i, 56.
3 J. Pinkerton (ed.), *A General Collection of the Best Voyages, etc.* (London, 1808–14), ix, 45.
4 Sir Thomas Herbert, *Some Yeares Travels, etc.* (London, 1664), 179–82.

5 J. Morier, *A Second Journey through Persia, etc.* (London, 1818), 362–6.
6 Sir William Ouseley, *Travels in Various Countries of the East, etc.* (London, 1823) iii, 550.
7 J.B. Fraser, *Narrative of a Journey into Khoransan* (London, 1825), 293.
8 A. Burnes, *Travels into Bokhara* (London, 1834), ii, 130.
9 J.P. Ferrier, *Caravan Journeys and Wanderings in Persia* (London, 1856), 59–60.
10 E.B. Eastwick, *Journal of a Diplomate's Three Years, etc.* (London, 1864), ii, 139.
11 G.C. Napier, 'Extracts from a Diary of a Tour in Khorassan', *Journ. R.G.S.* xlvi (1876), 70–1.
12 G.N. Curzon, *Persia and the Persian Question* (London, 1892), i, 293–7.
13 J. Rennell, *The Geographical System of Herodotus* (London, 1830), i, 229.
14 J.T. Wheeler, *The Geography of Herodotus* (London, 1854), 291.
15 J.B.B. D'Anville, *Compendium of Ancient Geography* (London, 1810), ii, 26.
16 G. Rawlinson, *The Five Great Monarchies of the Ancient World* (London, 1879), ii, 273.
17 A.F. v. Stahl, 'Notes on the March of Alexander the Great from Ecbatana to Hyrcania', *Geog. Journ.* xlvi (1924), 318.
18 R. Ghirshman, *Iran* (Harmondsworth, 1954), 65.
19 Ibn Khaldun, *The Muqaddimah* (London, 1958), I, 155.
20 G. Le Strange, *Mesopotamia and Persia under the Mongols, etc.* (London, 1903), 102.

THREE

Persian Influences in Mughal India

Agar firdaus bar ruyi zamin ast,
Hamin ast, hamin ast, hamin ast!

If there is a paradise on Earth,
It is this, it is this, it is this!

Persian couplet in the Diwan-i-Khas, Delhi

Throughout most of historical times Persia and India have been no strangers to each other; they were certainly mutually acquainted during the Achaemenid period, for Darius the Great caused to be inscribed at Bisitun and elsewhere in letters extant today that amongst the many countries under his sway was Gandhara, which then incorporated the western Punjab and the upper Indus valley, a region with which he was personally acquainted during his eastern campaigns at the beginning of the sixth century B.C., utilizing furthermore the services of Scylax the Greek to investigate that great river to its very mouth. Herodotus has certain things to say about India,[1] mainly concerning its people, its natural history, and its climate, so that during the fifth century B.C. India was already in danger of becoming documented, whilst in the following century Alexander led his Greeks to conquer the lands which extended eastwards to the Indus valley. During all these and subsequent incursions from the west, whether from Susa, Ecbatana, Macedonia, or Hellas, or via the ancient Gulf route, Persia was the inevitable link, affording a right-of-way for the passage of men and ideas, and in the process making her own contribution to the Indian world, whilst inevitably bringing back some influences in reciprocity.

In the course of almost two millennia to follow, India became increasingly known to her occidental neighbours, but it would be inappropriate here to relate the names of travellers from the western world who journeyed into India, usually with a percipient eye, to record what they had observed as they penetrated more deeply into the subcontinent to the farther shores of Bengal. Nor would it be appropriate to trace the whole course of Islamic infiltration into India from Transoxiana, from Persia, and from Arab lands, affording an impetus for fresh adventurers to invade and then establish their various regimes and dynasties in the centuries preceding Babur. These invaders, these infiltrators brought with them, it is true, the language and literature of Persia even if they were not Persians themselves, for Persian had become the civilizing medium of the hither East and thereby was borne along with the stream of ideas which were to affect so profoundly the course of Indian history. Of these early Muslim newcomers, those from Transoxiana and of Turkish stock were the most consequential, despite the previous Arab conquest and subsequent retreat from Sind; Mahmud of Ghazni, for instance, patron of Firdausi and Albiruni, was merely following in the footsteps of Archaemenids, Seleucids, and Sassanids in launching a fresh wave of Persian graces and civilization to which the Turkmans and Mongols had themselves succumbed. Sufficient evidence remains of their Persianized importations, cultural and architectural, to substantiate a pioneering claim which, once admitted, may be relegated to a position subordinate to the major theme, namely, the consideration of direct Persian influence in Mughal India from the advent of Babur to the death of Aurangzeb.

Concerning this later surge of cultural invasion and influence, the following passage of Lane-Poole comes to mind and will serve as an introduction to the argument. Babur, first of the Mughals, he states, 'is the link between Central Asia and India, between predatory hordes and imperial government, between Timur and Akbar. The blood of the two scourges of Asia, Mongol and Turk, Chingiz and Timur, mixed in his veins, and to the daring and restlessness of the nomad Tatar he joined the culture and urbanity of the Persian.'[2] Of this great spearhead of the Mughal dynasty he further observes that 'in Persian, the language of culture, the Latin of Central Asia, as it is of India, he was an accomplished poet',[3] for he had steeped himself thoroughly in the charms and refinements of Persia's legacy.

This vital link of Babur's may be said to have a twofold significance: it drew not only Persian-speaking Asia to India to achieve a new harmony of literature and the visible arts, but it joined also the earlier Indo-Islamic past to the more recent Timurid revival,

the whole union flowering into that luxuriant growth epitomized in
Mughal India.

During at least five centuries prior to the advent of Babur, India
had steadily been receiving a stream of immigrants from the west, and
these had brought with them fresh ideas, a new tongue, and a virile
religion, all instruments of persuasion and conversion. Such foreign
adventurers were chiefly either Turani (Turkic) or Irani (Persian), that
is to say, the former were Sunnis from the north-west, the latter Shi'a
and emanating often from Shiraz, comprising physicians, poets,
lawyers, and a professional class generally.[4] Their motives for
migrating eastwards varied according to time and place; the Mongol
invasions of these Muslim countries undoubtedly caused many to flee
in the direction of the comparative safety of the lands beyond the
Indus, others may have been lured by the accounts by travellers and
compatriots of once fabulous lands, whilst a persistent flow was
maintained by men of all professions who at sundry times found their
efforts producing little reward in their own countries, and who
thereupon travelled in search of more sympathetic patrons of their
talents and skills.

Persia had contributed largely to the last group and this tendency
had not been abated during the national resurgence of the Safavids; it
is interesting to observe that a mere quarter of a century separated
Isma'il's victory in Persia from Babur's later conquest of the India of
the Lodi dynasty. The Safavid period is perhaps the most brilliant in
the history of Islamic Persia, yet it is not to that dynasty that one turns
for appreciation of its men of letters but rather to contemporaneous
India, where the Mughal Court was adorned by a brilliant group of
Persians, in many cases neither settlers nor the sons of immigrants, but
those who had gone forth from Persia to enhance their fortunes and
then sometimes to return homewards when that object had been
accomplished. It has rightly been adduced from this that lack of
patronage rather than lack of talent had so markedly diminished the
literary scene in Persia; the Safavid loss was clearly a Mughal gain.[5]
Of this peaceful Persian invasion it is said that 'after Babur's time the
Musulman courts had many close family connections with Persia, and
in the seventeenth century Persian fashions were as much in vogue
with the Mogul aristocracy as Italian fashions were in France and
England'.[6] Of the many Persians who were eminent at the Mughal
Court it will suffice here to mention Hakim Abu'l Fath, foreign
minister of Akbar, Asaf Khan, prime minister of Jahangir, Shah Jahan,
'Ali Mardan, and Amir Khan, wardens of the marches, and Ruhullah

Khan, finance minister of Aurangzeb; and by such an agency the Mughal bureaucracy derived its system from that borrowed by Akbar from Persia, military in character and alien to Hindu tradition.

It is appropriate, in these circumstances, to consider first of all this revived and reinforced impact of Persian language and literature upon the Indian scene, for where language precedes other influences readily follow, as all imperial movements and aggrandisements have shown in the long course of history. Quoting from original sources, mainly Shibli Nu'mani, al-Badaoni, and those quoted in Sprenger, E.G. Browne produces the information that about 170 Persian poets had established themselves in India during the fifteenth and sixteenth centuries, fifty-one of whom arrived from Persia during Akbar's time, so that 'Ali-quli Salim is constrained to say:

> There exist not in Persia the means of acquiring perfection;
> Henna does not develop its colour until it comes to India.

thereby echoing Sa'ib who says:

> There is no head wherein desire for thee danceth not,
> Even as the determination to visit India is in every heart.[7]

Al-Badaoni devotes himself extensively to an exemplary review of the luminaries of Akbar's Court who wrote in Persian and who were mainly of Persian birth; when the poets, philosophers, religious teachers, and physicians are counted their numbers total almost three hundred,[8] a staggering enough figure by any standard, yet such was Akbar's empiricism that he must also have commanded a further formidable body of men learned in venacular tongues and of religious beliefs other than Islam.

Of Babur's own proficiency in Persian as well as in his native Turki there is no possible doubt, and it is said that he esteemed Jami above all other poets.[9] Akbar's literary credentials are open to some suspicion in that it has not been definitely established whether he was literate or not, but his appreciation of poetry is beyond question, for his great pleasure lay in having it read aloud to him and in commending to his memory Hafiz and Rumi, two great exponents of the school of Persian Sufism. Akbar's mother was Persian as was the celebrated Nur Jahan, wife of Jahangir, while young Mughal princes were brought up to read and write in both Persian and Arabic as part of their formal education. We learn, too, that Jahangir was disposed to bestow upon his sons Persian names: Khusrau, Khurram, Jahandar, Shahryar, and Hoshang, and this too must be indicative of Court trends at that time. It is hardly occasion for surprise, therefore, to discern an atmosphere highly favourable for the burgeoning of Persian influence and manners which permeated the Court and then, of necessity throughout the whole cultivated strata of Mughal society.

In the realm of philosophy and theology Muslim India was undeveloped; little original thought had emerged since Islam had not yet established itself on Indian soil; thus it had to borrow from Muslim sources further afield. There was therefore this profound difference between Persia and India: the former from the time of the Muslim conquest had been vested in the new religion, refashioning the garment to suit Persian shape and taste so that Shi'a theology and Sufi mysticism grew and flourished in that genial climate, Shi'ism being almost indigenous whilst Sufism was transplanted to blossom anew. There too Arabic studies and contributions were profound, scholarship was unquestionable, whilst deep down ran the undercurrent of earlier religious lore, so that the mysteries of ancient Khurasan flowed beneath the upper stream of the newer philosophy of Mesopotamia and Arabia. In India no parallel situation existed; the Muslims were foreigners in a strange and alien land, so in seeking their inspiration from the west they deprived themselves of initiative to devise and develop their own system and school of thought. The result is that, in the main, Indian Islam was but a mirroring of images from Persia and Arabic countries, devoid of originality and new concepts.

It is of interest to note that whilst the Mughal emperors were of Sunni persuasion, despite Akbar's religious flirtations and Humayun's Shi'a duress at the Safavid Court of Shah Tahmasp, the Deccani kingdoms were not only Shi'a but included the name of the Persian Shah in their *khutba* whereby they acknowledged his suzerainty, and it was not until the seventeenth century had progressed that Shah Jahan and Aurangzeb succeeded in effecting the compliance of these petty monarchs in acknowledging the Mughal emperor and in disavowing both Shi'a doctrine and the name of the Shah.[10] This is in marked contrast to Babur's earlier attitude a century or more before when, in gratitude to Shah Isma'il for his assistance in Babur's struggle against the Chagtai chiefs of Transoxiana, he put on the *Taj* or Persian head-dress, recited the *khutba* in the Shah's honour, and inserted the names of the twelve Shi'a imams on his coins, for in this respect Babur was echoing the Timurid tolerance of Shi'a doctrine which, in the case of Sultan Husain ibn Bayqara of Herat, occasionally manifested itself as an open declaration of that creed.[11] It was Babur who counselled Humayun to be tolerant in religious matters, saying wisely: 'Overlook

37

Figure 4 Dervishes Dancing in the Courtyard of a Mosque in the
Presence of Jahangir and his Suite
(Mughal School, Mid-17th Century)

the difference between the Sunnis and the Shi'as, otherwise the decrepitude of Islam would inevitably follow', to which he added, in this admonition called *Wasiyat Nama-i-Maklifi*, 'Cleanse the tablet of your heart of religious bigotry and administer justice in accordance with the prescribed manner of every community',[12] and in the subsequent departure from this sage advice has been proved its inherent truth.

This friendly disposition on the part of Babur had its roots in Shah Isma'il's routing of Shaibani Khan's Uzbeks, amongst whose captive host was Babur's sister Khanzada Begam, who was treated with due ceremony and restored to her brother's care; thus was established a cordial intercourse between Safavid and Mughal which was pregnant with future significance, especially for India. It was consolidated later by Humayun during his exile, whose tolerance became manifest in the inscription he caused to be made in the shrine of Ahmad-i-Jam, ancestor of Hamida Begam the wife of Humayun and mother of Akbar, at Turbat-i-Shaikh Jam in Khurasan:

O Thou, whose mercy accepts the apology of all,
The mind of everyone is exposed to Thy Majesty.
The threshold of Thy gate is the *qibla* of all peoples,
Thy bounty with a glance supports everyone.
A wanderer in the desert of destitution
Muhammad Humayun (A.D. 1544)

In this cultural resurgence science was not overlooked, for we read that Akbar issued a new command whereby all people should give up the 'Arabic Sciences' and should study only those really useful, namely, astronomy, mathematics, medicine, and philosophy, and since surgery was abhorrent to Hindus, the new skills of Persian and Arabic medicine were practised by those of like persuasion. The number of hospitals established between the reigns of Akbar and Aurangzeb was considerable, especially when it is recollected that few previously existed, whilst various systems and schools of medicine were practised.[13]

Akbar was zealous in furthering the education of his subjects, and to that end he encouraged literacy and understanding by reading. Writing of the imperial capital al-Badaoni remarks that there was 'no street or market in which the booksellers do not stand at roadsides selling copies of the *divans* of those two poets Urfi or Shiraz and Husain Sana'i, and both Persians and Indians buy them';[14] thus it would seem that books in Persian far outnumbered those in Sanskrit.

Of equal importance to the new-found industry of bookselling was the foundation of libraries at royal bequest, by no means exclusively for the Court use but also for research by scholars, teachers, and students. These imperial libraries were established at Agra, Delhi, and elsewhere, and the Spanish priest Fr. Sebastian Manrique who was in Agra in 1641 records that the library in that city contained 24,000 volumes.[15] Al-Badaoni amusingly tells of the diligence of royal librarians in seeking out defaulting subscribers, striking a familiar note today, for 'on account of the book *Khirad-afza*, which had disappeared from the Library . . . an order was issued that my *madad-ma'ash* should be stopped, and that they should demand the book of me *nolens volens*'.[16]

Such literary activity, in the days before the printing press was known in India, demanded skill in calligraphy, and this was not wanting. So much of the work was in Persian that the quill employed was styled *qalam-i-Irani*. It would be improper to suggest that this cursive art had been introduced by the Mughals, for that is not so; calligraphy had flourished in India from the earliest period of Muslim incursions, but it was not, however, until the Mughal period that it reached its highest state of development in India, and this, without question, was due to the patronage afforded by the Mughal emperors to immigrant Persian calligraphists who in turn influenced Indians – Muslims and Hindus – towards a proficiency in the art.[17]

It would also be incorrect to assume that literary influences at this period were all one way; a process of give and take applied, so that Sanskrit and Indian vernacular works were translated into Persian, thereby opening up new and wider horizons to the greater edification of Persian savants. Albiruni's *Tarikh al Hind* was an early compendium of Hindu studies; the *Mahabharata* was rendered into Persian by Abu Saleh bin Shuaib and Abu Hasan 'Ali, and again by al-Badaoni who further was entrusted by Akbar with a translation of *Simhasana Dvatriansat*; the *Ramayana* and the *Upanishads*, the *Puranas*, the *Bhagavad Gita* and other standard works were likewise translated into Persian. Further, the indigenous languages could not remain unaffected by this reciprocity, so that Persian words were welcomed within the fold of Punjabi, Bengali, Hindi, and other north Indian tongues, thereby enriching their vocabularies, and entire Persian and Arabic works were translated into Sanskrit and Hindi.

In the vicinity of the Court at Delhi there grew up a new language, a fusion of Hindi grammar and Persian vocabulary, and thus it was that the new *urdu* afforded a fresh medium for the transmission of ideas and idioms into the life of the northern plains and into the Deccan; with this new vehicle for expression and communication arrived new works and new authors, so that *Urdu* came eventually to stand as a language and repository of a literature in its own right. So, either directly from the older language of the conqueror or indirectly through the newer vernacular of the camp, Persian infiltrated into the literature and the common languages of the people, influencing them beyond conceivable measure and leaving its impress there until the present day.

Before proceeding to discuss the visual arts and architecture it is convenient to consider some of the less spectacular influences which owed their inception in India to the Court of the Mughals.

Concerning *chaugan* or polo, Abu'l Fazl 'Allami tells us that 'His Majesty [Akbar] is very fond of this game. Externally, the game adds to the splendour of the Court; but viewed from a higher point, it reveals concealed talents',[18] whilst of other sports and pastimes introduced during Akbar's reign it is as interesting as it is instructive to quote Abu'l Fazl further: 'The games of hockey [properly polo] and wolf-running for which Tabriz was famous, but which had been interdicted on account of riots, were revived by the Shah's orders for his Majesty's delectation',[19] and of Akbar's favourite sport of *ishqbazi* or pigeon-flying he adds, 'This occupation affords the ordinary run of people a dull kind of amusement; but his Majesty, in his wisdom, makes it a study. . . . Presents of pigeons are sent by the kings of Iran and Turan.'[20] Al-Badaoni confirms these sporting tendencies in even more concise terms.[21] Indoors, backgammon or *nard* was commonly played, and this pastime, known to Persians at a later date as *takht-i-Nadir Shah*, was, according to Ferishta, invented by Buzurj Mihr, minister of Nushirwan.[22]

No evidence exists to indicate that nose ornaments or *nath* were in use in pre-Mughal times, and it seems evident, from early miniature paintings, that their introduction into India followed but slowly the advance of the invader; perhaps it was not until the new imperial regime was soundly established that this form of ornament became more widely used.[23] In itself, this small and even trifling contribution is seemingly without significance, yet when it is recalled that these nose decorations are held in high esteem by the Indian masses today, it is salutary to reflect that a common Hindu practice owes its inception to an alien intrusion from a Muslim land.

It is perhaps almost unnecessary to recall that during the reigns of the first four Mughals diplomatic relations between India and Persia were close and cordial, despite their clash of interests over Kandahar, which city changed hands with remarkable frequency in accordance with the ascendancy now of Persia and then of India. Persian diplomatic intercourse with India was, of course, no new thing, for we read of embassies despatched to the Court of Vijayanagara between 1443 and 1512,[24] during which time more durable contacts were made with Gujerat and the principalities of the Deccan where Persian immigrants and ideas were accorded a ready welcome. Babur's goodwill towards Shah Isma'il has already been mentioned, whilst Tahmasp's hospitality to the exiled Humayun is so familiar that it hardly requires reference other than to observe that this was to have lasting effect in India, as will shortly be noted. The missions exchanged between the two imperial courts from the time of Shah Isma'il render a long catalogue of names, and despite misunderstandings and occasional clashes of interest it was not until the reign of Aurangzeb, that most intolerant of Sunnis, that a rupture occurred only to be healed on that Mughal's death.[25]

It is known that the garden existed in pre-Mughal India, for Firuz Shah is credited with having laid out over a thousand gardens whilst even before his time the Indian garden had existed; yet it is to Babur that we are indebted for the introduction of the *firdaus*, not merely for superficial nomenclature such as *Hasht Behesht, Chihil Situn*, and *Chahar Bagh*, but for the concept and design along typical Persian lines,[26] and we are informed too that the greatest contribution of the Mughals to Indian art was the spacious formal garden laid out by Persian or central Asian gardeners, giving an inception to the richness and beauty of Persian floral design in the decorative arts of India.[27]

Unquestionably, however, when tangible evidence of a flow of influences is sought in any country, pertaining to any era, then this must be looked for amongst the visual remains in the fields of art and architecture, and here the subject is so vast that compression performs scant justice, yet at the risk of *reductio ad absurdum* a brief, if necessarily perfunctory review, must be attempted.

Royal patronage had, as has been observed, a decisive effect in bringing into India both artists and craftsmen as well as scholars and professional men. Bihzad, called the 'Raphael of the East' and the greatest Persian artist of his time, worked under the protection of Sultan Husain ibn Bayqara; two of his most noted pupils and chief artists were Mir Sayyid 'Ali of Tabriz and Khwaja Abdus Samad of Shiraz, both of whom accompanied Humayun to India on his return from exile, forming the nucleus of the Mughal school of painting which flowered during Akbar's reign and again during Jahangir's time. Thus Humayun revived the Indo-Timurid school of painting introduced by his father Babur, infusing new life into Indian art traditions naturalized in China.[28] So, too, we learn, 'in Rajput painting, the geometric composition and sweeping outline, the flatness and simple contrasts of colour, and the chaste romantic atmosphere are all more characteristic of the Iranian than the Hindu tradition'.[29]

It was in miniature painting and portraiture that the greatest emphasis lay, inspiration at first being drawn from the manuscripts in the imperial libraries, and under the supervision of Mir Sayyid 'Ali the illustrations in the folio volumes of *Dastan-i-Amir Hamzeh* were completed, bearing an inescapable Safavid stamp. Thus it was that the earlier paintings have a marked Persian impress, though in the course of time and consequent upon the employment of Indian artists, both Hindu and Muslim, many of whom were recruited by Akbar from Gujarat, a newer style was achieved wherein the two elements were harmoniously blended.[30] Persian conventions of landscape and their delight in the beauties of nature, of animals and birds, were thus taken over and integrated into a less formalistic native tradition to the enrichment of both traditions until, under Jahangir, Mughal painting reached its zenith, the earlier stiff formality yielding to spontaneity and freshness, the subjects drawn from life rather than from the more circumscribed manuscripts.[31]

Since the days of the Ghaznavids northern India under Muslim rule had been constrained to develop an architectural style which, though exhibiting a degree of independence, nevertheless owed its inspiration to influences from the north-west, and Safavid Persia later left its notable mark upon the buildings of Lahore and other cities of the Punjab. This was virtually a renewal of contacts made during pre-Islamic Iran as far back as the times of the Achaemenids, and in the audience halls of the Mughals may be detected more than a chance resemblance to the *apadanas* of the ancient Medes and Persians. The Timurids in this respect as well as others were successors to the Ghaznavids, and thus it is seen that a constant flow of cultural stimuli washed the northern plains of India, watering the ground for Babur's successors and nourishing that soil from which the Mughals were to reap so rich a harvest.

Since Havell, improved knowledge and a more extensive survey of the architecture of India and the countries to the north and west have opened up new vistas and presented new proportions. Without doubt India is indebted to Persia for the structural concept of the dome (possibly in return for the Persian borrowing of the pointed arch), which had been brought to its final state on the Iranian plateau before being transported eastwards; thus the Imamzadeh Yahia at Varamin is considered to be the precursor of the dome of the mosque in the Purana Qila at Delhi, whilst the somewhat bulbous double dome exemplified in Timurid Samarkand was later introduced into early Mughal buildings, and so examples of the bulbous dome in India are evidently of a date anterior to that of the *madrasseh* of Mahmud Gawar at Bidur in the Deccan, *c.* 1472. The designer of the dome of the Taj Mahal was Isma'il Khan Rumi, probably of Turkish origin, whilst Ustad Isa from Persia was the supervising architect for the whole edifice; and despite the unfamiliarity of the white marble material it is unmistakably Persian, deriving partly from the nationality of its designers and again from familiar and established precedents in Humayun's tomb and that of Khan Khanan alongside it, thereby translating 'the gay and gaudy Persian taste into the dreamy, languid spirit of later Mughal art'.[32]

'The term "Mogul" as applied to architecture has its drawbacks,' Briggs has observed, 'but the fact remains that the buildings erected under the Mughal emperors were more definitely Muhammadan or "Saracenic" in character than those which preceded them and need to be classified as a separate school.'[33] It is not, in consequence, argued that these celebrated early Mughal buildings are wholly Persian, for that clearly is not so, but the dynamic concept, especially in the dome design and the interior chamber complex, certainly is, whilst indigenous ideas are revealed in the fanciful kiosks and the excellence of the masonry whereby they represent a synthesis of two great building styles.

An argument for the continuing Persian influence in Indian architecture has again been advanced by the example of the tomb of Khan Khanan at Delhi, post 1627, which reveals a return to the earlier Persian style introduced over half a century previously in Humayun's tomb, indicating that even after this period of time the influence was still active. Many arguments have been put forward concerning the style and spirit of Humayun's tomb itself, but no new facts here emerge; it is convenient therefore to restate that, under the auspices of his widow the Hamida Begam, who shared her husband's Persian exile, and under the direction of Mirak Mirza Ghuyas, an architect in the Timurid tradition, it assumed the scale and design of a Persianized prototype in Indo-Muslim architecture which was to serve as the inspiration of many of the buildings of the following two centuries.[34]

Akbar's deserted memorial, Fathepur Sikri, comprehends a variety of styles deriving mainly from earlier Indian origins, and it would be idle to propose that this great Mughal relic depended upon Persian influence, yet an exception must be allowed in the case of the imposing Buland Darwaza, one of the world's largest sacred thresholds. Here is a wholly Persian concept conveying immediately the grand design which characterizes the eminent mosques of Persia and Transoxiana, varying in surface detail only by the employment of an intermingling of marble with red sandstone, a pleasing innovation in a severe and majestic design, a happy blend used later and with great effect elsewhere in India.[35] The great *aivan* ornamented with pendentives or stalactites is one of Persia's great glories, though transferred to India in a more sober and restrained manner.

Prior to Akbar's reign we see a massive example of the acquired style from Humayun in the form of a mosque at Fathabad in the Punjab, embellished with enamelled tiles after the Persian fashion, whilst much farther east at Sahasram in Bengal the contemporary mausoleum of Sher Shah exemplifies the harmony and discipline inherent in the early Indo-Persian style, intermediate between 'the austerity of the Tughlak buildings and the feminine grace of Shah Jahan's masterpiece'.[36] In Sind, as in Gujarat and the Deccan, other interesting evidence is present; tombs and mosques built there during the latter half of the sixteenth century and the early seventeenth century betray an affinity with Persian principles not readily overlooked. One is singled out for special consideration: the tomb of Sharfa Khan near Tatta (1638), so remarkably conforming to the Persian idea in its general design, its fine brickwork, and the blue tiling of the dome that no doubt remains as to the source of its conception.[37]

In other fields, both utilitarian and artistic, the same influences are evident. It could hardly be doubted, for example, that the ornate multi-arched bridge over the Gumti at Jaunpur, built during the latter part of the sixteenth century by Hazara workmen imported from Afghanistan, is of the same school and spirit which inspired those celebrated bridges at Isfahan, whilst in domestic architecture, in gateways, in arcaded bazaars, and in caravanserais, the Persian hand is all too evident. The faience mosaic in the Lahore fort derives directly from a corresponding Persian decoration conceived two centuries earlier, and the use of the word *kashi* for ornamental glazed tile-work reveals its direct antecedent in the ceramic city of Kashan; one of the most celebrated examples of this work is to be seen in the early seventeenth-century tomb of Wazir Khan at Lahore. Chardin has given evidence from his travels that this enamelled pottery was exported from Persia, since at that time none was made in India.[38] Stucco work of the sixteenth and seventeenth centuries in Agra bears a marked resemblance to similar decorations in Isfahan, and a like parallel exists between the lamp niches of the great shrine at Ardabil and those in the 'Ali Qapu at Isfahan, later to be more elaborately repeated in the great forts at Agra and Delhi; the intrusion of Persian floral designs and motifs into arts and crafts has already been noted, and the art of inlaying precious stones has, on good authority, been ascribed to Arab and Persian origins.[39]

It has truly been said that in carpet weaving and other textiles, in painting and in pottery, the Mughals indented largely upon Persia,[40] and all other decorative forms are largely elaborations of these fundamental crafts. Abu'l Fazl tells us that Akbar had more than a hundred *karkhanajat* or workshops of arts and crafts attached to the royal household, a fertile source of inspiration and invention, wherein, as Fr. Monserrate confirmed, were practised 'the finer and more reputable arts, such as painting, goldsmith work, tapestry making, carpet and curtain making, and the manufacture of arms'.[41] In short, we are reliably informed by a distinguished authority, 'Persian contributions in Mogul times to the arts of painting, textile design, carpet weaving and garden planning are decisive. Persian poets, calligraphers, illuminators, designers, weavers, indeed master-craftsmen of all kinds, thronged the courts of Akbar, Humayun, Jahangir and Shah Jahan, and if their work was soon acclimated and later in a certain degree submerged by the density and pressure of the surrounding Hindu culture, it remained an essential element in Indian civilization and at the height of its power was responsible for many masterpieces.'[42]

The Iranian plateau has contributed greatly to the arts and achievements of India throughout historical times, whilst Persia herself has not been slow to receive in return. It was not, however, until the comparatively recent Mughal era that the immigration of men, skills, and, accomplishments reached its full flood into India from the west, borne along on the tide of a conquering dynasty which stayed at the full where its predecessors had receded; the influence was thus more profound and indelible. The Mughal period is therefore the supreme culmination of a process expressing a synthesis of two different forms of genius, Persian and Indian, interplaying to the enrichment of both and the delectation of the world.

That it could not last much beyond Jahangir is due to two interrelated causes, the first and most apparent being the constrained, xenophobic, and bigoted nature of Aurangzeb, whose repressive and puritanical reign discouraged a further flowering of the arts and graces inspired by his illustrious and more tolerant forebears. The second cause stemmed in part from the first, for if Akbar had indeed voiced the sentiment of 'India for the Indians', his great-grandson put it into full effect so that the vital flow from other and hardier lands ceased. It is almost axiomatic that the 'climate' of India is difficult for the foreigner, who tends to 'deteriorate' in this new environment, an argument persuasively developed by a noted Indian writer of our own times[43] and which the Portuguese and the British have themselves discovered. 'The only hope for the Mughal State of a vigorous life lay in the constant immigration of strong and capable men from the north-western hills and the countries beyond the passes . . . and so long as no obstacle was offered to the free immigration of these, and of the more cultured natives of Persia, the Empire flourished and the Mongol stock remained virile and vigorous.'[44] Only when this principle ceased to apply did torpor and atrophy set in, and though the last pitiable scion of a once noble house, Bahadur Shah, was removed from his rickety throne in 1857, the Mughal Empire as a cultured and artistic entity expired with Aurangzeb; to look beyond his reign, or even within it, is to observe the signs of a decadence whereby the whole world became the poorer.

Notes

1 Herodotus, *The History*, trans. G. Rawlinson (London, 1862), *passim*..
2 Lane-Poole, S., *Mediaeval India under Muhammedan Rule* (A.D. 712–1764) (London, 1906), 193.
3 Ibid., 194.
4 Edwardes, S.M., and Garrett, H.L.O., *Mughal Rule in India* (Oxford, 1930), 161.
5 Browne, E.G., *Literary History of Persia* (Cambridge, 1928), iv, 24–5; Abdur Rahim, 'Mughal Relations with India', *Islamic Culture*, viii (1934), 460–1. See also Taraporevala, V.D.B., and Marshall, D.N., *Mughal Bibliography: Select Persian Sources for the Study of Mughals in India* (Bombay, 1962), *passim*.
6 Havell, E.B., *Indian Architecture* (London, 1927), 156.
7 Browne, E.G., op. cit., 164–6.
8 Al-Badaoni, *Muntakhab-ut-Tawarikh*, trans. W. Haig (Calcutta, 1925), iii, *passim*.

9 *Memoirs of Zehir-ed-din Muhammed Babur*, trans. and annotated by Leyden, Erskine, and King (Oxford, 1921), 2 vols., *passim*.
10 *Cambridge History of India* (Cambridge, 1937), iv, 197.
11 Hasan Askari, 'Indo-Persian Relations in the Age of the Great Mughals', *Journ. Bihar Research Soc.*, xl (Dec. 1954), pt. 4, 325.
12 Husain, M., 'Cultural Aspects of Indo-Iranian Relations during the Mughal Period' *Indo-Iranica*, x (1957), iii, 5–6.
13 Al-Badaoni, op. cit., trans. W.H. Lowe (Calcutta, 1884), ii, 375.
14 Ibid, iii, 393.
15 Smith V.A., *A History of Fine Art in India and Ceylon* (Bombay, 1961), 186.
16 Al-Badaoni, op. cit., ii, 389.
17 Khan Bahadur Maulvi Zafar Hasan, 'Muslim Calligraphy', *Indian Art and Letters*, ix (1935), no. 1, 60.
18 Abu'l-Fazl 'Allami, *The 'Ain-i-Akbari*, trans. H. Blochmann (Calcutta, 1927), 309.
19 Abu'l-Fazl 'Allami, *The Akbarnameh*, trans. H. Beveridge (Calcutta, 1898), i, 443–4.
20 *'Ain-i-Akbari*, 310.
21 Al-Badaoni, op. cit., ii, 69.
22 Muhammed Kasim Ferishta, *History of the Rise of the Mahomedan Power in India till the Year* A.D., *1612* (Calcutta and London, 1908), i, 150.
23 Chatterjee, K.N., 'The Use of Nose Ornaments in India', *Journ. and Proc. Asiatic Soc. of Bengal*, xxiii (1927), 290–3.
24 Saletore, B.A., 'A New Persian Embassy to the Vijayanagara Court', *New Indian Antiquary* i (July 1938), no. 4, 229–39.
25 Manucci, N., *Storia do Mogor or Mogul India 1653–1708*, trans. W. Irvine (London, 1907), iv, *passim*.
26 Villers-Stuart, C., 'The Garden in Indian Art', *Indian Art and Letters* xxi (1947), no. 2, 71.
27 Havell, *Indian Architecture*, 157.
28 Havell, E.B., *Indian Sculpture and Painting* (London, 1908), 188.
29 Goetz, H., 'Persia and India after the Conquest of Mahmud', *Legacy of Persia* (Oxford, 1953), 92.
30 Pandey, A.B., *Later Mediaeval India: a History of the Mughals* (Allahabad, 1963), 511; Wellesz, E., *Akbar's Religious Thought Reflected in Mogul Painting* (London, 1952), 34–42.
31 Binyon, L., and Arnold, T., *The Court Painters of the Great Moguls* (Oxford, 1921), 67; Rawlinson, H.G., *India: A Short Cultural History* (London, 1943), 367–8; Edwardes and Garrett, op. cit., 323.
32 Goetz, op. cit., 112; Cresswell, K.A.C., 'Indian Domes of Persian Origin', *Asiatic Review*, v (1914), 475–83; Smith, op. cit., 160.
33 Briggs, M.S., 'Muslim Architecture in India', *Legacy of India* (Oxford, 1937), 146–7.
34 *Cambridge History of India*, iv, 532–4; Brown, P., *Indian Architecture: the Islamic Period* (Bombay, 1942), 92–3; Havell, E.B., *Handbook of Indian Art* (London, 1920), 133; Powell Price, J.C., *A History of India* (Edinburgh, 1955), 278; Briggs, op. cit., 248.

35 Havell, *Indian Architecture, pp. 21, 174; Smith, op. cit., 159.*
36 Smith, op. cit., 406.
37 Fergusson, J., *Indian and Eastern Architecture*, rev. Burgess and Spiers (London, 1910), 281–2.
38 Chardin, J., *Travels in Persia*, ed. N.M. Penzer (London, 1927), 268.
39 Fergusson, op. cit., 306 (ref. Havell's article in *Nineteenth Century and After*, iii (1903), 1039 ff.).
40 Havell, *Indian Architecture.* 174.
41 Abdul Qadir, 'The Culture Influences of Islam', *Legacy of India*, (Oxford, 1937), 296.
42 Pope, A.U., 'Some Interrelations between Persian and Indian Architecture', *Indian Art and Letters*, xi (1935), no. 2, 119.
43 Chaudhuri, N.C., *The Continent of Circe* (London, 1965), *passim.*
44 Edwardes and Garrett, op. cit., 354.

FOUR

Shi'a and Sufi

. . . When at the first in that far place
We came into the world of space,
Or soul by travail in the end
To that perfection shall ascend.

Fariduddin 'Attar: The Veil

The relevance of these two concepts, one theological and the other mystical, to Persian thought and history is sufficiently manifest to those who visit Persia today and who may chance to read some Persian literature in translation, especially the incomparable poetry. What traveller has failed to remark upon those splendid mosques, shrines, and madrassehs for which the country is renowned, each a monument to the Shi'a faith, and who can read the classic poets without being conscious of that profound mystical insight which is the essence of Sufism? Less readily apparent, perhaps, is the effect of religious particularism upon the history and politics of Persia, yet this point should not be overlooked. Persia's historical isolation is not simply a matter of geography, apparent though this is, but also of doctrine; the breaking away of the Shi'a Muslims from their Sunni co-religionists has left a cleavage which is far greater and less reconcilable than that between Catholic and Protestant, and even that analogy is hardly appropriate.

To most people the world of Islam seems united, the principles, doctrine and dogmas of the Muslim faith universal and undeviating, yet in truth that is far from the case since Islam has not been spared schisms, heresies, and sectarianism. Two broad divisions stand out, however: the 'orthodox' *Sunni* and the 'heterodox' *Shi'a*, the former being in the great majority throughout the world whilst the latter are confined mainly to Persia and adjacent countries, notably Iraq. Of

Persia's population most by far are Shi'a and in the more remote parts of the country it is considered almost inconceivable that one could be other than of that persuasion.

The Shi'a differ from the Sunni principally in their doctrine of 'apostolic succession' rather than in propounding a new theology, though it will be seen that in guidance and interpretation of the divine law the Shi'a have adopted an attitude differing from that of their opponents, but even this attitude itself has been subject to divergencies from the original conception. It will be recalled that on the death of Muhammad there was no male issue to succeed the Prophet; the claim of 'Ali, Muhammad's cousin and son-in-law (married to the illustrious Fatima) was advanced only to be scorned by the rival Syrian Arabs who championed Abu Bakr, father-in-law and companion of Muhammad, and he in due course was succeeded by Omar and Othman as second and third caliphs respectively. On the death of Othman, 'Ali was elected fourth caliph only to be deposed and subsequently murdered in A.D. 661. At this important point the Shi'a broke with the Sunnis, for the former held that 'Ali was, in fact, the first rightful caliph, his three predecessors being classed as imposters and usurpers; in Shi'a eyes the caliphate stemmed from 'Ali. Hassan and Hussein, sons of 'Ali and claimants to the caliphate on 'Ali's death, had their lives abruptly terminated, and the anniversary of the murder of Hussein at Karbala on the tenth of Muhurram A.D. 680 is today celebrated with a great show of mourning throughout the Shi'a world. At this juncture, too, the doctrine of the Imamate emerges, the Shi'a sects (for they, too, tend towards fragmentation) holding that 'Ali's successors composed the line of imams in whom reposed infallibility in the interpretation of the divine law; thus it is seen that the Shi'a (partisans of 'Ali) sustain a form of spiritual absolutism, whereas the Sunni (followers of the Companions of the Prophet) acknowledged the communal consensus of opinion in accordance with custom and under the leadership of the caliph. The majority of Shi'a, colloquially known as 'Twelvers', recognize twelve imams, the last being Muhammad al-Muntazar who disappeared about A.D. 833, and it is believed that this 'hidden imam', sinless and incorruptible, will appear at a second coming to deliver the faithful and restore righteousness. This Messianic vision was most probably inspired by the hopes of Jews and Christians of whose tenets the Muslims had some knowledge. Self-styled *Mahdis* or claimants to the imamate have appeared at various times in the last thousand years and we recall especially the Mahdi of the Sudan who overcame

General Gordon and, more recently, the 'Mad Mullah of Somaliland'. The Isma'ili sect of the Shi'a which embraced the Assassins of earlier times and of whom the Aga Khan is acknowledged leader regard Isma'il as the seventh Imam and so set themselves at variance with the majority 'Twelvers'; the Isma'ili, however, are of small consequence in Persia today.

It is important that the concept of the Imam should be fully appreciated, for it is here that Shi'a and Sunni diverge without much hope of reconciliation. Sunnis do, indeed, recognize an imamate but it is an office rather than the personification of quasi-divine attributes, and the Imam is regarded as Muhammad's successor as constitutional head and leader but not, of course, as prophet. In other words, this is the Caliphate with which perhaps we are more familiar. On the other hand, to the Shi'ite the Imam is the mystical mediator between God and mankind and only through the guidance and intercessions of this sinless being can men hope to avoid Divine wrath and punishment. Further, it is not necessary that the Imam should appear alive or visible to the faithful, and in his concealment from the world he still carries on his spiritual functions whilst his temporal power is vested in a legate deriving authority from the Imam. It is in this sense that the Shah of Persia was the Imam's viceroy and, as Grunebaum[1] has pointed out, 'as late as 1906 the first constitution of Persia embodied the statement that parliament was to be established with the agreement and consent of the (Hidden) Imam of the Age'. The Shi'a Imamate, if considered in its entirety, appears to have two distinct aspects in its genesis, the one political, the other esoteric. First and expedient, there was the desire for a legitimate leader of the community whose eligibility and authority would be beyond dispute, and then by development of the idea there was incorporated the age-old theory of the divine king whose sway is infallible. This has been adequately expressed by Wickens[2] who states that 'the nearest equivalent of the Shi'ite Imam is not, as has been often asserted, the Pope . . . but the Nestorian Christ'.

Political reasons have tended to favour the development of Shi'ism in Persia; the Iranians are of ancient non-Arab stock and were proselytes of Islam at the point of the sword. Shi'ism therefore tended to suggest differentiation from the rest of the Islamic fold not only in its sectarianism but also nationally, especially against the growing influence and intrusions of the Sunni Ottoman Turks. Early in the sixteenth century a new Persian dynasty under Shah Isma'il summoned anew this old nonconformist sect, establishing it as the national religion; that position it has held there to this day known as the Imami sect, otherwise Ja'farites, after the name of the sixth Imam who did much to codify Quranic law.

There is also a tradition that Hussein, son of 'Ali, married a daughter of Yezdigird III, the last reigning king of the Sassanid dynasty, and this would serve to confer a further sense of political legitimacy and continuity to the claim of the Imamate. That this doctrine of the Imamate was of great benefit to the incumbent of the Persian throne is indisputable, since the divine right of kingship was invoked; it has also assisted greatly in the shaping of a national consciousness which is paramount throughout Persia today. Indeed, it is not straining the point in stating that political stability and territorial integrity have been greatly fortified in Persia by adherence to Shi'ism, which has been the nation's rallying point in a rebellious and fissiparous Muslim world, even if it may have been at the cost of a self-imposed political and religious isolation. Reciting 'There is no God but God; Muhammad is the Prophet of God and 'Ali is the Friend of God' the Shi'ite entered the holy tomb of the Imam Reza at Meshed but before doing so delivered a kick upon the threshold of the shrine of the Sunni caliph Harun ar-Rashid which stands nearby. This not only epitomizes religious difference but is symbolical also of Persian pride in the face of a hostile world. Perhaps, too, it is a gesture of defiance against a religious creed 'imposed' upon them by the Arabs who, for their part, would scarcely tolerate the Gnosticism and other mystic cults of the ancient Near East which still have their vestiges in contemporary Shi'a thought and which are further discussed below.

Other practices have been associated with Shi'ism which distinguish it from the Sunni world and may here be briefly mentioned, though they are entirely subordinate to the major theme expressed above. Sacrifice and possibly atonement forcibly recalled in the slaughter at Karbala and the Prophet's daughter Fatima holding the world as a dowry are quite possibly accretions from the Shi'ites' early contacts with the Christians. There are practices such as the legitimacy of denying one's faith under duress, a disposition towards martyrdom, the reverence of saints and the system of temporary marriage. In these respects there is sufficient indication of a wide divergence from the views held by the Sunnis, so that the Shi'a are by no means Sunni without the validity of their orders but on the contrary have gradually built up their own characteristic corpus of law and practice.

From earliest times a strain of mysticism appeared in the uncompromising fundamentalist attitude of Islam generally professed

Figure 5 Minarets of the Shrine of Ni'matullah at Mahan near Kirman

and whilst mystics have been viewed with distrust by the more orthodox they have also acted as a necessary leaven. Shi'ism, with its belief in the hidden Imam, its esoteric doctrine and secret knowledge, has been a favourable breeding ground for mysticism and this connexion is greater than is generally supposed, although even the formalist Shi'ites have not hesitated to condemn the extravagances of mystical speculation. Muslim mystics are styled *Sufi*, a word derived from *suf* (wool), since the early mystics practised an asceticism which included wearing garments of undyed wool. Other attempts to derive the word from Sefavi (the dynasty founded by Shah Isma'il) or from *sophos* (Greek *wisdom*) cannot be considered successful. In common with mystics of other faiths they devoted themselves to austerity, ecstasy, prayer, and contemplation, qualities which would set them apart from their worldly and unascetic fellow Muslims, and which would suffice to incur the suspicion and hostility of orthodox theologians. However, it is their pantheistic doctrine of the unity of God and the world which is their distinctive attribute: all comes from God, all is directed towards God, nothing exists beyond God, all is God; this naturally leads to the desire for union of the individual soul with its Maker from whom it has been separated in long exile. The early mystic al-Hallaj, who suffered martyrdom for his heresy, summed up this idea in the words:

In that glory is no 'I' or 'We' or 'Thou'.
'I', 'We', 'Thou' and 'He' are all one thing.

This idea is in marked contradistinction to the orthodox dogma, for 'in thus setting man as it were face to face with God', writes Gibb,[3] 'without any mediating spiritual or personal elements, Islam necessarily emphasized the contrast between them'. Yet surely these mystics could turn to the Quran for legitimate inspiration, for is it not there written that 'Wherever you turn there is the face of God' and also 'We are nearer to him than the vein of his neck'?

Naturally the Sufi tended to band themselves together and in time established religious orders under spiritual directors and in accordance with a rule, though many continued to roam freely without corporate affiliation; in Persia the mystics are termed *darvish* and have been renowned for their bodily contortions and other physical manifestations when celebrating their rites which momentarily summon up visions of paradise. Veneration of saints, unprovided for in early Islamic ideas, is a Sufi concept which has spread far beyond its original confines and in common with the exaltation of the

Prophet and the practice of celibacy indicates the influence of Christianity on Sufi thought.

In a sympathetic and penetrating study of the subject, Fr. Rice[4] has indicated that the prime purpose of Sufism was to purify and spiritualize Islam from within and certainly in this respect al-Ghazali would provide more than adequate personal testimony. An interesting suggestion is further made by him that 'Persia's revenge for the imposition of Islam and the Arabic Quran was her bid for the utter transformation of the religious outlook of all the Islamic peoples by the dissemination of the Sufi creed and the creation of a body of mystical poetry which is almost as widely known as the Quran itself . . . In this way Persia has conquered a spiritual domain far more extensive than any won by the arms of Cyrus and Darius, and one which is still far from being a thing of the past.' This is a provoking corollary to the inference suggested above of the effect of Shi'ism upon Persian thought and attitudes.

The interplay between Sufism and poetry has been remarked upon by many authorities and leads to ambiguities in expression; immortality of the soul is postulated in the language of allegory to such a degree that it is difficult at times to distinguish between divine and earthly love, imagery and symbolism are given full play to dwell upon the essence of Sufism which is that God is the only reality, all else is illusion. A parallel with 'The Song of Solomon' and certain books of the Apocrypha comes readily to mind. In Persia especially some of the greatest poets – Jami, Rumi, Sa'di, Hafiz – have been greatly influenced by these mystical strains and all have drunk deeply at the well of al-Ghazali who is pre-eminent as theologian, philosopher, and mystic. Sufism is one of Persia's spiritual roots which has inspired much of the beauty of literature, painting and architecture through the ages. Sufism, as expressed by Persia's poets, is comprehensive and all-embracing in its tenets, there is no narrow exclusiveness and no assumption that the truth is reserved only for the elect. Hafiz, in Nicholson's fine translation, makes this manifest in his poem to the Beloved:

Love is where the glory falls
Of Thy face – on convent walls
Or on tavern floors, the same
Unextinguishable flame.

Where the turbaned anchorite
Chanteth Allah day and night,

Church bells ring the call to prayer
And the Cross of Christ is there.

whilst the mystical doctrine that everything of which we are conscious, good or evil, is in some way an attribute of the Divine is well expressed in Fitzgerald's quatrain from Omar Khayyam:

Heav'n but the Vision of fulfilled Desire,
And Hell the Shadow from a Soul on fire,
Cast on the Darkness into which Ourselves
So late emerged from, shall so soon expire.

In more recent times Sufism has experienced a revival of somewhat more orthodox tendencies; much of its more immoderate speculation has been modified and the inclination towards pantheism has been slightly abated, though its essential if subtle tenets remain unimpaired. Sufism, moreover, is to be found at all social levels, clerical and lay. The Murshid of Kerman, guardian of the shrine at Mahun and himself a Sufi, once expressed to Sir Percy Sykes[5] the comforting view that the Sufi teaching of universal love would sweep away ignorance and bigotry, creating instead an atmosphere of religious tolerance, which even the most ardent protagonist would be constrained to admit is not paramount in Islam today. Were that to be so, then the world's debt to Sufism would be beyond all doubt.

It may be said that in moulding the theology of Shi'ism and the mysticism of Sufism, Persia herself has of necessity been influenced reciprocally by these two complementary strains. Her politics, nationalism, culture, and above all her poetry have reflected these influences which are by no means dead things but are much alive today: one will encounter in some Persian street or garden a person earnestly reading Sa'di or Hafiz aloud. The key to understanding Persia today as yesterday is her theology and esoteric philosophy, for these have permeated the thought and conduct of her people down through the generations.

Notes

1 Grunebaum, G.E. von, *Islam: Essays in the Nature and Growth of a Cultural Tradition* (London, 1955), 12.
2 Wickens, G.M., 'Religion', *Legacy of Persia* (Oxford, 1953), 153.
3 Gibb, H.A.R., *Mohammedanism* (Oxford, 1949), 70.
4 Rice, C., *The Persian Sufis* (London, 1964), 11.
5 Sykes, P.M. *Ten Thousand Miles in Persia* (London, 1902), 197.

FIVE

The Persian Lut

The country of Persia is dry, barren, mountainous, and but thinly inhabited. I speak in general; the twelfth part is not inhabited, nor cultivated.

Sir John Chardin: Travels in Persia

It is appropriate to discuss the significance of the great desert plateau of central north-east and south-east Persia in both geographical and historical terms, since not only is this a most interesting subject in itself, but it must also be agreed that to appreciate Persia fully is to understand its geography; to do this attention must be paid to the vast central desert and its encircling mountain ranges. It will be shown that the desert of the plateau is itself of sufficient importance, in inverse ration to our knowledge of it, to warrant this attention, for not only does it occupy so great a part of the country but it has a significance embracing climate, habitability and communications.

Persia may be described as a great saucer. If one considers its contours, it is observed that the perimeter of the country comprises almost entirely a series of mountain ranges, the saucer's rim, whilst the great centre is a mighty depression. This is a simple picture of the mountains and deserts of Iran, the broad and predominant features of the country. The depression, however, is purely relative to the high mountain masses surrounding it; indeed, plateau is the more correct term, for it stands broadly at between 2,000 and 3,500 feet above sea level with subsidiary depressions and elevations, and like its great sister plateau of Arabia is almost entirely desert.

These Persian deserts are interesting, even fascinating places, not only because of their great extent, but also because of certain unique features. Those whose conception of desert is conventional and conditioned perhaps by the writings of romantic novelists will be speedily disillusioned in Persia. These vast wastelands are desert indeed, they certainly include sand dunes, but for the most part they are uninviting expanses of sand and stone, largely covered with saline deposits, and with frequent outcrops of rocky arid hills and even mountains interspersed here and there. Broadly speaking a great proportion of the country's surface, perhaps half, is strewn with saline mud and other deposits of recent geological time, thus generally concealing the older rocks which nevertheless protrude in places and give evidence of strong faulting. In parts these exposures of older rocks achieve mountainous proportions, sometimes as isolated masses, sometimes grouped in miniature ranges.

This short survey of *Persia deserta* will concentrate upon that great expanse of largely waterless country comprising the central and north-eastern parts of Persia, generally known as the Lut. Here we may pause to consider terminology which has exercised the imagination of geographers and cartographers over the past century or more. Conventionally, in European parlance this enormous area stretching from Tehran in the shadows of the Elburz to the borders of Pakistan has been divided into two regions with different names: in the north the Dasht-i-Kavir and in the south the Dasht-i-Lut. Properly, however, 'dasht' signifies an arid plain, 'kavir' is an expanse of saline mud (and this characteristic is frequently encountered in the northern wastes), whilst 'lut' refers to waterless desert. For the sake of simplicity and following current Persian vernacular usage, the whole region will be referred to as the Lut, whilst kavir will denote expanses of saline mud within the Lut.

Of all the world's great deserts, those of Persia have perhaps been the least frequented and explored. For this there is first of all an economic reason, since the great trade routes have of necessity skirted the desert, the most renowned of these ancient highways being the old Silk Road, a branch of which passed under the foot of the Elburz mountains linking the Black Sea ports with Turkestan and Cathay. Then again, the forbidding nature of central Persia invites few residents and fewer wayfarers, the temperatures and aridity of the Lut rendering travel at times unbearable, whilst the treacherous expanses of kavir provide an almost impassable barrier. Of this kavir Curzon wrote[1] that 'one of the most strange and funereal scenes upon which ever fell the eye of man lays its palsied hand across the middle part', and this is as apt a description as could be applied to this saline wasteland.

If attention is directed first of all to the great kavirs which extend across the northern Lut, the question arises: Why should this great deposit of salt be there at all? Geologists assert that the Iranian plateau in Permian times – that is, when red sandstone was being formed probably about 250,000,000 years ago – was part of the bed of an ancient sea, the Tethys, and indeed much of this sandstone with other sedimentary rocks is visible there today. During the Tertiary period, approximately 70,000,000 years ago, uplift took place and the waters over the present plateau were cut off from the rest of the Tethys by the higher ground of the present mountain ranges; finally, during the Quarternary period the drying-up process took place, so that after the last great Ice Age the configuration of Iran largely assumed its present appearance. In simpler terms, therefore, the Iranian plateau was once an inland sea, possibly later a series of extensive lakes, finally mud, after which desiccation took place; the salt would be a natural residue. Tradition asserts this and legends to this effect abound; earlier town sites on the edge of the northern kavir have the reputation of having once been ports, and even Jonah has been credited with having been cast up hereabouts by a much-maligned whale.[2] More substantially, it is interesting to note that during their traverses of the great kavir Sven Hedin,[3] at the turn of this century, discovered fossilized coral, whilst some years earlier Lieutenant Vaughan[4] found various marine shells, including those of oysters. I have noted countless specimens of well-rounded stones and pebbles which give every evidence of water-worn smoothness, and Vaughan, who took samples of the salt from the Darya-i-Namak (Sea of Salt) for chemical analysis, found these to be almost pure sodium chloride; this uniformity in salinity is a definite characteristic of marine salts and would suggest evaporation *in situ* rather than deposition by capillary action. Persia's few rivers, in the main and contrary to the general rule, flow centrewards to end inconclusively in this arid waste, the desert soaking up what has not been lost by evaporation, and so the silt brought down by drainage would also add to the salinity, though insufficient to cause it on such a vast scale.

The surface of the kavir presents different aspects in different parts and according to the narrator. In 1887 Lieutenant Galindo, for example, crossing the great kavir from south to north, experienced 'at first principally black mud with isolated patches of white salt, and slimy pools of green water', whilst a year later, somewhat to the westward, Vaughan described 'a vast frozen sea . . . salt-formed into one immense sheet of dazzling brilliancy, while here and there upon its

Figure 6 Salt, Sand and Mountain on the Way between Tabas and Yazd

surface pools of water . . . were visible'.[5] Hedin, in 1905, who traversed the northern Lut from Tehran to Seistan, states that generally, apart from the salinity aforementioned, the firmer surface of the kavir is a fine yellow mud or alluvial deposit; sand is not common. My own incursions into the Lut have led me to conclude that the kavir, according to locality, wears all three aspects described above; indeed, north-east of Kerman beyond Shah Dad I have seen salt deposits piled up so thick that men were shovelling it in great lumps into a lorry for sale in the bazaar. A common aspect of the kavir's surface is a division into polygonal sections of saline-mud crust beneath which a slimy mire exists, the corners and edges of these sections turning upwards rather like stale slices of bread. Elsewhere, excessive crystallization causes sharply defined little mounds to appear, but beneath is the treacherous ooze with drainage channels known as 'shatts'; into these can be engulfed man or beast. It has been assumed that the presence of magnesium chloride has kept the saline mud in a state of continual wetness and this is aggravated by precipitation during the cooler months. Undoubtedly, too, the underlying rocks are impervious and so the moisture is contained near the surface. A feature readily observed is the clearly defined 'shore line' of the kavir, for the change of surface from dry desert to kavir is abrupt, giving the impression of the edge of a mud lake, and so it is.

Evidence abounds therefore to support the theory that kavirs are the bed of a former marine depression, and that beneath the uninviting surface is an extensive water table which is freshened partly by precipitation from the winter and spring rains and partly by drainage from the encircling mountains. During the winter months temperatures in the northern Lut can be remarkably low, in the middle forties by day and dropping to freezing point by night, in marked contradistinction to the baking heat of the summer months. Nevertheless it is pertinent to remark that even the ebullient Sir Thomas Herbert, who visited Persia in the seventeenth century, found that the charms of this desert did not appreciably improve in the colder weather. 'We beheld the ground', he says, 'covered with a loose and flying sand which by the fury of the winter weather is accumulated into such heaps . . . that the track is lost and passengers (too oft) overwhelmed and stifled by that tempestuous tyrant'.[6] There will be occasion later to observe climatic conditions more fully, and also the possible consequences of bringing water to the surface.

The southern Lut, by contrast with the northern kavirs, has that evil quality which only apparently endless stony and sandy wastes can imply, though outcrops of more resistant rock at times add relief to the topography. These outcrops must however not be considered simply as hillocks, though in many cases that is so, as in places they achieve mountainous proportions. It is a cruel desert with very few wells or oases, and the chance drop of water can be so stagnant as to induce violent fits of vomiting and diarrhoea. Extending over the greater part of south-east Persia, it reaches its most formidable proportions in its southern half; the area eastwards of Kerman beyond Shah Dad or Khabis is largely unexplored and of such uninviting countenance that none but the most resolute would care to venture into it. In the heat haze visibly can be difficult and in the centre of this southern Lut is reputed to be the hottest region of the world. In the vicinity of Deh Saif north of Shah Dad I registered a June afternoon shade temperature of 130° F., but temperatures further to the eastwards in July and August are appreciably higher and can almost reach the limits of human endurance. As would no doubt be expected, relative humidity is low, averaging in the summer months about 15 per cent. Curzon again comes up with the apt phrase, 'for league upon league extends the appalling waste that has here stamped on Persia the imprint of eternal desolation'. Earlier travellers – Marco Polo, Friar Odoricus and others – have described it in similar terms.

Changes of diurnal temperature causing alternate expansion and contraction of the rock break up the surface and this erosive process is assisted by the scouring action of the wind which flings sand particles upon the rock. Consequently many fantastic forms have been sculptured in the more resistant rocks of the southern desert and these have been designated Shahr-i-Lut or Cities of the Lut, since they resemble the crumbling vestiges of former habitations. Elsewhere persistent northerly winds inducing dust storms have swept the sand into confused ridges of dunes concentrated mainly in the south and these have presented a formidable barrier to travellers as well as exciting their comment. Dr Gabriel,[7] during a traverse of the south-eastern corner of the Lut, estimated the sandhills there to cover an area of about 5,700 square miles and their height, from crest to trough, to be in excess of 700 feet.

It is not surprising that vegetation in these desert regions is slight. First, there is the general lack of surface water so that only xerophilous plants can exist, and this they do in parts where the water table is not more than 30 feet below the surface; where the depth is greater no flora exists. Second, there is generally the absence of a formed soil, and organic content is very low or almost nil. Where, however, water can be utilized on the surface and the soil permits, flourishing oases exist, producing wheat, dates, cotton, citrus fruits and other commodities, but the line of demarcation between desert and sown is clearly and abruptly defined. Broadly speaking, therefore, the natural flora of the Lut can be divided into two main types: halophytes or salt-resisting plants which exist in the region of the kavirs, and xerophytes or drought-resisting plants which exist in the more arid ground. All these stunted growths are widely spaced in their struggle for survival and can hardly be said to be competitors; their economic value to man is very low, if any at all. In much of the southern Lut where sandy stony rock bakes in the overpowering heat, where dust storms prevail and where water is non-existent, the landscape is entirely devoid of vegetation and this absence of flora completes the scene of desolation characteristic of this region.

The existence of oases has already been remarked upon and they illustrate the beneficial effects of sweet water upon the soil. Such water is derived either from wells which tap the water table at convenient depths, occasionally from springs, often by a peculiarly Persian system of irrigation engineering known as *qanats* or *kariz*. It is necessary to consider these life-lines in the arid landscape, for it is a water system which has existed for thousands of years and is almost entirely confined either to Persia as we know it today or over adjacent borders in lands which once came under the sway of the ancient Persian empire. The qanat system, in contrast to the vertical well, is a means of bringing water underground horizontally from its source to its required destination and this is done by sinking a shaft in ground higher than the village and at some distance from it where the existence of subterranean water is suspected. Where water is encountered by this means and by what is termed the master shaft at a depth not exceeding the height of ground on which the village stands, an underground tunnel is then constructed, usually commencing from the village end at surface level and then burrowing into the ground towards the base of the master shaft so that when this point is reached the water will flow towards the village. The spoil from the excavation is sent upward through a series of vertical shafts spaced at close intervals of about 60 feet and these of course are sunk parallel to the master shaft; they also permit ventilation. On completion therefore a vertical section of shafts, tunnel and sloping surface would roughly resemble a series of right-angled triangles, with the tunnel and shafts as adjacent sides of the right-angle and the ground surface as the hypotenuse. It is largely an hereditary occupation, crude but effective in bringing cold sweet water to where it is needed, and the mounds of spoil at the heads of the shafts are characteristic sights in the Persian scene, resembling diminutive slag heaps. Dimensions in this system can be almost incredible. Whilst the master shaft does not usually exceed 200 feet (and this is deep enough for only four men to work with primitive means, that is, two at the shaft head, one in the shaft itself and one in the underground passage), the master shafts at Gunabad in Eastern Persia measure nearly 1,000 feet, and in the vicinity of Yazd a tunnel has been constructed some 40 miles in length.

Two questions are pertinent at this stage and are of great interest and significance: first, has it always been so in recent geological time; and second, can irrigation works be extended to bring much more of this land under cultivation?

To take the first question; an examination of present climatic influences is required and it must then be seen if these have undergone change or modification within historic times. Generally in a country or region one great controlling climatic influence is the nature of the predominant air masses which encompass it; the British

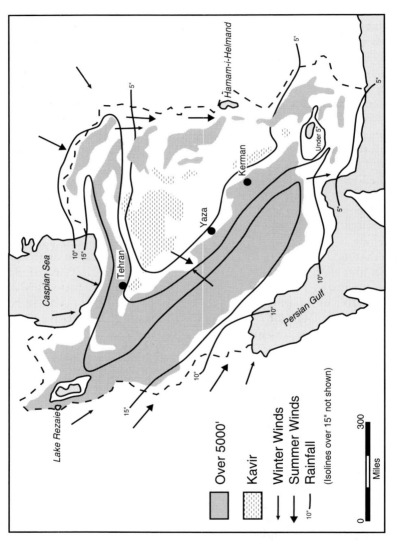

Figure 7 Map of climatic Influences in the Persian Lut

Isles, for instance, are generally subjected to moist and relatively warm air streams from the Atlantic which afford a humid soil, lush vegetation and a comfortable habitat. In Persia the winds are controlled by the pressure system of Central Asia which is low in summer and high in winter. This means that in the hot months the winds tend to blow inwards from a north-easterly direction, and as these inblowing winds are dry, either coming from the steppes of Central Asia or being an extension of desiccated monsoonal winds from the Sind depression, they have no rain-bearing qualities and therefore accentuate the aridity; these are known as the Sad-o-bist or winds of 120 days, prevailing between May and September. In the cooler months the winds blow mainly from the high-pressure areas of the north and, as is common with such winds from colder regions, their moisture-bearing content is low so that this largely negative humid quality tends to increase relatively as they penetrate into warmer land areas. Across the Caspian the northerly winds do pick up some moisture to be discharged mainly on the northern slopes of the Elburz mountains; also marine influences from the westward penetrate into north-west Persia, bringing moisture to those parts, so that rain and sometimes even snow occasionally affect the northern kavirs in winter though they do not proceed further south. From the great mountain ranges north and west of the kavir there is also considerable drainage from the rain and snow-melt which adds to the subterranean waters of the kavir. Orographical rains, that is those induced by air rising above mountains, do occur but are mainly local phenomena with no widespread effect. The low rainfall and the marked tendency towards inland drainage is accompanied by intense evaporation; winds tend to be scorchingly hot in summer and bitingly cold in winter and with velocities of over 70 miles per hour. Rainfall totals in the northern Lut average about 10 inches a year and this figure diminishes progressively southwards. These, it is emphasized, are averages over many years, but it may rain torrentially to the measure of a few inches in twenty-four hours in the course of one season whilst other years have no rainfall at all. The following quotation from the *Admiralty Handbook on Persia*[8] is succinct and apt: 'The southern Lut and the plains of Seistan are the epitome of arid Persia. An inch or two of rain a year coming in five or six showers, a blazing cloudless sky from late April to mid-November, a northerly blast, laden with salt and sand, rising at times to a fury, dreaded for its cold in winter and heat in summer, these are the climatic characteristics of desert Persia.'

Climatic conditions therefore have made these desert regions unaccommodating to man, since the rigours of the climate and the poverty of the soil render vegetation scarce and largely valueless with a corresponding paucity of animal life. This is a simple statement of cause and effect and is of profound significance in the study of Persian geography, since changes in climate, if such can be proved, are determining factors in the life of man. Evidence of climatic changes must necessarily be circumstantial since weather records in Persia and indeed for the great part of the Middle East and Central Asia are mainly confined to this century and are fairly scanty at that. Whether the air masses over Persia have appreciably changed their characteristics within the last few thousand years is conjectural, though it is just possible that they had a higher degree of humidity than now. One thing however which has attracted the attention of travellers is the existence of ruined settlements scattered throughout these barren regions, and conclusions have been drawn to the effect that conditions for human habitation were once more favourable than they are now. Over two thousand years ago on his return from the Indus valley Alexander marched a great army across the wastes of the Makran and the southern Lut, whilst his lieutenant Krateros marched a further army on a more northerly route westward through Seistan and Karmania. Arrian tells of hardship and privations accompanying Alexander's march, rightly describing the route as a difficult one, and whilst we are not here concerned with Alexander's motives for choosing such an inhospitable path, it nevertheless remains that he succeeded in bringing a large army with attendant camp followers through a region where today even a small caravan finds the going far from good. Even more astonishing is the performance of Krateros, who not only traversed the now waterless southern Lut to Kerman, but brought his elephants safely through with him. Elephants would stand a slender chance along that way today, where even camels are hard pressed. Ellsworth Huntingdon[9] made a special study of the climates of Central Asia and drew attention to two descriptions of the same province, that of Kerman, though two millennia separate the authors. A modern description is given by Sir Percy Sykes: 'The whole province can best be described as partly desert, pure and simple, and partly desert tempered with oases. . . . As may be supposed, the rivers are unimportant.' With this unflattering description my own observations there lead me to concur. On the other hand Strabo, the ancient geographer, conveyed a vastly different impression. 'Kerman', he says, 'lies more to the north than Gedrosia. This is indicated by its fertility, for it not only produces everything, but the trees are of large size . . . it is also watered by rivers.' Although contrasting descriptions of this sort are not necessarily conclusive, nevertheless it is hard to believe that both were describing the same region. From the signs of former prosperity in ancient times, the extensive ruins of flourishing settlements and the cultural remains indicative of a higher standard of expression than in our own times, one deduces the existence of a larger population throughout the Middle East than obtains today, and this would seem to suggest that rainfall or availability of surface water was greater then than now.

Further evidence of more pluvial times in the past can hardly fail to strike the contemporary traveller, and that is the existence of alluvial debris and large dried watercourses principally in areas of local elevation which clearly suggest the presence of abundant water in times past, though certainly not now. Two great if shallow Persian lakes, Rezaiyeh (Urmia) in the north-west and Hamam-i-Helmand on the borders of Afghanistan, show every indication of receding in extent, and if this persists they will leave only saline quagmires as evidence of their past existence, whilst even the Caspian itself is shrinking in volume and extent, and ports established on Persian shores are now unmistakably silting up. In Seistan the rate of evaporation of the Haman-i-Helmand during the dry summer months, when the river flow is minimal, has been estimated at 10 feet in the course of a year.[10] Ravages of war and man's depredations, on the other hand, can hardly be allowed as prime factors in the impoverishment of the land and the development of desert conditions, though in marginal regions such as that under review they would naturally be a contributory influence. Such age-old practices as deforestation, indiscriminate cropping and the destructiveness of the ubiquitous goat would also play their important part, and in this connection it is convenient to recall the formation of a dust bowl in mid-western U.S.A. following a wrong agricultural practice. Removal of vegetation, especially forest cover, can lead to soil erosion and a reduction of sub-surface water with consequent lowering of the water table, and thus a vicious cycle sets in with erosion and desiccation acting the one upon the other. As for war, if we consider Azerbaijan, one of the most fertile of Persia's provinces and the granary of the nation, it is noted that this has been a continual battleground since time immemorial and has suffered more from despoliation by foreign armies than perhaps any comparable region, and much the same may be said of north-east Khorasan. Kerman has been comparatively unimpaired by the invader in the course of a long history yet now it is a province largely of almost complete desolation.

Briefly stated therefore, and in general terms, hot climate regimes in continental regions as evidenced by the Persian plateau produce dry conditions which in turn determine the increasing paucity of vegetation; vegetation death precedes the encroachment of the desert, which in turn induces soil conditions unsuitable to the renewal of vegetation when more humid conditions return. History has amply shown how increasingly arid conditions have led to famine and the consequent distress has impelled migrations and other disturbances of far-reaching effect, and so it is seen that climatic changes have undoubtedly exerted a profound influence on man and his habitat.

It is tempting, therefore, to speculate that of the once great marine beds which the central desert basin comprised, the whole dried out gradually as emergence took place to form kavirs of tremendous proportions, then the southern Lut dried up completely since it enjoys persistently higher temperatures and negligible run-off from the mountains, finally attaining its present desiccated condition. By inference the northern kavirs would in course of time tend to follow suit and if so the pattern of desert formation of Central Asia would be followed. However, such simplifications may contain their own pitfalls and care must be taken, for want of more reliable evidence, not to stray beyond the bounds of reasonable conjecture.

This now leads to the second question: can such desert regions be recovered, if only in part, to wider agricultural use which past evidence has suggested? Could irrigation, if undertaken on sufficiently large a scale, render the desert productive? This is highly questionable, for not only is surface or sub-aerial water lacking, but soils are largely non-existent. Over vast tracts of land the surface consists of particles of various sizes of the bedrock, either eroded in their present state or transported by natural agencies past and present. Climate fashions soils, and here in a country where the hot season and the rains, if any, do not coincide, soil formations are slow and rock metamorphoses equally so. Small pathetic streams are occasionally encountered winding their way inconclusively into the desert, but their banks are often devoid of any vegetation whatever, indicating that soil poverty is as great a retarding influence as water shortage; sometimes this is aggravated by the salinity of the water itself. Beneath the surface of much of Persia and at varying depths are great reservoirs of water which if tapped and brought to the surface for distribution in areas to be irrigated (and this would be an engineering feat of considerable magnitude and expense if undertaken on sufficiently great a scale) might conceivably have beneficial results. However, evaporation would need to be contended with, for this, it is already noted, is excessive and the heat of the soil by day might well militate against plant life. In many cases the construction of qanats has led to a lowering of the water table, but on the other hand indiscriminate and over-enthusiastic efforts might at the same time elsewhere tend to raise the water table just where irrigation was most persistent, thereby inducing the twin scourges of waterlogging and salinity. A further consequence of increasing the supply of surface water may be a rise in the incidence of disease due to the attraction of insects. It has been observed[11] in Egypt and Iraq during this century that malaria and bilharzia have increased alarmingly as irrigation methods were extended, and whilst it does not necessarily follow that this is an automatic consequence wherever such engineering schemes are undertaken, it is a possibility which should be examined.

This survey of Persia's deserts is inspired with two motives: one, to re-state the formidable nature of this vast terrain in order to show how much of the country is wasteland (and it is stressed that the region now considered is confined to the great desert basins of the Lut, whereas mountain and desert combine elsewhere to increase the regions of desolation); and the other, to warn against expecting too much from it under assumed different circumstances, that is to say, by the engineering of extensive and expensive irrigation systems. A pre-requisite to such a venture would be a systematic soil survey, for on this all else would depend. Determination of the nature of the underground water would also require close consideration in order to avoid the hit-and-miss of earlier practices whereby saline water was made to flow over good soil or good water to flow over unproductive ground. Problems of slope and the siting of the water table, and the proximity of impervious underlying rock, are also other important considerations, and whereas one should avoid defeatism, the difficulties attendant upon flooding land with water, if it were procurable, in quantity must not be underestimated.

Finally, we are once more faced with the inevitable conclusion, expressed in its starkest terms, that geography is the basis on which history rests, the inexorable master shaping the destinies of men and which, as yet, has remained indifferent and immune to man's blandishments.

Notes

1 Curzon, G.N., *Persia and the Persian Question*, Vol. 1 (London, 1892), i, 178.
2 Stewart, C.E., The Herat Valley and the Persian Border (*Proc. of R.G.S.*, Vol. VIII, 1886); Curson, op. cit., ii, 247.
3 Hedin, Sven, *Overland to India*, Vol. 1 (London, 1910), i, 253.
4 Vaughan, H.B., Journeys in Persia (*Geog. Journ.*, Feb., 1896), vii, 166.
5 Curzon, op. cit., ii, 24–9.
6 Herbert, Sir Thos., *Travels in Persia, 1627–1629* (London, 1928), 142.
7 Gabriel, Alfons, Southern Lut and Iranian Baluchistan (*Geog. Jour.*, 92, 1938), 202.
8 Mason, K. (ed.), *Persia* (*N.I.D.*, Admiralty, 1945), 158.
9 Huntingdon, E., *The Pulse of Asia* (London, 1907), 319–20.
10 Sykes, H.R., The Lut, the Great Desert of Persia (*Jour. Man. Geog. Soc.*, Vol. XXIII, 1907).
11 Fisher, W.B., *The Middle East* (London, 1956).

SIX

Britain and the Gulf

I Prelude

No arm of the sea has been or is of greater interest, alike to the geologist and archaeologist, the historian and geographer, the merchant, the statesman, and the student of strategy, than the inland water known as the Persian Gulf.

Sir Arnold T. Wilson: The Persian Gulf

In considering three and a half centuries of British policy in the Persian Gulf, of which the maritime arm had been the chief instrument whereby the paramount interests of Britain and, until 1947, the Indian Empire in that region were conserved and advanced, an evolutionary process is to be discerned in which expediency fashioned policy despite clashes between contrasting philosophies both in Britain and in India from time to time. Throughout three hundred and fifty years military and mercantile priorities were intermingled, not only on the side of Britain but also by her European maritime competitors, though it has been well observed that most of the early activities in the Persian Gulf, even well before the times of which we are treating, were commercial rather than naval, but naval power must rest upon a prosperous mercantile marine so that in the early stages at least it is impossible, even if held desirable, to separate the one from the other.[1]

Thus, the naval supremacy of Britain in the Persian Gulf during those years does more than simply to illustrate Mahan's thesis concerning the influence of sea power upon history, and this survey incorporating and developing some earlier arguments more cursorily propounded[2] will trace the gradual development of British influence

73

in the whole maritime region and likewise the comparable degree of policies formulated to correspond with the growth of that influence. National aspirations and objectives, we are reminded, find their international expression in a reasoned and viable foreign policy.

It should be recalled, too, that the Persian Gulf had tended to be disregarded politically by its land neighbours – the Ottoman Empire, Persia, the Mughal Empire – in times before those with which we are now dealing despite its subsequent intrinsic significance for Britain and other major powers, as will be noted. Until comparatively recently it had also been largely overlooked in political studies. 'The fact that it does not feature so prominently in studies of British imperial policy', an Indian historian has observed, 'can be attributed to two reasons: the sheer complexity of the region in geopolitical terms and the predominance which Great Britain, with her overwhelming superiority on the seas, enjoyed over a region that was so susceptible to naval pressure.'[3]

It becomes readily apparent that from the early 1800s Britain was the dominant and indeed the only power in the Persian Gulf capable of imposing a maritime peace, and though she did not claim a form of paramountcy over the littoral Arab states such as she exercised in India, for the Gulf remained an international waterway accessible to all nations though patrolled by Britain, nevertheless her supremacy there was unquestioned and went either by default or despite other powers. The circumstances of how this came about will be evident from this narrative.

Notes

1 Eldridge, F.B., *The Background of Eastern Sea Power* (London, 1948), 97.
2 Standish, J.F., British Maritime Policy in the Persian Gulf, *Middle Eastern Studies*, III, No. 4.
3 Kumar, R., *India and the Persian Gulf Region, 1858–1907* (London, 1965), 2.

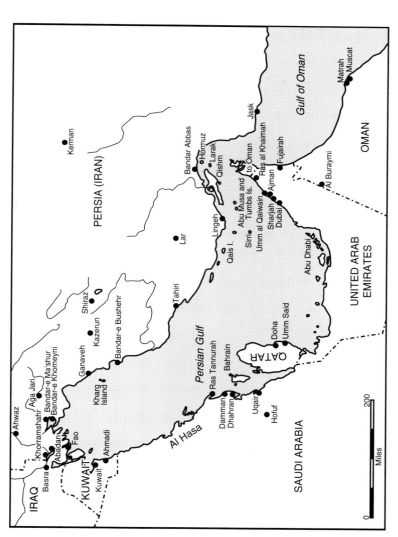

Figure 8 Map of the Persian Gulf

II British Beginnings

For we aim, not at gnats and small flies, but at a commerce honourable and equal to two mighty nations.

Sir Thomas Roe, 1617.[1]

From the earliest times of remote antiquity until the present the Persian Gulf has, by its very penetration into the heart of the Middle East, afforded maritime communications between those lands and the outer oceans, an arterial waterway linking Orient with Occident. Its neighbouring lands saw the dawn of Mesopotamian civilization and from those parts have gone forth men and ideas to leaven and ferment the greater world beyond. Assyrians and Babylonians sailed upon its waters, Alexander's admiral Nearchus traversed its entire length, the unknown author of the *Periplus of the Erythraean Sea* accorded it his notice, Chinese junks made their incursions there, Sassanid Persians tried ineffectually to become its masters, later yielding place to the Arabs who, borne on the tide of conquering Islam, established their dominance and founded Basra, city of Sindbad. Then came the Europeans in their quest for trade which had long excited their imagination, because the age-old traffic in silks and spices, 'splendid and trifling' as Gibbon described it, to a large extent passed from the farther East along the Gulf and thence to the cities and ports of the Levant. It was in the attempt to intercept this trade, much coveted by the West, and no doubt to acquire a monopoly as well, that the Portuguese arrived in the Gulf at the beginning of the sixteenth century, quickly establishing an ascendancy which for more than a hundred years denied those waters and their ports to rival powers and during which period it has been said that Hormuz, their principal port on the Persian shore, exceeded Amsterdam and Antwerp in the value of its trade.[2]

The Persian Gulf extends from its southern entrance at the strait of Hormuz to the delta area of the Tigris-Euphrates-Karun confluence, a distance of some 500 miles whilst its breadth is variable being 180 miles at its greatest extent and about 26 miles wide at the strait. To the west lie lands populated by Arabic-speaking peoples who combine mainly the orthodox Sunni tenets of Islam with those professed by Wahabis and Ibadis. To the east are peoples who, broadly speaking, may be referred to as Persians, though ethnic and linguistic strains vary, whilst the majority religion is that of the Shi'a Muslims. Thus the Gulf does more than divide the two great opposing plateaux of Arabia and Persia geographically; it has created a national and religious barrier which has also inhibited communications in each direction. It may therefore be appreciated that the Gulf has tended to favour the progress of communications along its greatest extent and with the lands and seas beyond rather than across its waters. Thus in this sense it may be compared with the Red Sea as a link between the Mediterranean and the Indian Ocean and it may also be observed that the ascendancy of the one as a route has usually been achieved by a relative decline in importance of the other.

Eastward from the strait of Hormuz stretches the Gulf of Oman which is bounded on the north by the Makran coast of Persia and thence Baluchistan, on the south by the mountains and sands of Oman, then finally losing itself to seawards in the Arabian Sea. Consideration of the Persian Gulf is incomplete without reference to the complementary Gulf of Oman, the doorway to Muscat and threshold of the Middle East.

Throughout most of the sixteenth century Britain had tried to establish adequate trading connexions with the East and accordingly had considered a route through Russia and the Caspian provinces. When that failed the Levant Company was formed and the countries of the Eastern Mediterranean were deemed to be the channels through which trade with the Orient might be conducted, but this venture met with only limited success. Finally, direct relations with Persia were sought, principally through missions led by Anthony Jenkinson and the Shirley brothers, and at the same time investigations of the Persian Gulf itself were undertaken.

The first Englishmen to visit the Persian Gulf – John Newbery, Ralph Fitch and others – did so between the years 1581 and 1583, two decades after Jenkinson had penetrated northern Persia to attend the Court of Shah Tahmasp at Qazvin and three centuries after Geoffrey de Langley's first English mission to Arghun Khan, the Mongol sovereign. They had been impelled by the same urge to reach India as that of their fellow countryman Thomas Stevens who had reached Goa in 1579 via the Cape route which was then controlled by the Portuguese, for Stevens' letters home had aroused great interest in the prospect of opening up trade with India.

In a narrative commenced in 1583 Fitch has recounted his passage southwards from Basra, which he had reached from Aleppo, to Hormuz of high repute. He was greatly impressed with the trade carried on at that port which comprised all sorts of spices, drugs, silk, cloth of silk, fine tapestry of Persia [i.e. carpets], great store of pearls, which came from the Isle of Baharim and are the best pearls of all others, and many horses, which serve all India.[3]

Fitch spent eight years travelling in the East as far afield as Malacca, including an enforced stay of sixteen months at Goa where, on arrival, he was cast into prison by the Portuguese who were antagonistic to any form of trading competition from rival European nations.

Nevertheless, it was consequent upon the enthusiasm, efforts and hardships of these and kindred Elizabethan merchant adventurers that trading connexions were established which ultimately led to the founding of the East India Company in 1600 and this great organization remained, during the succeeding two and a half centuries until the conclusion of the Indian Mutiny, the dominating commercial, military and political factor in the Gulf and its seaward approaches. Trading stations in Persia and in the Ottoman domains obviously followed, and thus did trade precede the flag which was inevitably to come into conflict with those of rival powers.

Britain made her political entry into those waters forty years after the arrival of Newbery and Fitch when in 1622 Hormuz was captured from the Portuguese thereby breaking their grip on that seaway since Albuquerque's first incursion there in 1506, and from that later date, despite no immediate advantage at that time, there was maintained in the Gulf region a British maritime presence which was inseparable from mercantile interests. Despite later technical developments of which aviation is perhaps the most notable, the maritime forces remained the prime arbiters in the preservation of peace and order over a vast field which comprehend both Constantinople and Calcutta and which Britain, as an emerging imperial power in the East, was obliged to sustain.

The circumstances leading primarily to the expulsion of the Portuguese were that that nation, by its harsh and oppressive measures against the principalities and peoples of the Gulf, had rendered itself obnoxious and especially so to the rising Safavid dynasty of Persia whose nominal authority extended along the whole of the northern shores together with a tenuous claim to certain coastal areas and islands on the Arabian side. Furthermore, unlike other and later European rivals, notably the British and the Dutch, Portugal conducted her foreign trade not by means of a mercantile company but on the basis of a royal monopoly, and this undoubtedly accounted for much of the sensitivity displayed by that nation's emissaries who were disposed to treat the Gulf as a Portuguese colony.

At the end of 1621, therefore, when the English Company's ships had arrived at Jask which had been established as a trading post two years previously while others had been founded at Shiraz and Isfahan in 1617, and all due largely to the labours of Sir Robert Shirley who was at that time in the service of Shah Abbas I, the Persian governor forbade the merchantmen to work their cargoes until such time as the English captains would be willing to render military assistance against the Portuguese whose headquarters were at Hormuz.[4] Portugal was nominally at peace with England, being at that time united with Spain under the Spanish crown, though local conflicts in the East and especially in the waters stretching from the Shatt-al-Arab to India had for the previous two decades been endemic between the ships of the two rival nations for the commerce of the Orient. Any hesitancy which the ships' captains may have entertained was dispelled by the fact that the monsoon was then unfavourable for an immediate return voyage to Surat and therefore, with an eye towards a resumption of trade in the future and with assurances from the Persians that their commercial status and privileges at Hormuz would be enhanced, they embarked a Persian force, setting sail for Qishm and Hormuz. By the following year both places were in Persian hands and the English Company established at the mainland port of Gombroon, as Bandar Abbas was then styled. The Portuguese were finally dislodged from the Gulf and the immediately adjacent waters in 1650 when they were obliged to evacuate Muscat, but despite loss of territorial jurisdiction the Portuguese fleet contrived nevertheless to make their presence felt from time to time until the turn of the following century. Thus did Britain commence a long and eventful supremacy in the Gulf which, though seriously disputed by other European contestants and even local powers, remained until 1971.

The defeat of the Portuguese was noteworthy also as indicating for the first time in the British era the naval inadequacy of the Persians. In 1845 Sir John Malcolm had noticed the dread and abhorrence of the sea held by the Persians 'of whom all classes have an unconquerable antipathy to that element',[5] and this undoubtedly accounts for the Arab chiefs at that time and later holding in their possession all the islands and almost all the harbours on both sides of the Gulf whilst at best the Shah was obliged to remain content to impose a merely nominal obedience. This lack of organized sea power by any country or shaikhdom occupying a portion of the Gulf littoral had been a decisive factor in Gulf politics from the advent of the Portuguese until more recent times.

Throughout the century and a half which followed, events ultimately favoured the Company, though the contest with Britain's rivals, the Dutch and the French, was sternly drawn out and at times by no means decisive. The fluctuating fortunes of these countries in the Gulf and immediately beyond merits brief consideration.

Of the two powers opposing Britain, the Dutch proved to be the more formidable, both commercially and militarily, and they secured an early foothold in the Gulf by establishing themselves at Gombroon not long after the dislodgment of the Portuguese from that area. The first point of dispute was the Dutch refusal to pay to the English Company the customs dues to which the Company was entitled under a privilege conferred by Shah Abbas after the expulsion of the Portuguese from Hormuz in 1622. The growing Dutch threat to British interests in the southern part of the Persian Gulf induced the English Company to commence trade with Basra and in 1635 their first ship arrived at that port. Ten years later the Dutch followed suit and at the same time attacked Qishm with a view to consolidating their trading position with mainland Persia. As if things were not proceeding adversely enough for the Company, England was greatly distracted in Europe during its war with the Dutch in 1653 and 1654 which placed the latter at an advantage overseas whilst concurrently English relations with Persia were worsened by the constant refusal of the Company to lend to the Persians ships and maritime assistance against their enemies.

This situation whereby the Dutch were enabled to get the upper hand prevailed during most of the remainder of the seventeenth century with alarming repercussions upon British trade and prestige. This was evident in 1677 when Dr John Fryer on visiting Bandar Abbas recorded that the Dutch dominated the trade of the port whilst 'the English Company's Trade is but small there, only carrying off some few Drugs, Carmania Wool, Goates, Dates and Horses.'[6] However, in 1688 events nearer to home resulted in an alliance between England and Holland, and thus the maritime relationship between the two countries tended to become more balanced whilst concurrently the position of Holland as a continental power declined. Repercussions were gradually felt abroad, notably in a diminution of Dutch naval strength, whilst Shah Husain in 1697 granted a new *firman* to the English Company conferring upon them Persian privileges at the expense of the Dutch.

The eighteenth century saw the Dutch in the process of a slow but stubborn retreat from the Gulf. In 1754 they had established a factory at Kharg and for a time offered vigorous opposition to English trading interests in the northern part of the Gulf but this success was short-lived for they were obliged to abandon that position eleven years later after an assault by Mir Mahanna, the Governor of Bandar Riq, whilst a few years earlier in 1759 they withdrew from Bandar Abbas. Their dislodgment from Kharg may therefore be considered as the point of Dutch withdrawal from active participation in the affairs of the Gulf.

The decline of Dutch influence in the Persian Gulf during the mid-eighteenth century may be ascribed to three reasons: the gradual reversal of their military fortunes *vis-à-vis* the English; internal difficulties within the Dutch East India Company itself which inhibited favourable development overseas except where the Dutch had established themselves territorially as in Java; and, not least, their propensity, like that of their Portuguese predecessors, to alienate native powers and peoples by an excessively martial disposition which overrode considerations of trade and lasting tenure. Sir Thomas Roe had observed this last characteristic more than a century earlier when, after delivering a stricture against the Portuguese, he went on to remark in his *Journal*: 'It hath been also the error of the Dutch, who seek plantation here by the sword. They turn a wonderful stock, they prowl in all places, they possess some of the best; yet their dead pays [i.e. wages to wounded, non-active soldiers] consume all the gain.' For good measure he concluded with the homily: 'Let this be received as a rule that, if you will profit, seek it at sea, and in quiet trade; for without controversy it is an error to affect garrisons and land wars in India.'[7]

The French arrived later upon the scene and it was not until 1665 that their trading company, founded by Colbert, the gifted finance minister, opened a factory at Bandar Abbas, though at that time its trade was slight and the French were of no great consequence in this field of international rivalry until the following century was well advanced. Thus the middle of the eighteenth century had almost arrived before France presented a military threat to British interests in India and the Gulf, and this was occasioned by the War of Austrian Succession (1740–1748) when opposing sides were taken by England and France. This encouraged Dupleix, the Governor of Pondicherry, to pursue an expansionist policy in southern India and such a distraction caused the English Company to devote more attention to affairs within the subcontinent with a corresponding weakening of their position in the Gulf.

French influence in the Persian Gulf was confined mainly to the harassment of the English rather than the advancement of their own mercantile interests, and this they contrived to do with some continued success, but by 1763 after the conclusion of the Seven Years' War the British position in India improved as that of France declined and so the English Company found itself increasingly free from continental distractions to such an extent that they were able to reinforce their position in the Gulf, though the French menace remained until the defeat of Napoleon in the early years of the following century.[8]

In this context it is important to note that it was largely the military threat posed by the French stemming from the policy of aggrandisement advocated principally by Dupleix which caused the English East India Company gradually to transform a position up to that time purely commercial into a political attitude as well, and thus it was that the Company developed thenceforward to become gradually the ascendant military and political force in India and the Persian Gulf.

It follows, therefore, that since the sixteenth century and up to recent times, as will later be seen, one or other of the great naval powers of Western Europe has dominated the Persian Gulf. In those waters Britain had succeeded in maintaining a predominance, even if at times precariously, first to protect her Eastern trade and then, by consequence, as an instrument of diplomacy and strategy. It should not be assumed, however, that throughout all that period the English flag was commonly to be seen in the Gulf since that was an area ancillary to the major trading region of India where the Company's activities were concentrated. Even so, up to the second half of the eighteenth century the Gulf region and especially Persia formed a market which was receptive to English manufactures and in particular to woollen goods for which no comparable demand existed in India. Indeed, it was at times difficult to maintain an adequate maritime presence between Bombay and Basra. By the terms of their engagement with Persia after the expulsion of the Portuguese the East India Company undertook to keep two men-of-war constantly for the defence of the Gulf, as much in the Persian interest of their own, but even that undertaking was difficult to fulfil, for the Council at Surat in 1661 is found complaining that 'whereas our Honble. Employers were pleased . . . to promise a supply of three ships this yeare for the prosecution of the aforesaide affairs and on further consideration have sent forth only one, our want of shipping is first and principally to be considered.'[9] This admonition was to be repeated only three years later when, owing to outrages committed by the Persian governor at Gombroon, the Council declared that 'in our opinion nothing but a visible power can possibly redeeme and bring us to our former repute',[10] whilst as if nothing had been learnt in the meantime barely a century later in 1759 the French found it convenient to destroy the English factory at Bandar Abbas which was then quite unprotected by any maritime force other than one small sloop, and in consequence of this event and other concurrent local problems that factory's operations were in 1763 transferred to Basra.[11] Such parsimony at home was to become painfully apparent throughout the following centuries and this has not been the only circumstance in imperial history when private enterprise overseas was accorded a grudging support from the seat of government.

The year 1668 had seen the first convoys formed for merchant traffic in the Persian Gulf and Red Sea as a safeguard against piracy and also interference from the growing naval power of Muscat, and this protection was afforded mainly by the Company's Marine formed in 1613; further reference will be made to British efforts to quell the hostile tribes whose depredations were to play havoc on both sides of the Gulf for want of an adequate maritime police force. In 1739 Nadir Shah, who had only three years before elevated himself to the Persian throne, invaded India and sacked the imperial capital of Delhi, so in consequence the Mughal Empire was gravely weakened; thereby too he assisted the expansion of British power on the subcontinent. His plunder included a vast amount of money in coin, which appreciably increased his spending power and facilitated external trade in which the Gulf ports participated. Two years later Nadir unsuccessfully attempted to build his own ships at the newly-constructed port of Bushire (abu Shahr) from timber grown in the Caspian provinces, but this proved to be an impossible undertaking so he resorted to buying ships from Europe and Surat and with this newly-acquired naval strength he was able to annex Bahrain and to bring Muscat under his control. After Nadir's death in 1747 Persia relapsed into a state of anarchy during which both the commerce and the peace of the Gulf suffered, and there was a renewal of piratical acts by Arab maritime tribes who assaulted Bandar Abbas and other Persian ports. Three elements may therefore be discerned in this upsurge of disorder in the Gulf: the removal of any effective Persian check when their naval forces disintegrated after Nadir's death; the corresponding decline of British naval power due to graver preoccupations in India; and the renewed disputes among Persian local authorities on the relaxation of strong central control at the Persian Court.

During these troublous times consideration had been given to the possibility of moving the Company's Agency from Bandar Abbas to some island in the Gulf, this exciting some flow of correspondence between the Agent, Bombay and London, but in 1754 the decision was reached for the factory to remain at Bandar Abbas, partly for reasons of trade with Persia and partly from the desire not to appear to encourage territorial expansion by the Company in the Gulf.[12] Despite repeated applications at that time (and these were renewed during the following century) for British naval assistance, either by the Shah in support of various enterprises contemplated against Muscat and lesser Arab chiefs, or by the Turkish authorities with similar intent, the Company in the main evinced reluctance to provide ships for a hostile purpose or to become embroiled in the internecine quarrels in the Gulf.[13]

At this time it had been considered politic for the Company to establish direct representation among the major littoral powers and in 1763 Karim Khan, who had succeeded in restoring a measure of order and stability in Persia, was induced to grant a *firman* enabling the Company to set up a factory and residency at Bushire which the Agent and Council in Persia had considered to be the best port for the Company's trade in the Persian Gulf since it was not only full of inland merchants but there was also 'one conveniency attending Bushire, that a person there need have no connections or caress anyone but the Shaikh himself.'[14] This at the same time conceded to the English an almost exclusive right to trade in Persian dominions, and since this *firman* was renewed by another in 1788 it becomes apparent that British influence and prestige were now so firmly established in the Shah's domains as virtually to exclude all other claimants. In the latter half of the eighteenth century British Residents had also been appointed at Basra and Baghdad within Ottoman territory and thus the headwaters of the Gulf and the principal points of continental entry were subjected to increasing British influence. Indeed, so important had Basra now appeared in the eyes of the Company that in 1764 they contrived that their Agent there should also be recognized as British Consul, a matter unprecedented in the Company's history, and this may be viewed as a possible first step in the political development within the Gulf whereby the East India Company was accorded a diplomatic agency by the home government. Such was the growing extent of British influence that in 1798 the Resident at Bushire was required to arbitrate in a dispute between the Pasha of Baghdad and the Sultan of Muscat, a role to be increasingly adopted in succeeding years, for Bushire had by this time assumed the status of British headquarters in the Persian Gulf and seat of the Political Resident.

Nevertheless, all was not plain sailing, for in a review of recent demands for the Company's support in territorial disputes and of current policy, the Court of Directors advised the Agent at Basra in 1768 that 'you must avoid if possible going upon any expedition on shore . . . for you may be assured they [the local powers] will leave the whole work to be done by our Forces . . . in short, avoid any alliance with the Arabs otherwise than to be on Friendship.' They concluded with the sage advice: 'Always remember that the Promises or even Writings of Persians or Arabs will no longer be Validity than their interest coincides with them.'[15] This counsel was no doubt tempered by consideration of the shortage of shipping available throughout the whole of the eighteenth century since London, and not for the last time in the history of British interests east of Suez, clearly expected maritime policy and defence to be carried out with slender resources stretched to the utmost. The Company had frequently remonstrated, as in the preceding century, to the Government in London that 'the Maritime Reputation of the East India Company in those parts has suffered extremely from their inability to cope with the Naval Strength of other powers against them', to which they were obliged to add, 'these misfortunes . . . can, in your Memorialists' apprehension, only be remedied by the appearance of Ships of War.'[16] The latter part of that century first saw ships of the Royal Navy operating in the Gulf and neighbouring seas to reinforce the Bombay Marine in support of the East Indiamen, and *H.M.S. Seahorse* arrived at Bushire in 1775 bearing in her complement Midshipman Horatio Nelson, but notwithstanding the assurance in London that 'His Majesty is graciously pleased to promise you that support which your affairs seem to require . . . and restore matters in the Persian Gulph to a state of tranquillity and security'[17] this promised reinforcement was not readily forthcoming. Thus it is noted that attacks upon the British flag were common, especially in the case of unarmed or unescorted vessels, until the early part of the succeeding century.[18]

Yet the fact remained, and almost paradoxically, that despite the continual concern for lack of adequate naval support, the Company's trade in the Gulf during the last quarter of the eighteenth century was on the decline. This was due mainly to disturbances on land, piracies at sea, a disastrous plague in Turkish Arabia in 1775 and a manifestation of commercial ineptitude by the Company itself in restricting its imports of textiles from Persia at a time when money in that country was in short supply. A disengagement at that time from the Gulf might have seemed justified were it not for the fact that in the course of that century the Company had assumed obligations and responsibilities for the protection of sea-borne commerce to and from India, duties which once assumed could not be lightly shed. Events at the turn of the following century were to reinforce those obligations and impose fresh ones so that mercantile interests steadily became subordinated to those of politics and strategy.

British relations with Kuwait had commenced at this time by a diversion there of mails from the Gulf to Aleppo in 1775, since Basra was then being besieged by the Persians, and this arrangement continued for the next four years until Basra was able to resume that traffic. Nevertheless the Company's connexion with Grane, or Al Qurain, as Kuwait was then known, continued to grow in the succeeding years despite Turkish claims to the sovereignty of the shaikhdom, repercussions of which were to be experienced two centuries later on the occasion of the threat made by Iraq in 1961 and the later assault in 1990. The first attempt at nautical surveying in the Gulf was made by Lieutenant John McCluer of the Bombay Marine in 1783 who 'determined with the limited means he possessed to make up defects [in the existing charts] and to rescue from darkness the navigation of coasts frequented from the remotest ages of antiquity'.[19] His resolution to chart the waters which were then hydrographically almost *mare incognitus* and his initial success in the northern area were followed during the ensuing 150 years by officers of the Indian and Royal Navies who have placed all seafaring nations in their debt in presenting a faithful delineation of the shores and waters of the Gulf and its seaward approaches, and of the great rivers debouching into what was to become recognized as a British lake, for 'the charts of the Gulf are solely the result of English Enterprise.'[20]

A century and a half of precarious supremacy at sea therefore found the British at the close of the eighteenth century custodians of their hard-earned if dwindling trade; their period of guardianship of the peace and prosperity of the Gulf had yet to begin.

Notes

1 Sainsbury, W.N. (ed.), *Calendar of State Papers (East Indies) 1617–1621* (London, 1870), 15. Sir Thomas Roe to William Robbins (agent to Sir Robert Shirley in Persia), 17 January 1617.
2 *Persia* (N.I.D., Admiralty, 1945), 282.
3 Locke, J.C. (ed.), *The First Englishmen in India* (London, 1930), 74.
4 *Calendar of State Papers, 1622–1624* (London, 1878), 304. Court Minutes of the East India Co., 25 July 1623.
5 Malcolm, Sir John, *Sketches of Persia* (London, 1845), 20.
6 Fryer, J., *A New Account of East India and Persia, etc. 1672–1681* (Hakluyt Society, 1909–1912), II, 163–4.
7 Thompson, E. and Garratt, G.T., *Rise and Fulfilment of British Rule in India* (London, 1934), 12.
8 Toussaint, A., *History of the Indian Ocean* (London, 1966), 150 ff.
9 *Selections from State Papers, Bombay, 1600–1800* (Calcutta, 1908), 18. Consultation in Surat, 25 October 1661.
10 Ibid., 24. George Oxinden and Council at Surat to Court of Directors, 28 January 1664.
11 Abdul Amir Amin, *British Interests in the Persian Gulf* (Leiden, 1967), 42–52.
12 *Factory Records (Gombroon Diary)*, Vols. 6 & 7. 1750–55.
13 *Selections from State Papers*, 48. Public Dept. Diary No. 9, 22 October 1735; ibid., 52. Public Dept. Diary No. 10, 25 February 1737; ibid., 54–56. Public Dept. Diary No. 4, February 1740; ibid., 282. Henry Moore (Agent at Basra) to Pasha of Baghdad, 20 February 1774.
14 *Selections from State Papers*, 151. Public Dept. Diary No. 38, 30 January 1762.
15 Ibid., 246. Court of Directors to Agent and Council at Basra, 2 March 1768.
16 *Factory Records (Persia and the Persian Gulf)*, vol. 21. Memorial of Chairman etc. of East India Co. to Lord Weymouth, 23 February 1769.
17 Ibid., Lord Weymouth to Chairman etc. 8 May 1769.
18 Ibid., Report on the British Trade with Persia and Arabia, 15 August 1790.
19 Low, C.R., *History of the Indian Navy* (London, 1877), I, 188.
20 Fraser, L., Some Problems of the Persian Gulf, *Proc. of Central Asian Soc.*, 8 January 1908, 5.

III The Trucial Years

The British Government, in its operations in the Gulph having in view the preserving of its tranquillity – as it was owing to the wars among the powers who inhabit its shores that the growth of piracy was encouraged – applied its whole attention to bring about a reconciliation . . .

Warden (Bombay) to Jukes (Bushire), 1821[1]

From the early seventeenth century and during the succeeding two hundred years British policy in the Gulf, directed from the East India Company's factories first at Surat then later, in 1688, at Bombay, had aimed principally at an expansion of peaceful trading, the suppression of maritime aggression, the confinement of competition, the need for security and expediency in communications between Britain and India and, initially, an avoidance of entanglements on land among disputatious factions. Nevertheless, even as early as the founding of the establishment at Bombay this latter hope appeared illusory, for increasing territorial and diplomatic responsibilities with the approval of the Home Government had caused the Court of Directors to note presciently that

> The increase of our revenue is the subject of our care, as much as our trade: 'tis that must maintain our force when twenty accidents may interrupt our trade; 'tis that must make us a nation in India; without that, we are but as a great number of Interlopers, united by His Majesty's Royal Charter, fit only to trade where no body of power thinks it their interest to prevent us.[2]

This pronouncement, anticipating perhaps a novel form of Anglo-Indian nationhood, foreshadowed by nearly a century Pitt's India Act of 1784 which had reinforced the Regulating Act of 1773, whereby was created a Government Department in the form of a Board of Control whose functions lay in the supervision of the political, financial and military commitments within the East India Company's territorial possessions and also in the delegation to the Governor-General of greater powers and responsibilities, thereby laying the firm foundation of an imperial policy of which India was the core. The price of empire, however, is in part the cost of safeguarding frontiers against alien powers, whether physical or ideological, and thus at the end of the eighteenth century the incipient British Empire in India found itself confronted by an enemy within and yet another without.

At this time the Company's most formidable foe was Tipu Sultan of Mysore who, with his late father Haidar 'Ali, had been conducting a series of wars in India against the English since 1767. Tipu was a resolute warrior and the Mysore wars were sternly contested whilst in 1798 he recruited a considerable number of French mercenaries from Mauritius, receiving in the following year from Napoleon written assurances of his support.

In addition, the news of the landing of Napoleon's French expeditionary force in Egypt in 1798 was alarming, since a land threat to India by a strong and sophisticated European power posed a new and formidable problem, even if those fears were to be alleviated shortly afterwards by the destruction of the French fleet by Nelson at Abukir Bay. Last, there was Sultan ibn Ahmad of Muscat who was then under suspicion of entertaining intrigues with the French and who was also known to be in communication with the court of Mysore. It was expedient, therefore, to make every effort to secure the western approaches to India and to ensure that no support should be accorded to Napoleon by Indian or Arab potentates, for such a combination presented alarming possibilities.

That there could be no compromise with Tipu was apparent since even the moderate Arthur Wellesley, future Duke of Wellington, had observed that the logical prosecution of this war was necessitated by 'the consequence of this alliance with the French and in order to punish Tippoo for a breach of faith with us.'[3] That Tipu, in his letter of congratulations to the Governor-General, Lord Mornington, on the outcome of Abukir Bay, took the occasion to hope 'that the French, who are of a crooked disposition, faithless, and the enemies of mankind, may be ever depressed and ruined'[4] was of no avail; war to the end was inevitable and that end came in May 1799 when Tipu was defeated and killed at Seringapatam. With him disappeared the main agency for French interference in India.

Whilst it is true that, during the Napoleonic wars, at this stage the Persian Gulf itself formed only an insignificant part of the theatre over which Anglo-French rivalry struggled for supremacy in Eastern waters, nevertheless for so long as the French operated from their base at Mauritius and elsewhere in the Indian Ocean, then for so long were British naval forces severely extended in the attempt to contain the enemy. Therefore in 1798 Britain, through her new Resident at Bushire, Mirza Mehdi 'Ali Khan, had induced the Imam of Muscat, as

Sultan ibn Ahmad was then styled by the British, to enter into an agreement always to take the side of Britain in international matters and to deny any commercial or other foothold in his dominions to either the French or the Dutch during such time as they might be at war with Britain,[5] whilst in the following year Malcolm's first mission proceeded from Bombay to Tehran via Muscat with a similar purpose in view as well as to counter the designs upon India by Zaman Shah of Afghanistan, being more successful on this occasion than on his second mission in 1808. Thus did Napoleonic France help to shape British policy in the Middle East, imposing upon the region, as earlier noted during the time of Dupleix, an enhanced political and strategic significance and thereby reinvigorating Britain's diplomatic influence within the whole Gulf region.

Consequently, and in view of current French intrigues in Persia which might even imply a potential landward threat to India herself, in 1808 Lord Minto, Governor-General of India, expressed his views thus to Sir John Malcolm, who headed the second mission from India to Persia:

> A further object of importance to obtain from Persia is the exclusion of the French from an establishment in any of the ports or islands in the Persian Gulph subject to the authority of that Government, or from any commercial establishment within the limits of the Persian dominions . . . [The British] Government is desirous also of knowing your opinion with regard to the expediency of undertaking at an early period an expedition on a small scale, for the purpose of preventing the French from occupying a maritime station on the coast or of dislodging them if they should already have obtained possession of such a post.[6]

Not surprisingly, Malcolm reported from Muscat on his way to Persia that Saiyid Sa'id, who had succeeded his father Sultan ibn Ahmad, too must stand clear of any advances made by the French

> whether in India, the Red Sea, or the Gulph, and he should in no extremity . . . allow the French to take possession of any port or island in the Gulph, or to land in any place that was occupied by the troops of his Government . . .[7]

and thereby the imposition of sanctions upon the French was to become widened and extended. Notwithstanding this firm resolve his mission to Persia on this second occasion met with little success owing to his failure to reach Tehran due to matters of self-imposed protocol.

The set-back was temporary, however, for in the following year an Imperial mission headed by Sir Harford Jones reached the Shah's Court and succeeded in effecting a treaty whereby Britain's diplomatic and commercial relations were considerably enhanced to the detriment of those of France. This success fortunately was not negatived by the extraordinary occurrence in 1810 when the Shah found two opposing British plenipotentaries accredited to him; Harford Jones representing the Home Government and Malcolm representing the Government of India, a situation which was terminated only when Malcolm withdrew after some unseemly exchanges between Jones and himself. This occasion was nevertheless portentous for it marked a turning point in Anglo-Persian relations which had hitherto been conducted from the British side by the Government of India and generally Gulfwards and commercial in intent; now these relations were increasingly if erratically to be conducted by the envoys of the Home Government appointed to Tehran and they were to assume added political significance. It was not until 1835, however, that Palmerston put this change finally and formally into effect by his appointment of Henry Ellis as British ambassador on the accession of Muhammad Shah to the Persian throne.

It was not until the surrender of Mauritius in 1810 that the French naval menace came to an end, for until then 'the security of British trade east of the Cape depended on the systematic concentration of merchantmen under convoy escort'.[8] However, while Britain's attention had been directed against Napoleon's presumed oriental ambitions which presented a continued grave threat, heightening the strategic importance of the Gulf, a more general and deep-seated state of disturbance and insecurity was manifesting itself in the Persian Gulf, the causes of which might be described as: the propensity of the maritime Arabs to lawless pursuits, the naval ambitions of Saiyid Sa'id of Muscat, the ascendancy of the Wahabis in central Arabia, the irresolution of the Sublime Porte in Turkish Iraq, the impotency of Persia and the vulnerability of Bahrain. The whole environment was eminently favourable to the Qawasim pirates whose activities now knew no restraint and whose attacks upon British shipping increased until a belated blockade in 1806 undertaken by joint British and Muscati naval forces employed against them induced the Qawasim to agree to a truce of temporary duration, return their spoil, and respect the flag and property of the Company and its dependents. This modest victory was unfortunately to be short-lived.

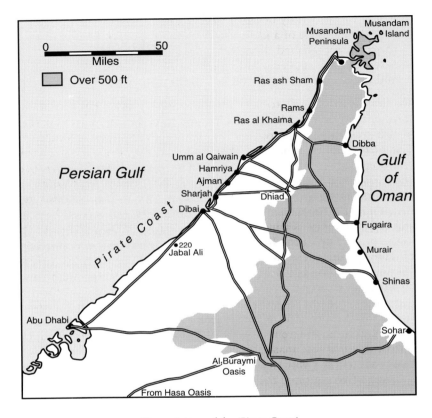

Figure 9 Map of the 'Pirate Coast'

It is necessary, then, to direct attention to the continued acts of piracy which for centuries had been a means of tribal livelihood in the Gulf and elsewhere around the Arabian shores and with which British ships, as representing the only organized maritime force, had become increasingly involved. The principal tribe was that of the Qawasim (at times referred to as Jawasim or Jawasmis), of whom it is recorded that 'Their occupation is piracy, and their delight murder . . . for they are descended from a Houl, or monster'.[9] Their main port was at Ras-al-Khaimah but ancillary ports and strongholds extended along the coast from Khor-as-Shem or Elphinstone's Inlet for 150 miles in a south-westerly direction. 'The towns of this coast', said Low, which was generally designated 'The Pirate Coast', are all built near the entrance of a *khor*, or salt water inlet, and the maritime robbers, established here from a very remote period . . . extended their depredations along the southern coast of Arabia, and even to the shores of India and the Red Sea.[10]

We first hear of those tribal pirates gaining an ascendancy over the ships of the Bombay Marine in 1770 when the *Britannia* and another British vessel were captured and detained; these may have formed the first prizes though it has already been noted that the convoy system had been instituted a hundred years earlier when East Indiamen had been assaulted in the Gulf and the Arabian Sea. The Court of Directors, however, were reluctant to engage in hostile measures which might involve them in practical difficulties throughout the Gulf and especially with Karim Khan in Persia, so they suggested recourse to the protection of the Royal Navy and to a resumption of a system of convoys in those waters.[11] Further attacks were nevertheless continued against the British flag during the next thirty years since resolute naval action was not forthcoming, a series of inconclusive wars in India and distractions by the French there having imposed a severe and protracted strain upon the Company's resources. A limitation of a different nature, however, had been placed upon British ships, whose masters had been enjoined not to interfere with piracy as such but only to act in self-defence. Thus the Qawasim were encouraged to continue their activities even to the point of deception and treachery. When, therefore, the position of Saiyid Sa'id became precarious and repeated attacks had been made upon British ships, despite the truce of 1806, the Bombay Government furnished an expedition in 1809 to punish the pirates, who were accordingly engaged and a part of whose fleet was destroyed; the results were nevertheless inconclusive. The instructions given by Bombay to commanding officers on this occasion were as interesting as they were explicit:

> The object of your expedition is . . . to be directed to the destruction of these pirate vessels, the operations of the forces under your command being, excepting in cases of particular emergency, limited to the sea, neither are the troops or crews of the ships meant to be employed on shore against any land forces in the service of the Wahabee Chiefs, unless their being so should be found essentially requisite, either for the destruction of the

piratical boats or to recover for the Imaum of Muscat some of the seaports between Rasat Nud and Mussendum, at present in the hands of the piratical Joasmees.

Directing attention towards the opposite shores of the Gulf, the Government's orders continued more circumspectly:

> . . . but in any case you need not hesitate to proceed to destroy the maritime equipment of the pirates on that state of the Gulph . . . taking care to proceed in all such cases with the utmost practicable respect towards the undisputed right of His Majesty the King of Persia . . . without the slightest intention to occupy any part of the territory . . .

Notwithstanding these injunctions to apply their attention to confining hostilities at sea, the captains were further enjoined:

> The Governor-in-Council would also be happy to be favoured with your opinion in respect to the most eligible island in the vicinity of the Joasmee ports which it would be advisable for us to occupy as a maritime station of Residency in preference to Muscat, with the view of more effectually commanding the entrance of the Gulph and checking the future depredations of the pirates . . .[12]

and thus it becomes apparent that despite the narrowness of immediate aims, a grander design was already forming in the minds of the governing councils in India.

The year 1809 provided a turning point in other respects, for clearly from that time onward an attitude of *laissez faire* could hardly be longer maintained; either Britain was to exercise her foreshadowed role as policeman in the Gulf, or face a complete withdrawal. The dispute between Persia and Bahrain was nascent and was to cause bedevilment into the twentieth century, trade and security were threatened by belligerency at sea, whilst Britain's ally Saiyid Sa'id was menaced on either side by the Qawasim and the Wahabis to such an extent that a little extra pressure might drive him from the one to seek the dubious support of the other. Not only here but elsewhere along the Arabian shores and the oases of Oman was the threat continually posed by the Wahabi tribes, notably that of the Sa'udi amirate of Najd, a militant and fundamentalist Islamic sect which had assumed a vigorous proselytizing role amongst fellow Muslims and which was under strong suspicion of instigating acts of piracy amongst the coastal tribes. The British quandary was not long to remain unresolved and action was taken to subdue the pirates, support Saiyid Sa'id and keep the Wahabis in check. That this simple set of decisions was to have far-reaching implications and consequences of an international character could hardly have been foreseen at that time, nor was it to be fully appreciated that the end of the Napoleonic regime, in freeing British India from distractions which had their genesis in Europe, would cause Britain to assume a greater burden of responsibility concomitant with the rise of empire and the relatively peaceful disposition then subsisting within her domains and beyond her borders.

The state of affairs in the Oman peninsula at that time should now be considered. This eastern extremity of Arabia, in which Muscat occupies a commanding position to seaward, stands isolated from its neighbours by sea and sand so that its inhabitants have tended to remain aloof, both socially and politically, from those of the rest of mainland Arabia. Oman early, at about A.D. 700, inherited the doctrines of the extremist Khawarij sect and these tenets in due course became modified by the Ibadiya, who were noted for their sober disposition and an insistence on the electoral quality in the Imamate, an office in which sacerdotal and secular functions soon became intermingled. Thus to geography was allied an ecclesiastical isolation, first from the legitimist 'Abbasid caliphate then later from the Sa'udi Wahabis and other Muslim sects, so that Oman became cut off from the greater world of Islam though, as if to establish balance, its Rulers adopted an expansionist policy which led them to engage themselves not merely in territorial adventures and acquisitions along the opposite Persian coast but also in colonizing activities in East Africa and the islands off that coast.

Contrary to the elective principle a leading chief, Ahmad ibn Sa'id, on his assumption of the Imamate in 1749 succeeded in founding a dynasty in which the office of Imam became hereditary, and this continued until about 1811 (the exact year is uncertain) when, on the death of the then incumbent, and consequent upon family feuds, the Imamate was allowed to lapse and was not seriously revived until the twentieth century. Sultan ibn Ahmad, on ascending to the throne in Muscat in 1792, was entitled 'Saiyid' and much later his successors were to be known as 'Sultan', though by the Company's servants the Ruler was still styled 'Imam' until well into the nineteenth century.[13]

Thus it was that Saiyid Sa'id and his dynastic successors could not claim the religious adherence of the Omanis who, from that time, have been divided in their allegiance between the source of temporal power at Muscat (or wherever the Ruler at the time might be) and the claims of religious obedience by contestant Imams. Saiyid Sa'id was accordingly confronted with disputes and insurrections within his borders which he was as anxious to allay as were his adversaries, within and without his frontiers, to foment.

It has already been observed that the disturbance in the Gulf was favourable to piratical activities, and further contributory factors may be considered. First, there was the terrain of the Qawasim, which was noted by Captain Robert Taylor, Assistant Political Agent in Turkish Arabia at that time. 'The extreme general sterility of those parts of the continents of Persia and Arabia', he observed, 'which confine the intervening Gulf has contrived to present to the view of its Natives the life of a freebooter in a more inviting form than could have been given to it had they been situated in a country of greater resources.'[14] Next, there was the interminable warfare between the tribes of the Arabian mainland, which had led to a state of instability both politically and economically, this having been enhanced rather than otherwise by a temporary eclipse of the Wahabi Arabs, then hard pressed by the Egyptians under Mehemet 'Ali, whose drive eastwards towards the Gulf, commencing with an assault upon the Hijaz in 1811, was accompanied by disturbing claims to sovereignty over the lands along the Arabian shores. Finally, there was the role of the East India Company itself. This was also a time of marked transition in both the affairs and the administration of the Company, for its trade monopoly in its corporate capacity was abolished in India and adjacent countries in 1813, whilst two years beforehand the Gulf trade had been thrown open by a Resolution of the Bombay Government, and after 1819 there appear to be no references to the Company's trade. Separate and mutually independent Political Residencies were maintained by the Government of India at Baghdad, Basra, Bushire and Muscat, though all were under the administration of the Bombay Government.[15] The Company and its Marine, therefore, were not induced to subdue the pirates and police the Gulf merely in defence of narrow commercial interests, but had assumed that degree of supervision by virtue of the inevitable acquisition of the status of an international power.

Acting in conjunction with the Government of India at Calcutta, who at that time were now freed from the distractions of wars within the Indian subcontinent, Bombay was forced to the conclusion that nothing short of punitive measures of an unmistakeably forceful character and lasting nature would bring peace to the Gulf, whereupon an expedition was formed in 1819 under the command of Sir William Grant Keir. This assaulted the pirates so vigorously and so completely annihilated their fleet and strongholds that they were forced to accept the terms offered. To see the situation through the eyes of those who were responsible for determining events at that time, it is necessary to quote from contemporary documents which are self-revealing. Indicating the line of policy which Bombay proposed should be followed in Persian Gulf affairs, Mountstuart Elphinstone, Governor of Bombay, advised Lord Hastings, Governor-General of India, that

> We are of the opinion that we should abstain from . . . the pretensions which are advanced to the occupation of Bahrein . . . [giving] a distinct explanation to the Shaikh of that island that so long as he restrains his tribe from the prosecution of acts of aggression on the high seas . . . he may rely on experiencing from the British Government every degree of encouragement and friendly intercourse . . . Every vessel of a warlike character will no doubt be destroyed by the armament, and only those to be employed in commerce should in future be allowed to navigate . . .
>
> In regard to the Imam of Muscat we should hope that little difficulty would be experienced in convincing him of the policy of consolidating and strengthening the possessions and resources which he commands, instead of weakening them by an extension of his territories. We might derive very material aid from the co-operation of His Highness's vessels and boats, in the future protection of the Gulph, [and British supervision would] aid us in securing the future tranquillity of the Gulph, acting in conjunction with our own cruisers.
>
> The interest of Persia would as it appears to us be materially promoted, by our interposition in restoring the Gulph to its former state of security.
>
> The suggestion of forming an establishment in the Persian Gulph in a more central situation will engage our attention . . . It is our intention to station as large a marine force in the Gulph as we can spare, with some armed boats for the purpose of visiting different ports, and guarding against any vessels being equipped of a warlike character. The presence of this force [under Keir] combined with the salutary effects . . . are the measures which appear the best calculated for the general suppression of piracy.[16]

To Henry Willock, the British Minister at Tehran, Elphinstone at the same time sent a long letter acquainting him with these views, since the Persian Government might well have viewed with some apprehension such forcible action in the Gulf by the Company's Marine.

> You cannot afford the Persian Government a more satisfactory proof of the disinterestedness of our intentions than by an appeal to the nature and result of the last expedition [of 1809] on which occasion the most positive orders were issued for confining its operations to the destruction of the piratical craft and on no account to extend them to the interior of the country. These instructions having been fulfilled, the expedition returned to Bombay.

Elphinstone then pointed out that these expectations, however, had not been realized and consequently the Qawasim continued their depredations due to the absence of the constant presence of a marine force in the Gulf. He continued:

> You must be fully aware . . . that the influence of the [Persian] Government on the various tribes inhabiting the ports on the shores and islands of the Gulf of Persia has been completely annihilated since the ascendancy of the Wahabee power, and that it has not commanded the means of controlling those piratical habits which have been encouraged and protected by Sheikh of that tribe. Under these circumstances the British Government was at full liberty to pursue whatever measures it might consider necessary for the protection of its own subjects and the general trade of India against future annoyance . . .

and he concluded by impressing upon Willock that Britain desired to maintain an attitude of strict neutrality in the Gulf, but that the Persian Government must endeavour to establish the most effective control over its own coasts, prohibit the outfit of private armed vessels and lay down maritime regulations.[17]

Finally, Keir was addressed upon the ultimate arrangements that might be necessary to maintain the security of navigation in the Gulf.

> The Governor-in-Council is satisfied that the object thus contemplated cannot, from the distracted state in which the Gulph has so long continued, arising out of the decline of the influence of those authorities which formerly exercised a control

over it and of the ascendancy of the Power whose avowed views had been the prosecution of piracy, be attained without the interposition of the British Government in a more active degree than it has hitherto been our policy to adopt . . .

whilst in conclusion Bombay stressed the necessity for the promulgation of a code of maritime regulations to be observed by the different tribes of the Gulf.[18]

These documents accordingly lay bare the purpose and intentions of the British authorities in India and which, pursued unremittingly in the years to follow, formed the basis of British policy in the Persian Gulf until recent times. The extent of modification necessary in applying that policy and the degree of success attained become apparent with the passage of time.

Keir's expedition was successful, resulting in the General Treaty with the Arab Shaikhs for the cessation of plunder and piracy by land and sea. This was signed on 8 January, 1820, a similar undertaking being entered into by the Shaikh of Bahrain the following month,[19] and it is important to note that these engagements did not prevent open and lawful warfare but were directed specifically against piratical enterprises including the traffic in slaves. Keir was able to report that 'the impression made throughout the Gulf by the complete success of the expedition is palpably very great, and must, while it is maintained, produce the most beneficial consequences.' He cautioned, however, against running the risk of weakening the ascendancy thus acquired, for paper agreements must be backed by an obvious ability to deliver prompt punishment to transgressors.[20]

As an indication that these were no idle protestations, the policy of non-intervention by land was firmly applied, as is to be noted in the case of the Bani Bu 'Ali tribe. These belligerent Omanis had rebelled against Saiyid Sa'id and killed an emissary of Captain Thompson, the Political Agent at Muscat, whereupon the latter joined forces with Saiyid Sa'id, marching into the interior in order to exact retribution. For this adventure Thompson was admonished and removed from his appointment in 1820 as having transgressed against the declared policy of the Bombay Government which, it stated,

has repeatedly and expressly been declared to be, to confine our views strictly to the control and suppression of piracy where it actually subsists, and to abstain from taking part in disputes of the States in the Gulf, even when within reach of our maritime power, further than was absolutely necessary for the accomplishment of that object.

Elphinstone added the final reprimand:

> Your co-operation with the Imam, on the other hand, was calculated to persuade the Arab powers that we were inclined to pursue our enemies into the interior, and to interfere in their internal disputes for the professed purpose of guarding against prospective dangers at sea. The natural consequences of such an opinion would be to generate distrust and suspicion of our ultimate objects, and to draw into confederacies against us even the tribes and powers who are least entrusted in protecting pirates.[21]

Thompson, co-architect of the 1820 Treaty, was nevertheless to establish a precedent whereby Britain was to become drawn more and more, inevitably albeit unwillingly, into the mainland disputes of the Arab states.

The Persian impotency at sea was again made manifest when Fath 'Ali Shah vainly demanded of Saiyid Sa'id and later Keir that ships be provided for the purpose of carrying an army to assault Bahrain, though this request hardly accorded with the Persian claim that the Gulf comprised Persian territorial waters and that foreign ships-of-war should seek permission to enter the Gulf.[22] It is a fair comment on the state of affairs along the Persian coast that several times the Resident at Bushire had been approached by the Governor of that town requesting British co-operation in keeping order in his port and also to undertake the prevention of any aggression by sea.[23]

The signing of the 1820 Treaty marked the commencement of a period during which the Gulf enjoyed comparative peace although the British naval forces were hard pressed at times in seeing that its terms were observed. Inevitably, however, the other and open form of warfare persisted, and it was difficult also to distinguish acts of piracy from petty sea wars, whilst Saiyid Sa'id continually appealed to Bombay for support against maritime incursion by the Qawasim, though to no avail since this was contrary to expressed policy. It became clear to Bombay, therefore that nothing short of a cessation of all forms of maritime warfare would secure that state of tranquillity which the Government so earnestly desired. It is convenient here to pursue this aspect of peace-keeping at sea to its conclusion three decades later, and so a hardening of attitude at Bombay is discerned in the Government's instructions to the Resident at Bushire in 1828, in which he was informed that the Marine in the Gulf was established there to preserve peace, which was 'a most desirable object and one of equal consequence in an economical and political view.' It was deemed appropriate that the Government should look upon themselves as the head of a naval confederacy for the entire suppression of piracy (though indeed it formed the whole corpus of such an hypothetical union); nevertheless, the letter continued significantly,

> It is desirable still to abstain from all interference in any wars not arising from piratical causes, but as the attainment of our principal object, that of gradually introducing peaceable habits amongst the various tribes in the Gulf, will greatly depend upon their ceasing to have recourse to arms upon every occasion, I am directed to observe that while you continue most cautious in not giving guarantees or involving Government, you are to take every opportunity of impressing the different chiefs with our desire of their remaining at peace with each other . . . The pearl banks during the season should not be the theatre of war to any of the Arab chiefs, and the party infringing this rule by commencing an attack, should be treated as a pirate.[24]

The years 1834 and 1835 were nevertheless marked by a great number of disturbances in the Gulf, occasioning both acts of piracy and associated hostilities at sea in which the Bani Yas Arabs, subject to the Shaikh of Abu Dhabi, and the Qawasim of Sharjah jointly distinguished themselves, but an effective blockade of that latter port by Samuel Hennell, the Resident, had the effect of restoring order. This uprising by the Bani Yas was violent and protracted, lasting for five months during which shipping was attacked, trade in the Gulf suffered and the pearling fishery, on which the livelihood of so many Arabs depended, was subjected to menace and loss. It was quite apparent that repetitions of this undesirable activity, where the distinction between overt war at sea and covert piracy was finely drawn, could have damaging and lasting effect upon the whole economy of the Gulf. In 1835, therefore, the shaikhs were induced to enter into a maritime truce for a period of six months coinciding with the pearling season in the waters mainly surrounding Bahrain and Qatar, with the understanding that the British forces would not interpose themselves in tribal quarrels on land. Such was the effect of this truce that it was renewed during the following two years for eight months thence annually until 1843, and then from that time for a period of ten years. On the expiration of that agreement in 1853 a treaty of perpetual peace was effected, providing for a complete cessation of hostilities at sea between the shaikhdoms, and also that in the event of aggression by sea no retaliation should be undertaken but that reference should be made to the British authorities and that Britain should watch over the peace of the Gulf to ensure that all times the treaty was observed.[25] Thus did the Pirate Coast become appropriately redesignated the Trucial Coast of Oman. The year 1853 accordingly marks a triumphal stage in British policy in the Gulf, setting the seal on nearly half a century of patient diplomacy to exact by agreement that which would have been costly and perhaps unattained if attempted by force.

At this time it was obvious that the desire for peace and concord in the affairs of the Gulf was offset by a reluctance to become embroiled politically to any extent other than that of bare necessity. Even at that date it is apparent, as always, that the further authorities were from the scene the more unrealistic was their appraisal of trends and policy, whilst the active work of pacification and consolidation was left in the hands of the Residents, usually men of ability and initiative, who have left their indelible stamp upon the history of the Gulf. For example, Saiyid Sa'id had as usual been apprehensive of invasion of his territory by the resurgent Wahabisn and also of being engaged in hostilities with tribes under their control or influence. He pressed Bombay for an avowal of their policy in such an emergency and this in turn was referred to Calcutta. In their reply of 1 February 1834 the latter observed that they were

> . . . not prepared to sanction the employment of the British arms for the purpose of maintaining the integrity of the continental possessions of the Imam of Muscat. If we were once to commit ourselves by a declaration of our intention to support that Chief, this line of policy must be followed up at any expense, and it is impossible to set limits to the waste of blood and treasure which might ensue in consequence . . . Our only concern is with the maritime commerce of the Gulf, and as long as this is not molested, it matters not to us whether one power or another holds dominion on its shores . . . But even if the worst contingency that can be supposed likely to take place, were actually to happen, and the Wahabees were not only to acquire possession of the port of Muscat but also to commit acts of piracy upon the Gulf trade, it is conceived that it would be cheaper and easier to chastise them under these circumstances,

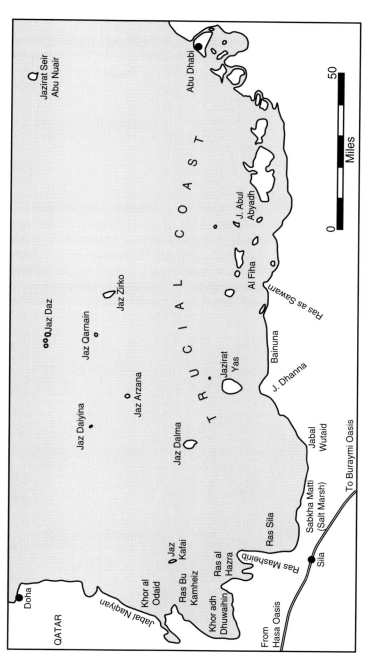

Figure 10 Map of the 'Trucial Coast'

than to take up the question in its present state and constitute ourselves the guardians of the possessions of the Imam of Muscat against his enemies.[26]

Distance lent a false perspective which was further distorted by the remoteness of London, for in April the Court of Directors, in acknowledging the above dispatch, had occasion to review the whole policy in regard to the Arab tribes of the Gulf and also to Saiyid Sa'id. In expressing entire concurrence with the views of the Government of India and having regard to the requirements for the protection of commerce and the enforcement of engagements already entered into, they further observed that

> . . . the Arab tribes on the Gulph would not be averse to our assuming protection over them, which would be implied in our prohibiting wars and becoming the arbitrators of all their disputes. We entirely concur with you, however, in considering the assumption of such a power, and indeed, any more intimate connexion with those States than at present exists, to be wholly inadvisable.[27]

Today these words have a familiar ring, expressing as they do the desire to secure maximum achievement for minimum cost, an improbable alliance of parsimony and peace. That the price must be paid and further political involvements accepted and pursued was to be borne out fully in the ensuing years.

This desired detachment from direct entanglement on the mainland was first rudely shaken by Egyptian ambitions in Arabia, which conflicted with British interests since the affairs of Turkish Iraq were an object of concern to Britain on grounds both economic and political. In 1812 the title of Resident at Basra had been changed to that of Political Agent in Turkish Arabia, and this latter official was to reside at either Baghdad or Basra as convenient, whilst in 1831 the Secret Committee in London directed that the Political Agent should fix his residence chiefly at Baghdad, thus indicating the importance which that pashaliq had assumed, despite or perhaps because of the Egyptian Ibrahim's rapid advance into Syria, which was a manifest threat to the integrity of the ailing Ottoman empire. The need for a better system of postal communications with India had long been apparent, quickened by the earlier Napoleonic hold on Egypt, and thus the great waterways of Turkish Mesopotamia linked with the Gulf had suggested an obvious and convenient route considerably shortening that round the Cape and, it was hoped, with less hazard than via Egypt and the Red Sea.

Between the years 1829 and 1832 surveyors were dispatched to examine the feasability of the Euphrates for steam navigation which was then in its vigorous infancy, and Lieutenant Ormsby of the Indian Navy was engaged in a survey of that river; his resultant charts produced in circumstances of incredible difficulty were nevertheless of the first order. At about the same time Colonel F.R. Chesney, who had first been occupying himself in examining communications via Egypt, was turning his attention to the Euphrates as a possible alternative, and between 1831 and 1832 he had traversed the entire length of that river by raft and so convinced himself of the advantages of what was to be known as the 'direct' route to India as opposed to the 'overland' route via Cairo. Chesney's argument, reinforced by the consideration that command of this riverine line of communication would serve also to outflank the Russians in any design to advance towards the Gulf, impressed Palmerston, then Foreign Secretary, and as a result in 1834 Chesney was commissioned by Parliament to lead an expedition along the Euphrates valley to examine in greater detail the navigable practicability of the project.

Despite protracted delays the expedition got under way and succeeded in hauling across the Syrian desert the iron hulks of two river steamers, the *Tigris* and *Euphrates*, designed to make the descent of the great river. The former vessel foundered soon after the descent began and almost ensured the deaths of Chesney and Lieutenant Lynch, I.N., Chesney's able assistant and subsequent successor in leading the enterprise. By 1842, when the expedition was disbanded, although the rivers Euphrates, Tigris and Karun had been well investigated, it was clear that the route presented more difficulties than conveniences and accordingly it languished just as that via Cairo and Suez prospered.

Nevertheless, it should be mentioned that well before this time and from an early date in the eighteenth century postal communications of a desultory kind had been maintained between Bombay and Basra by means of cruisers of the Bombay Marine. Between Basra and Aleppo, under the supervision of the Company's Agent, a dromedary post was kept up, and from Aleppo a horse post to Constantinople. It is interesting to observe that in 1798 Nelson, after the battle of the Nile, communicated the intelligence of his victory to the Bombay Government by this route.[28]

Meanwhile, in Arabia itself the Egyptians had been consolidating their position in an attempt to carve out an empire independent of the

Porte. In 1824, after armed disputes lasting for over six years, Mehemet 'Ali was obliged to recognize Turki ibn 'Abdullah, the Wahabi chief, as ruler of Najd (Central Arabia). Turki's reign lasted for ten years until his assassination in 1834 when his son Faisal succeeded to the Amirate; this occasioned a renewal of Egyptian designs and of assaults upon the house of Sa'ud. By 1838 Faisal had been defeated by Khurshid Pasha, commander of the Egyptian forces in Arabia, who had now advanced as far east as Hasa and Qatif (at the western coast of the Gulf), whilst early in the following year Khurshid dispatched emissaries to Bahrain and Kuwait, demanding supplies from the latter and the submission of the former.[29]

In London, Palmerston had at first been content to observe the progress of affairs in Arabia with equanimity but later viewed with growing alarm the distinct possibility that the Arabian littoral of the Gulf might become subjected to rule from Cairo and that the Mesopotamian basin might fall into Khedival hands. His anxieties had been aroused in particular by the memorandum presented to him in 1833 by Henry Ellis, now a member of the Board of Control in London, who had noted that it was contrary to British and Indian interests that a strong Muslim state should command lower Mesopotamia and the adjacent Arab lands and thus, by means of extended communications, be enabled to 'excite the attention and unsettle the minds of our Indian subjects'.[30] In the following year Palmerston was out of office though he returned to his former ministry in 1835; but confronted then with other distractions it was not until the end of 1838 that the news of the Egyptian advance to Hasa renewed his misgivings. Hennell was accordingly instructed to enter a protest to Khurshid and to keep a watchful eye on the maritime chiefs[31] whilst Campbell, Consul-General at Cairo, had been advised by Palmerston in November 1838 that he should ascertain from Mehemet 'Ali whether it was his intention to establish himself upon the eastern shores of Arabia and to occupy Bahrain. Campbell was further instructed that

> You will add that Her Majesty's Government hope and trust that he [Mehemet 'Ali] will, upon full consideration, abandon any intention of establishing himself on the Persian Gulf, because, as you have already declared to him, such a scheme on his part could not be viewed with indifference by the British Government.

At the same time like representations were made to Campbell from both Calcutta and Bombay.[32]

Hennell's instructions from Bombay were no less explicit. The acting Governor, James Farish, stated unequivocally that Hennell was to inform Khurshid that if his threat to subdue Bahrain were persisted in, then the whole future relations between Britain and Egypt would be at stake.[33] To add reinforcement to the argument Maitland, Commander-in-Chief East Indies Station, was ordered in June 1839 to dispose his squadron within the Gulf and to offer Hennell all support.[34] In that year, too, Britain acquired the insignificant port of Aden. This move was designed to offset Mehemet 'Ali's drive southwards into the Yemen.

So, until late 1840, affairs in the Gulf oscillated between Egyptian and British advances with anxious Arab chiefs disposed to incline towards apparent strength; then the Egyptian position deteriorated and their forces were rapidly withdrawn to defend Syria against a combination of British and Turkish forces. By the end of that year Mehemet 'Ali's imperial vision was shattered and his hopes of advancing into Arabia receded forever. Nevertheless he was careful to leave behind a Wahabi chief, Khalid ibn Sa'ud, as Amir of Najd and Hasa, who in turn made his submission to the Porte and was accordingly appointed *vali* of Najd. Thus it was that the Turks reinforced their subsequent claims to sovereignty over Central Arabia, ineffectual though in practice this was to prove.

An Ottoman assertion of dominion over Arabia would have been as unwelcome as that of Mehemet 'Ali, even if backed by an adequate show of force, but to allow an ineffective Turkish authority over the Arabian littoral would have been worse for it would have negated the whole policy of maritime peace and security in the Gulf. So Turkish attempts to bring these areas within the dominion of the Porte were strenuously resisted throughout the remainder of the century. In this connexion Stratford Canning, British Ambassador at Constantinople, had advised Lord Aberdeen, the Foreign Secretary, that

> the Information which I am directed by one of Your Lordship's instructions to obtain respecting the extent of the Sultan's legitimate Sovereignty in Arabia, is not easy of access. The Turks, even those in office, know little or nothing of the remote parts of [their] Empire, and the conjecture of the most learned among them would not fail to support the Sovereign's claim to the utmost possible latitude.[35]

Maitland's naval dispositions within the Gulf were no passing phase, for not long after these events Bombay issued instructions early in 1841 to the Superintendent of the Indian Navy that the authority of the Resident at Bushire was declared to be paramount in the Gulf to the extent that the entire squadron which might at any time be stationed there was to be placed at his disposal. Accordingly, the Navy was declared to be an instrument for implementing policy under the increasing power and prestige of the British representative in the Gulf.[36]

Britain still desired to maintain the *status quo ante bellum*, and the possibility of any realignment of interests with other powers, or territorial gains on her own behalf, were barely contemplated. Hennell deemed it expedient to inquire concerning the foreseen extent of British military presence in those waters, and in return the Government of India stated unequivocally that

> . . . now that the ambitious designs of the ruler of Egypt have been checked, it would be more prudent and conformable to our general views of policy in that quarter to avoid mixing ourselves up with the contests of the native powers, and far preferable that we should confine our interference to the constant maintenance of our maritime supremacy over the tribes of the coast.[37]

Rawlinson at Baghdad received his instructions in like vein. His appointment in 1843 as Political Agent in Turkish Arabia was made

> in the earnest desire to preserve peace between Persia and Turkey, and in the confidence that you will most zealously devote all your exertions to the accomplishment of this object; you will feel that your efforts can only be effectually aided by the reliance of both Governments upon your perfect impartiality in every question which exists or which may arise between them, and you will so act as to induce them to place their reliance upon you.[38]

Nine years later Rawlinson was able to report in a despatch that

> I have thus considered it my duty, since my nomination to the Political Agency of Turkish Arabia, to adopt a general conciliatory conduct, and to strengthen and extend our local influence, as far as that end may be attainable without giving umbrage to the Turkish authorities. In the prosecution of these objects, too, my hands have been greatly strengthened by the presence of the Hon'ble Co's armed steamer upon the river, and by the success of her commander in cultivating friendly relations with the Arab tribes.[39]

Other events on the farther side of the Gulf conspired to engage British attention during the years 1837 and 1838. The Shaikh of Sharjah, Sultan ibn Saqar, had in the former year desired British assistance in obtaining satisfaction from the people of Kharg, whereupon Hennell informed him that in no circumstances could the Arab chiefs be permitted to interfere in the affairs of the Persian coasts, adding that 'you may rest assured that if you attempt to send over a force ... you will incur the displeasure of the British Government.'[40] Britain was not, however, to restrict herself to guarding Persian shores from aggression but was also to assault them on her own account soon afterwards. In November 1837 a Persian army led in person by Muhammad Shah had invaded Afghanistan and besieged the city of Herat. To the Persians this was simply a resumption of the lands of eastern Khurasan which had earlier formed part of Persian territories, but the British governments both at home and in India viewed the matter in a far different light. Russia had steadily been encroaching upon Persian soil and extending her influence there; consequently, it seemed, any Persian thrust eastwards into Afghanistan would bring Russia closer to the threshold of India. Palmerston had prophesied that the clash between Russia and Britain would occur in Central Asia[41] and this dismal prospect had, during the years since the Treaty of Turkmanchai in 1828 which conceded Russia an advantage in the Caspian regions, exercised the minds of political prophets. Formal protests by Sir John M'Neill, the British Minister at Tehran, being unavailing, a naval expedition including the *Hugh Lindsay*, the first steamer to ply in the Gulf waters, left India for the Gulf and occupied Kharg and this event, coupled with heavy Persian losses before the walls of Herat, induced the Shah speedily to conclude his campaign and to retire within his own borders.

History was to repeat itself identically twenty years later when Nasr-ud-din Shah besieged Herat once more, thus giving cause to Sir James Outram's campaign in the Persian Gulf which was successful in effecting a second Persian withdrawal; a fuller account is given in Chapter 8. An inescapable conclusion from these various episodes is that the Persian coast was undefended and indefensible, placing that nation at the mercy of any power capable of providing an effective maritime force.

A further consideration of marked significance was the threat continually posed of Russian penetration in the north, for since the Treaty of Turkmanchai the Tsar had profited by the weakness of the Shah to extend his rule in Central Asia, and the British and Indian

Governments were not prepared to regard with indifference a potential Russian menace to India's northern borders. Whilst Russia's policy in Central Asia lies properly beyond the scope of this present study, nevertheless it coloured the outlook in Calcutta and conditioned certain reflexes there which were to persist throughout the following hundred years or more, and to induce Britain to counter that threat by strengthening her resources in the Gulf. The spectre of a southward drive by Russia, whose search for a warm water port was assiduously pursued, had confronted Britain since 1833 when Turkey signed the Treaty of Unkiar Skelessi with Russia. If it were the Russian ambition to extend that country's influence down the Euphrates valley to the Shatt-al-Arab then Britain would be powerless to counter that move and her whole strategy in the Middle East and beyond to India would be jeopardised. The East India Company were fully aware of this, for 'all our interest', said Thomas Love Peacock, Chief Examiner of India House, giving evidence before the Select Committee on Steam Navigation to India,

> in the way of guarding against Russia, lies in the Persian Gulf
> . . . They have now steam boats on the Volga and the Caspian.
> They will soon have them on the sea of Aral and the Oxus, and
> in all probability on the Euphrates and the Tigris . . . They will
> do everything in Asia that is worth the doing, and that we leave
> undone.[42]

In these circumstances it was not surprising that Palmerston afforded every encouragement to Chesney's enterprise to open up the river route through Mesopotamia, and a re-echo was heard half a century later on the eve of the Second Afghan War when the Foreign Secretary, Lord Salisbury, foresaw the Russians on the march again. 'Are you prepared to see the allegiance of the people of Asia given up to the advancing Power?' he demanded. 'If so, what chance is there of maintaining the loyalty of the people of India, if they know Russia to be dominant on the Tigris and Euphrates?'[43]

It is fashionable today to decry nineteenth century British apprehensions of the Russian menace in the East, but that these fears were not groundless may be seen from a memorandum presented to the Tsar in 1838.

> It is certain that as long as the English hold the key to the Persian
> Gulf, they can dispose at will of Persia's tranquillity, and
> maintain the prince who governs it in fear, humiliation and

dependence. These considerations are so grave that we believe there is no need to insist further on one fact that dominates all others; namely, that it is in Russia's well understood interest to use all her efforts to dislodge the English, if possible, from the position they have seized in the Persian Gulf.[44]

Concurrent with piratical activities had been an extensive traffic in slaves brought from Africa to the shores of Arabia and Persia, but the 1820 Treaty was inadequate to prevent this trade despite the fact that an article in that treaty had declared the carrying off and transportation of slaves to be piracy. Much, of course, depended on the interpretation of this article and any attempt at that time to force the issue too far could well have given rise to fresh disturbances within the Gulf as an indication of the maritime tribes' resentment at excessive interference with a substantial portion of their tribal economy. A separate approach had therefore to be made towards its suppression, and the first success was scored in 1822 when Saiyid Sa'id was prevailed upon to enter into an agreement for curtailing the sale of slaves within his dominions and forbidding their transportation to European ports and possessions. This year also saw the establishment of the Moresby Line which defined the eastern limits in the Indian Ocean for the movements of slavers. In 1838 and 1839 the maritime chiefs likewise acceded to the wishes of the British Government in confining their slaving activities, whilst in the latter year the Moresby Line was moved further to the westward in the Arabian Sea so that the movement of slaves from East Africa to Arabia and the Gulf was virtually restricted to coastal traffic and thereby afforded easier means of surveillance.[45]

Robertson, then acting Political Resident at Bushire, correctly assessed the situation when he communicated his views to the Secret Committee in London. 'The tranquillity we have given to these seas', he observed, 'although injurious to the Arab pirates . . . enabled them to recover much of their lost ground, and the employment of their men and boats . . . will still further increase their resources for extending that traffic which we wish to suppress.' He further expressed the view that the Arab chiefs would abandon this trade only through fear of British intervention, rightly concluding that the only way to prevent it effectively would be to impose a thorough check on the East African ports whence it originated.[46]

Robertson then addressed the Bombay Government on the necessity for consolidating the British position in the Gulf to the benefit of the tribes and countries bordering it since, he argued, 'The peace and prosperity of the Gulf has been hitherto maintained solely by our Maritime ascendancy, and the constant presence of a powerful Naval Squadron. The same means, and only the same means, can secure the same benefits for the future.' He concluded with a final altruistic observation. 'The expanse of our Naval Armament has been borne entirely by us – the benefit of it has been shared by Persia, Turkey and Arabia. If we have protected our own Commerce and Merchants, much more have we protected theirs. Where our Government has gained one, by duties of export and import, these Governments have gained four.'[47]

By this time, Palmerston had come to the conclusion that direction of anti-slavery efforts, to be effective in all waters, must be transferred from the Government of India to the Foreign Office. Consequent upon renewed British pressure, direct and indirect, the maritime chiefs finally undertook in 1847 to abolish completely the slave trade in their ports and in that year too Saiyid Sa'id agreed reluctantly to cease the export trade from his East African territories. In 1848 the Shah forbade the importation of slaves into Persia by sea, augmenting this decision in 1851 by empowering British ships to detain and search Persian vessels suspected of carrying slaves. By a later convention of 1882 the Persian agreements were confirmed and fortified. In 1847 the Porte issued *firmans* granting British ships the right of search of suspected slavers sailing under the Turkish flag and in 1873 the Sultan of Muscat entered into a similar agreement and in effect undertook to abolish slavery in his dominions. In the same year the Sultan of Zanzibar was pressed to conclude a treaty whereby the export of slaves from the East African mainland was to cease. A marked weakness in the earlier 1847 agreement with Saiyid Sa'id had been that a great deal of traffic flowed from Kilwa on the mainland to Zanzibar and this during the years 1862 to 1869, when statistics were more carefully compiled, averaged over 15,000 slaves annually, most of whom made clandestine passages to the north-east and on to Arabian shores. The only means of preventing this traffic was to sever the link between Kilwa and Zanzibar, so by confining the trade to the mainland the onward seaward passages were effectively stopped.[48] Accordingly, all the littoral powers of the Gulfs of Persia and Oman had engaged themselves to a cessation of this traffic, though it was not until 1927 when, by the Treaty of Jeddah, Ibn Sa'ud undertook to co-operate with Britain in suppressing the slave trade in Central Arabia. Though it was carried on clandestinely for some years following the signing of the agreements, nevertheless the vigilance of British-Indian ships, and of that control alone, kept the traffic down until it had become virtually extinguished. The gain to Britain was nil; the cost was excessive, for apart from maintaining effective anti-slave patrols in the Gulf and elsewhere around the Arabian coasts and in the Indian Ocean, slaves thus manumitted were expatriated to Bombay where they became a burden upon the funds of the Imperial Government.[49]

It is not out of place here to consider in retrospect the slave trade in Arabia as it existed during the first half of the nineteenth century in order to establish some sense of proportion and perspective. The main source of supply was East Africa and transport was by sea mainly during the south-west monsoon; it has been estimated that a *dhow* would carry as many as 150 slaves on a voyage which might take just over a fortnight to reach the Gulf of Oman.[50] In Eastern Arabia the principal entrepot ports were Muscat and Sur along the Batinah coast, and from thence the black cargoes were trans-shipped mainly to ports within the Persian Gulf and especially to Bushire. This latter port in itself was an entrepot serving the markets of south-west Persia and Turkish Arabia. On the other hand, the traffic to India was slight and the combination of legal deterrent and the cheapness of local indigenous labour made that market economically unattractive. Statistics at that time are variable, but from the evidence of observers such as Atkins Hamerton at Zanzibar, Commodore Brooks, I.N., Colonel Robertson at Bushire, and Captain Cogan, I.N., it seems likely that exports of slaves from Zanzibar, the main port of supply, during the 1840s approximated those of the 1860s cited above, that is to say, not less than 15,000 a year.[51] British repugnance towards this trade was induced not so much by inhuman treatment meted out, for undeniably many an African slave in an Eastern household enjoyed infinitely more status and comfort than his free compatriot in native African domains, as by the evangelical zeal and purpose engendered by Wilberforce and his colleagues in their principled campaign against slavery, and here they were fortunate in having in Palmerston a most formidable ally.

During the 1830s and 1840s British efforts were directed towards the preservation of peace and good order. Kharg, which had been fancied as a naval base, had been occupied, relinquished and reoccupied, to be finally abandoned in 1842, save for the subsequent punitive occupation in 1856 aforementioned, a proposal for its purchase by Britain having been turned down by the Government on the ground of the pretext which might thereby be afforded to Russia for corresponding action in the north.[52] In 1845 Sa'id ibn Mutlaq, acting on behalf of his master the Amir Faisal of Najd, threatened Muscat with aggression but forcible remonstrances by Hennell and a strong British naval demonstration off the Batinah coast brought the matter to a peaceable conclusion,[53] whilst in the following year Hennell again interposed to keep the peace between Saiyid Sa'id and the Prince Governor of Fars.[54] During this period and later, attempts were made by various powers – Persian, Turkish and Arab – to assert their authority over Bahrain, and indeed in 1851 Faisal ibn Turki managed to extort a *zakat* of 4,000 thalers annually from the reluctant Ruler of that island, but these attempts were successfully countered by British diplomacy, since the independence of that strategic shaikhdom was not only to be upheld *de jure* by Britain but was also essential for the preservation of maritime peace in the Gulf. The Ruler of Bahrain accordingly remained in a state of anxious independence until 1861, when a treaty of perpetual peace and friendship was effected between Britain and Bahrain whereby the former assumed the role of protecting power. This was the first positive step taken in that direction (a fuller narrative is given in Chapter 7) – it indicates the difference between insular Bahrain and the mainland shaikhdoms, for British naval power could adequately protect the former whilst protection of the latter would necessarily entail those commitments on land which had been as consistently shunned as they were difficult to fulfil.

At the turn of the half century British power in the Gulf had been established and consolidated and a few years of quiet – disturbed only by Sa'udi claims against the Khalifah ruler of Bahrain, disputes within the Khalifah family and a clandestine traffic in salves – then followed. Events outside the region, however, first in Europe, then in Central Asia and finally in India itself conspired to disturb this state of calm, events which were to have their repercussions within India, in relationships between Britain and India, and in the foreign policy of the British-Indian Empire. Such matters did not and could not remain unnoticed in the Gulf so that alignments there loosely arranged were now by force of circumstances to be refashioned and reinforced. The second half of the nineteenth century therefore marks the zenith of Imperial purpose and power, and for the Persian Gulf a period of peace and order.

Notes

1 *Enclosures to Bombay Secret Letters Received*, Vol. 7. Enclos. to Sec. Letter No. 3. Warden to Jukes, 10 May 1821.

2 Wilson, Sir Arnold, *The Persian Gulf* (London, 1928), 170.

3 Thompson and Garratt, op. cit., 202.

4 Ibid., 203.

5 Aitchison, C.U., *A Collection of Treaties, Engagements and Sanads relating to India and Neighbouring Countries* (Calcutta, 1933), XI, 287–8.

6 Saldhana, J.A., *Précis of Correspondence regarding the Affairs of the Persian Gulf, 1801–1853* (Calcutta, 1906), 10. Secret and Political Diary No. 263 of 1808. Minto to Malcolm, 7 March 1808.

7 Ibid., 11. Sec. and Pol. Diary No. 237 of 1808. Malcolm to Minto, 1 May 1808.

8 Graham, G.S., *Great Britain in the Indian Ocean* (Oxford, 1967), 40.

9 Malcolm, op. cit., 15.

10 Low, op. cit., I, 310 ff.

11 Lorimer, J.G., *Gazetteer of the Persian Gulf, Oman and Central Arabia* (Calcutta, 1915), I, 143.

12 Saldhana, op. cit., 46. Pol. Dept. Diary No. 339 of 1809. Bombay Govt. to Commanders of the Expedition against Pirates in the Gulf.

13 Shaikh Mansur, *History of Seyd Said, Sultan of Muscat* (London, 1819), 1; Salil ibn Razik, *History of the Imams and Seyyids of Oman*, trans. G.P. Badger (Hakluyt Soc., 1871), Appendix A; Palgrave, W.G., *Narrative of a Year's Journey through Central and Eastern Arabia, 1862–1863* (London, 1865), II, 285.

14 *Selections from Bombay Government Records*, XXIV, 38. Brief Notes by Captain Taylor, 1818.

15 Lorimer, op. cit., 1,213.

16 *Factory Records (Persia)*, Vol. 34. Elphinstone to Hastings, 15 December 1819.

17 Ibid., Elphinstone to Willock, 15 December 1819.

18 Saldhana, op. cit., 118–9.

19 Aitchison, op. cit., XI, 245, 248.

20 Saldhana, op. cit., 121.

21 Ibid, 132; Moyse-Bartlett, H., *The Pirates of Trucial Oman* (London, 1966), 99 ff.

22 *Factory Records (Persia)*, Vol. 34. Keir to Willock, 6 January 1820; ibid., Prince of Shiraz to Keir, 9 January 1820; *Enclos. to Bombay Sec. Letters*, Vol. 7. Enclos. No. 5 to Sec. Letter No. 2. Persian Ministers to Willock, 17 December 1820.

23 Saldhana, op. cit., 264.

24 Ibid., 172–3.

25 Aitchison, op. cit., XI, 252–3.

26 Saldhana, op. cit., 179–80.

27 Ibid., 181.

28 Saldhana, J.A., *Précis of Turkish Arabia Affairs, 1801–1905* (Simla, 1905), 197.

29 *Enclos. to Bombay Sec. Letters*, Vol. 14. Enclos. to Sec. Letter No. 87. Hennell to Willoughby, 18 May 1839 enclos. letter from Jabir ibn 'Abdullah to Hennell, 10 May 1839; Ibid., Hennell to Willoughby, 30 May 1839 enclos. letter from Khurshid Pasha to Hennell, 3 April 1839.

30 *Factory Records (Persia)*, Vol. 48. Memorandum by Henry Ellis, 9 January 1833.

31 Aitchison, op. cit., XI, 184.

32 Saldhana, *Précis of the Persian Gulf*, 202. Palmerston to Campbell, 29 November 1838.

33 *Enclos. to Bombay Sec. LEtters*, Vol. 14. Minute by Farish, and Willoughby to Hennell, 1 April 1839.

34 Bartlett, C.J., Great Britain and Sea Power (Oxford, 1963), 129.

35 *Secret Letters from Turkey, Egypt and Syria, 1842–1848*, Vol. II. Stratford Canning to Aberdeen, 26 February 1842.

36 Lorimer, op. cit., I, 232–3.

37 Saldhana, *Précis of Persian Gulf*, 226.

38 Saldhana, *Précis of Turkish Arabia*, 99.

39 Ibid., 58.

40 Saldhana, *Précis of Persian Gulf*, 269.

41 Webster, Sir Charles, *The Foreign Policy of Palmerston* (London, 1951), II, 738–9.

42 *Parliamentary Papers*, 1834. Vol. XIV No. 478. Appendix I, 10. Report of the Select Committee on Steam Navigation to India.

43 Seton-Watson, R.W., *Disraeli, Gladstone and the Eastern Question* (London, 1935), 497.

44 Mosely, P.E., Russia's Asiatic Policy in 1838, *Essays in the History of Modern Europe* (New York, 1936), 56.

45 Aitchison, op. cit., XI, 249, 289.

46 *Secret Letters from the Resident in the Persian Gulf, 1842–1843*. Robertson to Secret Committee, 10 March 1842.

47 Ibid., Robertson to Willoughby, 31 March 1842.

48 *Parliamentary Papers*, 1871, c. 420, xiv–xv. Report from the Select Committee on the Slave Trade (East Coast of Africa).

49 *Bombay Selections*, XXIV. Suppression of the Slave Trade in the Persian Gulf by Lieut. A.B. Kemball, 1844; Saldhana, J.A., *Précis on the Slave Trade in the Gulf of Oman and the Persian Gulf, 1873–1905* (Calcutta, 1906) – Appendix: Reports on the Slave Trade in the Persian Gulf, 1852–1858 by Captain H.F. Disbrowe; Aitchison, op. cit., XI, 251–2 and XIII, 73–6; *Secret Correspondence with Persia, 1859*. Wood to Rawlinson, 15 December 1859; *Slavery in the Persian Gulf* (Pol. and Sec. Dept. Memo, 29 December 1928); Coupland, Sir Reginald, *The Exploitation of East Africa* (London 1939) passim.

50 Colomb, P.H., *Slave Catching in the Indian Ocean* (London, 1873), 44–5.

51 Coupland, Sir Reginald, *East Africa and its Invaders* (Oxford, 1938), 316–20, 500; *Enclos. to Bombay Sec. Letters*, Vol. 45. Enclos. to Sec. Letter No. 58. Robertson to Willoughby, 4 March 1842; Colomb, op. cit., 49–51; Sulivan, G.L., *Dhow Chasing in Zanzibar Waters and on the Eastern Coast of Africa* (London, 1873), 19–20.

52 Lorimer, op. cit., I, 225.

53 Aitchison, op. cit., XI, 184.

54 Saldhana, *Précis of Persian Gulf*, 238–9.

IV Pax Britannica

If we are no longer prepared to continue the performance of the tasks we have undertaken, we must withdraw altogether; but the consequences of such a step would be so disastrous . . . to the peace of the Gulf . . .

Mayo to Argyll, 1870[1]

The outbreak of the Crimean War in 1854 compelled Britain to exercise a form of diplomacy in the Middle East different from that previously undertaken. In this case the British aim was to prevent the conflict from spreading eastward where the frontiers of India might be imperilled, coupled with the desire to contain the conflict in Europe. It had at that time appeared likely that Turkey and Persia might readily be induced to take opposing sides in the dispute, Persia siding with Russia. The Persian Governor of Dizful had seized the initiative in massing his forces on the frontier at the Shatt-al-Arab with the avowed intention of assaulting Basra and this in turn inspired the Turks to make a show of resistance; at the same time they were also negotiating with Shaikh Jabir of Mohammerah to join them against the Persians at the outbreak of hostilities. The tension was broken, however, by the dispatch of the British gunboat *Auckland* to Basra and so an uneasy peace was maintained between the two Islamic powers.[2] Palmerston had strongly expressed the view that in the event of Persia moving into the Russian camp a British expedition in the Gulf coupled with the seizure of Kharg would undoubtedly result,[3] and this punitive action was indeed to occur late in the following year though in the entirely different circumstances concerning Persia's advance upon Herat. For another reason in 1854 Britain was obliged to intervene to prevent hostilities again breaking out between Persia and Muscat, arising from differences concerning the lease of Bandar Abbas which up to that time had been held by Saiyid Sa'id, whilst during the three years following the Resident, Captain Kemball, used force to prevent warfare between Sultan ibn Saqar and the Shihiyin tribe of Omanis.[4]

In 1856 the doughty old ruler of Muscat and Zanzibar, Saiyid Sa'id, died. After a protracted series of disputes the former united sultanate was divided into two separate parts, Muscat and Oman going to Thuwaini, Sa'id's eldest son, whilst Zanzibar and the adjacent territories on the East African mainland went to another son, Majid. It was not, however, until the arbitration of the Governor-General of India was accepted that the dissension between Muscat and Zanzibar was resolved and in 1862 therefore the Canning Award put the seal upon the separation. Nevertheless, this division of Sa'id's former realms had a marked effect upon the economy of Muscat which was greatly dependent upon the revenues deriving from the East African colonies and on the returns from the lucrative slave trade there, while concurrent with the decline in prosperity was the gradual diminution of Muscat's status as a naval power.

The Canning Award of 1862 was signed by both the British and French Governments as guarantors of the independence of the two emergent sultanates and it was agreed upon between the two European powers that neither would seek to gain advantage of the other in either of the two sultanates. That this was to have later repercussions in Muscat could hardly have been foreseen at that time though the subsequent disputes between Britain and France in the Gulf of Oman had their formal origin in this joint declaration.

It has been observed with appropriate relevance that Britain's need to underpin and buttress Turkey in the interests of the security of the Straits of the Dardanelles was matched by the desire to ensure as strategic necessities the territorial integrity of Persia, the security of the Gulf and the denial of Turkish expansion along the Arabian littoral. 'The inland sea', it had further been noted,

> that marked the eastern boundary of the Arab world was part of the maritime frontier of India. Any relaxation of British control in the Persian Gulf, whether by formal concession to Persia, or by neglect of Russian military infiltration into Persia or Mesopotamia, might imperil not only an overland route to India, but the political stability of India itself.[5]

Therefore there is evidence of a notable reinforcement in policy whereby to the pacification of the waters and littoral of the Gulf was added the cardinal necessity for safeguarding the approaches to India.

The Indian Mutiny had, amongst other things, demonstrated the pressing need for administrative reform within those parts of the subcontinent subject to Company rule, so in 1858 the Crown assumed the powers of the Government of India and of the subordinate presidency governments. After two and a half centuries of trading, administration and imperial expansion the Honourable East India Company ceased to exist. Five years later the flag of the Indian Navy, so renamed in 1830, was hauled down and ships of the Royal Navy took over the duties of policing Eastern waters, and so was terminated that distinguished naval force to which 'we are mainly indebted for the breakdown of the Portuguese power on the Persian Gulf, the protection of British commerce against the rivalry of the Dutch and the French, the suppression of piracies and the establishment of maritime peace, and security of navigation by its surveys in the Gulf.'[6] The reconstituted Bombay Marine, later restyled the Indian Marine, was not a fighting force but rather a fleet auxiliary, its main duties comprising political, police, lighting and other services, the maintenance of gunboats on the Euphrates, the transport of troops and the carriage of mails. It was also responsible for the laying of the marine portion of the Indo-European telegraph between Basra and Gwadar.[7]

The assumption of new duties by the Royal Navy did not work out as well as had been expected. The limits of the East Indies Station were too extensive for the fleet units available, calls made upon it by local authorities were so numerous that they could not be adequately met, and the climate, especially in the Persian Gulf and Red Sea, was detrimental to the health of sailors accustomed to more temperate regions. It is noteworthy that even prior to the closing down of the Indian Navy manned by men familiar with such an exacting torrid zone, eight commodores in succession had to be appointed in fifteen years to the command of the Gulf station, of whom four died at their posts, while during the same period eleven other officers died and of the remainder no less than four-fifths had to take sick leave.[8] It is interesting to compare these statistics with those of the following century when the Senior Naval Officer Persian Gulf stated that at Bahrain in August 1926, of his total complement of eighty-eight officers and men, over forty were on the sick list at the same time.[9]

At no time during the Company's history had the naval forces available for service in the Gulf been adequate for the performance of their duties and only the lack of a competitive sea power had enabled them to succeed, but the abolition of a locally raised marine and of its officers who possessed invaluable local knowledge imposed further difficulties. Following general Outram's dispatch concerning the defeat of the Persian army at Borazjan in 1857 and in reply to Outram's complaint that reinforcements had been delayed in their arrival from Bombay, Canning had minuted,

> But this has been unavoidable. Of all the steam vessels which the Government of India possesses or can obtain on hire for service

in Persia . . . two only are on this side of India, each engaged on a duty which admits of no interruption or postponement. Two are in China, and every other vessel is in use between Bombay and Bushire . . . and in any case it is certain that the steam vessels at the disposal of the Government of India are not sufficient for the purpose of moving a little more than six thousand men, with its proportion of followers and horses, from Bombay to Bushire with the rapidity which the shortness of the seasons for operations whether by sea or land render desirable.[10]

Colonel Pelly, the Resident, had been constrained to observe that he had not possessed the means during the past year of 1862 of seizing slaving craft entering Gulf waters, and though the Government had expressly constituted the holder of his office as the arbitrator in all differences arising amongst the chiefs of the Arab coast, in reality he was powerless to perform his functions in the absence of suitable means of transport. This was evident in 1865 and 1866 when only one vessel, the *Highflyer*, was available to Pelly, and that for a limited time. It was not surprising that Pelly felt disinclined to initiate operations in support of Muscat against attacks by the Wahabis when a successful conclusion was doubtful. 'To act otherwise', remarked Pelly, 'would be to confirm the impression, already too prevalent, of our absence of naval power, and we would leave our ally the Sultan more than ever liable to Wahabee aggression.' Pelly had further occasion during the succeeding two years to deplore his powerlessness to fulfil his functions in relation to the Treaty chiefs. 'The one way to provide for a maritime police of the Gulf', he advised Bombay, 'is to have an armed vessel to be adapted for coasting work, to be efficiently armed and manned from England, and to be under the orders of the Indian Government.'[11]

Nasr-ud-din Shah, during this time, had leisure to note that the British naval absence almost matched his own utter inability to defend his coasts. He then deemed it appropriate to recommence negotiations with a view to obtaining some British warships under the command of English officers. Alison, the Minister at Tehran, had been solicited by Farrukh Khan, prime minister to the Shah, thus:

Your Lordship will observe how anxious His Majesty is to receive an early reply from Her Majesty's Government respecting the purchase and equipment of ships for service in the Persian Gulf, and how earnestly he invokes the moral interposition of Great Britain to prevent any unlawful aggression on the part of the Emam of Muscat against the Persian territory.[12]

Concurrently the quarrel between Persia and Muscat over Bandar Abbas had been flaring up again and this promised once more to disturb the fragile peace of the Gulf, difficult to maintain without adequate naval backing.

To the Shah's proposal the Government of India understandably saw objections, echoing Pelly's sentiments concerning the establishment of a small marine force for exclusive use in and around the Gulf waters. 'Such a force', Calcutta informed London in June 1868,

> would more effectually secure the Shah's real interest than any force of his own, while it would give stability to our ascendancy in the Gulf, which, ever since the abolition of the local navy, there has been some risk of our losing, and it would exclude all pretext for the intervention of other powers . . . It is chiefly from the absence of such a force that present political complications between the Governments of Persia and Muscat and between several of the maritime tribes have arisen, and it is in our opinion impossible for the peace of the Gulf to be maintained and trade protected unless the Resident at Bushire has at his command the means of enforcing the terms of the maritime truce . . .[13]

Neither the Admiralty nor the Foreign Office would initially concur in this proposal since it was considered advisable to maintain the newly-instituted system of marine policing, but a year later their objections were waived after receipt of repeated warnings from Calcutta and Bushire. A small force was accordingly detached from the East Indies Station, its main object being to police the Gulf waters, restrain all forms of piracy and hostilities at sea, and to suppress the slave trade.[14]

As for the quarrel between Persia and Muscat, the Viceroy instructed Pelly in June 1868 to continue his attempts to mediate between the two parties and furthermore Pelly should note that

> Under no circumstances can His Excellency in Calcutta countenance a resort to hostilities by either party, and should the Sultan of Muskat commit aggressions on any of the Persian ports, the Resident should insist on the cessation of hostilities, pending a settlement of the dispute by mediation, for which the British Government have already tendered their good offices.[15]

The resumption of a permanent marine force in the Gulf, and a successful conclusion of Pelly's attempts at mediation, induced the Shah to lose interest, for the time being, in creating his own navy, deeming that it would prove an unnecessary expense and a costly failure. 'As regards the proposed creation by Persia of a flotilla in the Persian Gulf,' Pelly was able to inform Calcutta, 'the Prince [Governor of Fars acting for the Shah] said he entirely concurred with me . . . He said Persia entrusted the peace of the Gulf entirely to the British Resident, and that he would be prepared to issue any orders I might draft in view to my securing full support and prompt communication from the local Governors along the Persian coast line.'[16]

As usual, the British desire for peace and good order was ill-matched by the other desire to avoid financial commitments inherent in imperial aims. In the wider context of maritime dispositions:

> Because Britain remained generally confident of her naval supremacy *vis-à-vis* France and Russia the influence of a parsimonious Exchequer on broad naval strategy tended to be considerable, if not paramount. Admiralty Lords during the latter half of the nineteenth century tended to accept the Foreign Office aphorism – let satisfied dogs sleep. Bases, like overseas squadrons, were therefore at the mercy of Treasury watchmen.[17]

The year 1868 was memorable, for it also saw a further consolidation of British relations with the Arab littoral states when the Resident prevailed upon the Shaikh of Doha, the most prominent of the Qatar chiefs, to enter into the undertakings already binding upon the Trucial chiefs. This was occasioned by outbreaks of violent warfare when the shaikhs of Bahrain and Abu Dhabi assaulted Qatar in 1867 in an attempt to attach Qatar to the island shaikhdom. Pelly was still powerless to act, other than to remonstrate, since he lacked any naval forces whatever to give effect to his remonstrances and it was hardly surprising therefore that in the succeeding year Qatar retaliated upon Bahrain since no redress could be expected from the Resident. Clearly the trucial system so patiently and painfully evolved was in danger of collapsing through want of naval power to police that system. It became imperative, if disaster were to be averted, to detach naval vessels from Indian waters to reinforce the Resident's sagging authority. A squadron of three vessels with Pelly on board sailed first to Bahrain where Muhammad ibn Khalifah was deposed in favour of his brother 'Ali, and then proceeded to Waqra on the Qatar coast where peace with Bahrain was enforced, and an agreement entered into in September 1868 whereby the Resident would be called upon to mediate in all future disputes at sea. Aitchison, the Foreign Secretary at Calcutta, felt obliged to observe to the Bombay Government that the correspondence relating to these incidents 'will be forwarded to the Secretary of State as additional evidence of the impolicy of the abolition of the Naval force in the Persian Gulf'.[18] Barely twelve months were to pass by before the dispossessed Muhammad ibn Khalifah returned in force to Bahrain and only a naval blockade of the island under Pelly's direction, and with ships temporarily detached from the East Indies Station for that purpose, had the effect of remedying the situation and restoring order.

Ever since Mehemet 'Ali's drive across Arabia culminating in his subsequent withdrawal in 1840, the Indian Government had been confronted with a southward advance of Ottoman forces, for that prospect was never far removed. This endemic Turkish threat to the Arab coastal tribes and the endeavour to substitute a shadowy land authority for a firm maritime presence was coupled with the parallel threat to the validity or enforcement of the engagements entered into with the trucial chiefs. In 1861 Dammam on the Hasa coast had been bombarded by the Resident, Felix Jones, in order to dislodge Muhammad ibn 'Abdullah who was sheltering there, this Muhammad being a contestant to the suzerainty of Bahrain against his kinsman Muhammad ibn Khalifah, whereupon the Turks entered a protest on the ground that Dammam was within Ottoman territory and jurisdiction. Arnold Kemball, the British Consul-General at Baghdad, expressed the view that had the Turks been able to control the province of Najd, to which they laid claim, and keep the Wahabis and pirates under restraint, then such action would have been welcomed as reducing the burden on Britain of having to try to maintain a constant and costly marine surveillance.

> But in point of fact the Porte has not the power to punish or coerce its tributary; not a single Turkish functionary exists in the country; and to judge from my own experience of the duties of the British Resident in the Persian Gulf, I feel assured that, were the relations of that officer with the Amir of Nejd to be disturbed in a manner to withdraw the Wahabi Coast from his immediate supervision, the effect must be highly prejudicial to the policy which has hitherto obtained under the orders and sanctions of H.M. Indian Government in that quarter.[19]

That the Government of India still had no desire to become embroiled in disputes on the mainland and would be willing to yield that duty to strong Ottoman authority is evident even in the next decade when, in 1871, Aitchison had noted to the Viceroy, Lord Mayo, that

> . . . it is a matter of absolute indifference whether these quasi-independent tribes [claimed to be dependent on the Amir of Nejd] are sovereign or absolutely controlled by Turkey. Probably the establishment of a strong Turkish influence in their internal administration would be rather an advantage than otherwise . . .

Aitchison then proceed to review the treaty relations existing between Britain and the maritime chiefs:

> It follows, therefore, that our position at sea in respect to these tribes is in no way affected by their quarrels on land either among themselves or with Turkey. There is nothing, therefore, in our maritime position to call for our interference on land. Is such interference required by other considerations? I think not. I think it would be rather an advantage than otherwise to establish firm Turkish rule along the coast . . .[20]

Mayo, who at the same time had been considering Bombay's expressed fears of an extension of Turkish influence with the littoral tribes and Arab states together with a recommendation that a more decided tone towards Turkey should be adopted, was inclined to favour Aitchison's reasoning. Not without some equivocation, he minuted that

> I always thought that it was one of the well-known maxims of diplomacy that a Government who desired peace should not initiate the discussion of complicated and difficult subjects, and should not reply to anticipated questions until they were put. I see no necessity whatever for expressing any opinion as to the boundaries of Nejd, Muscat, any portion of Oman, or the littoral of the Persian Gulf, though we are perhaps in a position to offer a sounder opinion on those subjects than any other Government, administration or power . . .[21]

Whilst these exchanges were taking place the Turks were proceeding to dispatch some troops by sea transport from Basra and these subsequently arrived at the Hasa oases where they were obliged to remain in a state of impotency due to the debilitated condition of the soldiers and to the watchfulness of Sa'ud ibn Faisal who kept them pinned down in that area. There the Turks remained anxiously but by 1874 they were withdrawn, leaving a nominal authority in a chief of the Bani Khalid tribe. In the following year they proclaimed Hasa to be part of the *sanjaq* of Basra whilst at the same time they were directing their attention once more to Brahrain and Qatar, a matter of great solicitude to the British authorities who were apprehensive of any renewal of disturbances in those shaikhdoms with whom they had entered into treaty relations.

But in any case, the mounting of a Turkish naval expedition and movements of troops by sea within the Gulf posed a novel situation for the Government of India. Whether the British could claim any right to deny these movements which ostensibly were for the purpose of subduing a so-called province of the Ottoman Empire was highly questionable, undesirable though they were, but in addition there was the distinct possibility of the adverse effect that these movements would have along the coast. Echoes of the anxieties engendered by this new Turkish activity were to be heard some years later when, in 1879, Lord Lytton, then Viceroy, addressed a long dispatch to Lord Cranbrook at the India Office. After making an extensive review of the circumstances attendant upon these Ottoman claims, he considered that the consequential extension and predominance in the Persian Gulf of Turkish power could only tend to a modifying of the distribution of power and influence in the Gulf and accordingly affect relations between Britain and Persia as well.

> One result of accepting the charge of the police of these waters has been to render the naval power of the British Government supreme in the Gulf; and any change in this respect might be undesirable. But we could not require the Turkish Government to fulfil its increased responsibilities in the Gulf without also obliging it to increase considerably its naval force; and it may be remarked that the Persian Government, which at present maintains no ships-of-war in the Gulf, would hardly view with indifference the operations of Turkish cruisers, and the presence of a strong Turkish fleet in these waters.[22]

Clearly, Lytton's apprehensions were not merely concerned with a Turkish challenge to British influence but also with the prospect of the building-up of a naval arms race in the Gulf with a consequential breaking down of the state of tranquillity which it had been the British purpose to maintain.

After the withdrawal of Turkish forces from Hasa in 1874 the Porte nevertheless continued, even if ineffectually, to maintain a nominal overlordship of the Hasa coast until the following century when in 1913 a convention between Britain and Turkey defined the limits of Ottoman authority as being confined to the region north and west of 'Uqair situated on the mainland opposite Bahrain, that island and the littoral east of the line being recognized as remaining under British influence. In the war that broke out in 1914 Turkish authority and interest were to disappear completely from the Arabian peninsula.

A further change in the political interests of India occurred in 1873 when the responsibility for the Political Residency in the Persian Gulf was transferred from Bombay to Calcutta. It is significant of the times that, in recommending this change to London, Mayo had observed during the previous year that '. . . there is no part of the countries referred to which cannot be communicated with as quickly through the telegraph, and nearly as quickly through the post, by the Government of India as by the Government of Bombay . . .' Thus the independent role for so long played first at Surat and then Bombay came to an end.[23] It is necessary, therefore, to describe the development of communications within and beyond the Gulf, and of the encouragement to trade.

The Company's factories, established solely for trading purposes, were naturally dependent upon means of communication with the outside world, these being provided initially by the East Indiamen. In their wake came Agents and Residents whose commercial functions were gradually augmented then superseded by political obligations and responsibilities. Mails were first diverted via Aleppo and Basra during the Seven Years' War and later the route down the Euphrates valley was essayed. This in turn paved the way for the firm of Lynch & Company who likewise opened up the Karun river to commercial enterprise. Indian post offices dominated the Gulf ports during the latter part of the nineteenth century, the first being opened in 1864 at Muscat, and at various intervals during the following thirty years British-Indian post offices were established at Bandar Abbas, Lingah, Gwadar, Jask, Bahrain, Bushire and Mohammerah. In Ottoman territory similar postal facilities were set up in 1868 at Basra and Baghdad, whilst Kuwait entered into an exclusive postal agreement with Britain in 1904. National policy and military strategy, arising from the Crimean War and the Indian Mutiny, determined that the international telegraph should link India with Britain, this vital link being completed within the century. By early 1865 the Persian Gulf section of the Indo-European Telegraph was completed linking Basra via Fao with Karachi by means of a submarine cable so that England and India could at last communicate directly with each other by this means; another forty years were to pass by before the land line across Persia was able to afford a similar facility. Wireless telegraphy within the Gulf region was proposed by the Political Resident at Bushire in 1908 in order to afford a diplomatic communication link, to facilitate the quarantine service, to assist operations for the suppression of the arms traffic, and to provide a ship-shore wireless link with merchant shipping. This network was completed in the following eight years. These enterprises, deriving from British initiative and expense, supervised and protected by the Indian Marine and by detachments from the Indian Engineers, whilst serving to fortify British hegemony in the Gulf, were nevertheless available to the world at large and thereby became international utilities.[24]

Technical developments, improved communications and an enforced maritime peace combined to encourage more tangible forms of prosperity. Trade flourished within the whole region and this expansion of commerce was generously and impartially distributed, Persia being a marked beneficiary. It is significant that during the middle part of the century, from the late 1830s to the late 1860s, the trade of the Gulf more than trebled its value.[25]

In 1883 Nasr-ud-din, infused once more with visions of maritime glory which were undoubtedly inspired by his unprecedented visit to England and the capitals of Europe, again laid plans for a Persian marine force in the Gulf. Two years later two small vessels arrived from Germany, the *Persepolis* designed for duties in territorial waters and the *Susa* for service as a dispatch boat on the Karun. Possibly the Shah's nautical ambitions were fired by the acquisition of this fleet for soon afterwards he began pursuing an aggressive policy in the Gulf. In these circumstances the Resident considered it to be expedient to ensure the continued loyalty of the maritime Arab chiefs. In 1887 all six chiefs addressed letters to the British Government giving assurances of their intention to maintain their existing status which it was the Persian intrigue to disturb.[26] This situation was further improved in 1892 when the shaikhs undertook not to enter into any agreements or correspondence with any power other than Britain; not to admit the agent of any government; and not to part with any portion of their territories save to the British Government.[27]

Two other forms of diplomatic activity were in motion at this time. First, there was the Turkish attempt to assert the Porte's authority upon Mohammerah, the principal town on the Persian side of the Shatt-al-Arab and lying on the western extremity of the province of Arabistan, now Khuzistan, an area occupied largely by Arabic-speaking people and more than once under dispute between Ottomans and Qajars. In 1893 Turkish officers at Fao suddenly began to levy customs duties on the cargoes of vessels from abroad bound up the river to Mohammerah, these authorities advancing the reason for this action being that they had received orders to treat Mohammerah as a Turkish port. Acting on the request of the Shah – who, though claiming the shaikh of Mohammerah as his vassal, was nevertheless powerless to reinforce his own remonstrances – the British ambassador lodged a strongly-worded protest at Constantinople, though principally in the interest of freedom to navigate that stretch of the river, whereupon the Turks withdrew. The autonomous shaikh Khaz'al deemed it prudent to seek British protection along the lines already afforded to the Rulers of Bahrain and Muscat (a non-alienation bond having been entered into between Britain and Muscat in 1891) by the signing of an exclusive agreement. In 1897 he secretly endeavoured to ally himself with Britain, though without success. The British Government remained reluctant to become entangled in mainland affairs and especially where no advantage seemed to be forthcoming, so the shaikh remained a nominal client of the Shah. Khaz'al renewed his request the following year and again as late as 1913. In 1914 the India Office recommended that a protective agreement should be concluded with him but the outbreak of war and the fact that Anglo-Persian diplomatic relations were involved made this proposition difficult to entertain. Had such an engagement then been entered into, its repercussions could well have been evident forty years later in the Anglo-Persian oil dispute, since the island of Abadan had in those earlier years come within Khaz'al's jurisdiction.[28]

The other event of diplomatic consequence concerned Kuwait. In 1896 when Mubarak succeeded to that shaikhdom after having murdered his kinsman Muhammad ibn Sabah, the new ruler attempted to negotiate an agreement with Britain similar to that applying to the trucial chiefs. Nothing came of this at that time since, as was the case of Mohammerah, Britain did not desire to be implicated in mainland affairs and in a possible clash with the Turks. In 1898 however Britain's interest in the proposition had been kindled for by then it had become clear that Kuwait might well become the terminus of the railway through Asia Minor. Early in 1899, therefore, and under strong recommendation from Curzon, now Viceroy, an agreement was signed with Mubarak whereby the shaikh bound himself, his heirs and successors not to treat with foreign powers nor to alienate any portion of his territory without British consent. By the end of the century, a chain of agreements extended from Muscat to Kuwait along the whole of the Arabian shores – though with the exception of Qatar – binding those littoral principalities in the Persian Gulf to accept the mediation and influence of Britain in their external affairs and in their relations with each other.[29]

That year 1899, too, was marked by the appearance of bubonic plague in India, and quarantine posts accordingly were set up in the Gulf. The only power capable of establishing and maintaining such posts was the Government of India, with the result that the Persian Government confided all such quarantine arrangements at their ports to British agency, this subsequently being followed by Bahrain and Muscat.[30]

A clandestine activity which had persisted during the latter part of the nineteenth century was the traffic in modern arms, this first attracting British attention during the Second Afghan War. In 1880, in the course of the campaign, it became clearly evident that large quantities of ammunition were reaching Afghanistan from India, and the Government thereupon placed a complete embargo on the supply of arms to Persian Gulf ports. The flow of arms was nevertheless stimulated by the suppression of the traffic on the East coast of Africa in accordance with the international (Brussels) conference of 1890, a diversion of that trade being effected into northern waters since Arabia and the region of the Persian Gulf were not subject to the limitations set by the conference. The consequent gun-running was considerable despite prohibitions placed, at repeated British insistence, by Persia (1881), Bahrain (1898), Kuwait (1900) and the Trucial States (1902). Local inquiries indicated that about 60 per cent of those imports found their final market in Persian territory where 'Martini Khan' was the recognized arbiter in tribal disputes, whilst about 25 per cent were absorbed through Turkish territories in the Gulf, and the remaining 15 per cent by non-Turkish Arabia. Such was the alarming proportion of the trade in Persia that in 1891 the Shah was induced additionally to confer upon British warships the right to search all vessels under the Persian flag which were suspected of carrying arms or ammunition, and at British insistence a similar promulgation was made in 1898 by the Sultan of Muscat, though only in respect of arms destined for India or Persia; elsewhere he retained that prerogative until five years later when he was obliged to concede the British right to search Muscati vessels suspected of carrying arms on the high seas. By 1903 the arms trade had been nominally prohibited at all ports in the Persian Gulf region with the partial exception of Muscat and Oman where an internal traffic was carried on, though as noted later the French flag allowed a continuation of the traffic until 1913. The onus of seeing that the agreements were enforced and respected and that the trade stopped rested entirely upon British naval supervision, and the search and blockade costs amounted then to about £125,000 annually.[31]

By the close of the nineteenth century British maritime predominance in the Gulf was clearly evident. In 1900, out of 327 steamers that entered those waters all but six were British, and of the whole tonnage over four-fifths were likewise British. Between them, Britain and India accounted for half the exports from the Gulf region whilst approximately two-thirds of goods imported came from the same two countries, the whole being the result of commercial enterprise and the ability to improve upon advantage gained.[32]

No more apt or fitting summary of the labours and achievements of British endeavour over the centuries under review as viewed at the turn of the century could be made than by quoting the dispatch of the Viceroy, Lord Curzon, to the Secretary of State for India on 21 September 1899, wherein he discussed British interests in the Gulf and the measures to be taken to maintain those interests. These Curzon considered to be commercial, political, strategic and telegraphic, for since Persia had been drawn into the vortex of European politics she was equally of Imperial as of Indian concern. The dispatch then defined the *de facto* and *de jure* positions in the Persian Gulf as follows:

> The *de jure* position in the Persian Gulf is that of a sea open to the flag of all nations . . .
>
> The *de facto* position upon the waters and on the shores of the Persian Gulf reflects a more positive British predominance than the preceding paragraphs might indicate. In the early years of the present century, the slave trade was rampant in the Gulf, and the vessels of the Indian Marine were engaged in a long and arduous struggle with the Arab pirates who infested its southern coasts. This conflict, which was conducted entirely by British agency and means, without any help from the Persian Government, resulted in the establishment of treaty relations with the great majority of the Arab chiefs, under which they

130

bound themselves to observe perpetual peace and to refer all disputes to the British Resident at Bushire. The *pax Britannica*, which has ever since, with rare exceptions, been maintained, is the issue of these arrangements and is the exclusive work of this country. Of similar origin were the soundings of the channels and the surveys of the shores of the Persian Gulf, which the navigators of all nations owe to the labours of a long line of naval officers of the Indian service. Meanwhile, British trade has acquired almost a monopoly of the foreign commerce of the Gulf ports . . .

During the last thirty years the maintenance of the submarine cables of the Indo-European Telegraph Company from Fao to Jask, and of the land lines from that place to Karachi, has also devolved upon the Indian Government and has tended to increase an already preponderant influence over both the waters and the shores of this sea. Latterly there has been a deliberate but necessary consolidation of our influence in certain quarters where trouble threatened or where rivalry was feared [here Curzon refers to engagements with Kuwait, Bahrain and Muscat] . . . Such, briefly summarized, is the position that has been won by Great Britain, not without the expenditure of many millions of money and the sacrifice of many valuable lives, in the Persian Gulf . . .

[With regard to the advance of Russia] . . . we could not contemplate without dismay the prospect of Russian neighbourhood in Eastern or Southern Persia, the inevitable consequence of which must be a great increase of our burdens; while the maritime defensibility of India would require to be altogether reconsidered, were the dangers of a land invasion to be supplemented by the appearance of a possible antagonist as a naval power in waters contiguous to Indian shores.[33]

Towards the close of the century it was apparent that various European powers were interested in the waters of the Gulf and the lands adjoining. The interests of France had been aroused in Oman largely because it offered a staging-post and *point d'appui* between her possessions in Africa and those farther East. In 1844 France had concluded a commercial treaty with Saiyid Sa'id and later, in 1862, she had joined Britain in a mutual declaration on Oman and Zanzibar concerning 'the right to engage reciprocally to respect the independence of the Sovereigns'[34] whilst in 1894 a French consul was appointed to Muscat. In the following year the Compagnie des Messageries Maritimes commenced operating a steamer service from France to Basra and other ports of the Gulf.

The seeds of dissent sown between France and Britain were therefore threefold: the granting of French flags to Omani vessels, the French attempt to establish a coaling depot at Bandar Jissah south of Muscat in 1898, and French participation in the arms traffic. The flag question was a long-drawn-out affair arising in 1891 and was regarded by Britain as an attempt to grant these vessels immunity from search with regard to the transport of slaves, and as a definite attempt to extend French influence along the littoral. It was not until 1905 that the Hague Tribunal finally disposed of this vexed matter and brought the practice to a close. The affair of the coaling station, ostensibly to refuel the new steamer service, was regarded by Britain as further evidence of French intrigue and was to exacerbate feelings between the two governments without a clear-cut victory emerging for either side. It was symptomatic of British sensitivity to any intrusion by another European power into the hegemony exercised by her in the Gulf and Oman that such intrusions should be resisted by all means at her disposal. Finally, the French traffic in arms was an enterprise in which French merchants and vessels under the protection of the French flag combined to conduct a flourishing trade, both overt and covert, and it was not until the onset of the First World War that France renounced her right of invoking privileges in connexion with the contraband trade in arms and ammunition at Muscat.[35]

Russia's interests were more imperial than those of the French. From the Black Sea through Central Asia they ended at the shores of the Pacific and for long that country had sought a warm-water port as an alternative to the winter ice-blocked ports of the North and the Far East, those of the Black Sea being in almost land-locked water. Therefore a base in the Gulf linked by land communications across the Middle East provided an obvious attraction. The proposal of Count Kapnist in 1898 to link the Mediterranean with the Gulf at Kuwait was therefore most disturbing to Britain, for Russia also lay athwart the north-west frontiers of India. The mere suggestion of an arc of Russian influence extending from the Gulf to the highlands of Central Asia presented a spectre that haunted British statesmen of that period, for the defence and security of India might be impaired.

The maintenance of the territorial integrity of Persia as well as Afghanistan was part of a policy, however inconsistently pursued, of ensuring the western land flank of India against Russian encroachment. Command of the Persian Gulf could not, obviously, guarantee the safety of the North-West frontier. None the less, this inland sea that marked the eastern boundary of the Arab world was part of the maritime frontier of India.[36]

The further suggestion of a Russian rail link to either Bandar Abbas or Chahbar across Seistan did little to allay suspicion, and British apprehensions were well stated in Curzon's dispatch above. Then again, there was the question of Russian naval visits to those waters linked with the possibility of Bandar Abbas becoming a Russian coaling depot, and finally the formation in 1901 of a steamship line to operate between the Black Sea and the Persian Gulf. These fears continued to be expressed and to agitate British minds until 1907 when an agreement was reached with Russia to divide Persia into spheres of Russian and British influence. During negotiations with Russia in August 1907 the Foreign Secretary, Sir Edward Grey, drew fresh attention to 'the special interests possessed by Great Britain in the Gulf, the result of British action in those waters for more than a hundred years', and stated that 'the Russian Government have in the course of the negotiations . . . explicitly stated that they do not deny the special interest of Great Britain in the Persian Gulf, a statement of which His Majesty's Government have formally taken note.'[37] Nevertheless, the Anglo-Russian Agreement of that year provided that the whole of the Persian littoral from the Shatt-al-Arab to Bandar Abbas should be within the Neutral Zone, a situation which was surprising considering the force of British statements previously expressed concerning her interest in those shores. The same year also witnessed the introduction of a new constitution for Persia to be followed soon after by an abortive revolution. Thus the year 1907 conceded Russia firm control in northern Persia, British influence being restricted to the south-east of that country, whilst an impotent Persian Government at Tehran surveyed the whole.

German interest in the region had its real beginnings at this time when in 1897 the trading firm of Wönckhaus was established at Lingah, shortly to be followed by the opening of a German vice-consulate at Bushire. Later in 1906 came the service of the Hamburg-Amerika shipping line linking the Gulf ports with those of North-West Europe. In the same year a German mining concession was granted at Abu Musa. Finally there was the construction of a railway southwards through Asia Minor towards the Gulf. The aims of Germany were ostensibly commercial, but they were marked by more than one effort to obtain a definite territorial footing within the Gulf. During Curzon's Viceroyalty a Belgian shipping and trading syndicate was proposed to operate in direct competition with British interests, whilst in 1899 the Belgians assumed control of the Persian customs administration and thus established themselves at ports along the Gulf. This period, when the distraction of the South African War had been disposed of and consequent political tensions in Europe had been eased, was characterized by a vigorous effort to maintain and advance Britain's interests in the Gulf, calling for a reappraisal of the strategic position from the points of view of both Britain and India, with attendant redispositions.[38]

In the House of Commons, Lord Cranborne, Under Secretary for Foreign Affairs, declared on 22 January 1902 that 'Our rights [in the Gulf] and our position of ascendancy, we cannot abandon . . . our ascendancy is not merely a question of theory, but a question of fact. Our position of ascendancy is assured by the existence of our maritime supremacy . . .'[39] and in the following year Lord Lansdowne, the Foreign Secretary, made this observation in the House of Lords:

> The noble lord asked me for a statement of our policy with regard to the Persian Gulf . . . It seems to me that our policy should be directed in the first place to protect our British trade in those waters. In the next place, I do not think that he suggests, or that we should suggest, that these efforts should be directed towards the exclusion of the legitimate trade of other powers. In the third place . . . we should regard the establishment of a naval base or of a fortified port in the Persian Gulf by any other power as a very grave menace to British interests, and we should certainly resist it with all the means at our disposal.[40]

The Resident, Colonel C.A. Kemball, at the same time reviewed British relationship with the trucial chiefs, which he deemed to be one of tacit predominance.

> Our overlordship so far as it refers to the maintenance of maritime peace, to the protection of our traders and to the observance by the Chiefs of their various engagements with us, is clear and accepted by the chiefs without demur. In regard to

internal affairs, our policy has been not to interfere unless internal disturbances led to the breach of maritime peace or injury to British residents, but our predominant position on the Arab coast enables us to offer advice in internal disputes, which is welcomed and obeyed cheerfully as a rule.[41]

The opening of the twentieth century, when British power and influence in the Gulf was at its zenith and a state of majestic calm prevailed, may once more be summed up by Curzon. In 1903 he made a viceregal tour of the Persian Gulf, thereby not only presenting a manifestation of British prestige but also evincing again that profound interest he had always taken in Persian affairs. To the Indian traders present at Bandar Abbas he declared that 'The great maritime highway of the Persian Gulf has never failed to attract these nations who held, or aspired to hold, the ports of India; and having embarked upon the Indian enterprise in which they ultimately outdistanced all other competitors, it fell naturally to the British to pursue their successful activity in this direction . . .'[42]

On the previous day Curzon held a public *darbar* at Sharjah and he remarked in his address on that occasion to the assembled Arab chiefs:

Out of the relations that were thus created (over the past hundred years) and which, by your own consent, constituted the British Government the guardian of international peace, there grew up political ties between the Government of India and yourselves, and you have relations with no other Power . . . Sometimes I think that the record of the past is in danger of being forgotten, and there are persons who ask, why should Great Britain continue to exercise these powers? The histories of your States and your families, and the present condition of the Gulf, are the answer. We were here before any other Power in modern times had shown its face in these waters. We found strife, and we have created order. It was our commerce as well as your security that was threatened and called for protection. At every port along these coasts the subjects of the King of England still reside and trade. The great Empire of India, which it is our duty to defend, lies almost at your gates. We saved you from extinction at the hands of your neighbours. We opened these seas to the ships of all nations and enabled their flags to fly in peace. We have not seized or held your territory. We have not destroyed your independence, but have preserved it. We are not now going to throw away this century of costly and triumphant enterprise; we shall not wipe out the most unselfish page in history. The peace of these waters must still be maintained; your independence will continue to be upheld; and the influence of the British Government must remain supreme.[43]

Today such sentiments are unfashionable but that in no way detracts from the validity of the statement. Two facts stand out: the period of Curzon's viceroyalty coincided with the moment of greatest calm until then achieved in the Gulf; that page of history might indeed be described as unselfish if, against the gradual paramountcy of Britain, might be weighed the cost in men and money which had been expended over the previous century and more in the attempt to bring peace where none was and order where that word was not understood.

Notes

1 *Persian Gulf Gazetteer, Part 1*. Historical and Political Materials: Précis of Bahrein Affairs, 1854–1904 (Simla, 1904). Government of India to Secretary of State, 20 May 1870.

2 Lorimer, op. cit., I, 231; Saldhana, *Précis of Turkish Arabia*, 21.

3 *Board's Drafts of Secret Letters to India*, Vol. 21. Clarendon to Murray, 22 October 1855.

4 Saldhana, J.A., *Précis of Correspondence regarding Trucial Chiefs, 1854–1905* (Calcutta, 1906), 11–17.

5 Graham, G.S., *The Politics of Naval Supremacy* (Cambridge, 1965), 89; *vide* also Kumar, op. cit., 5–6, 247.

6 Saldhana, J.A., *Précis on Naval Arrangements in the Persian Gulf, 1862–1905* (Calcutta, 1906), 1.

7 *Cambridge History of India* (Cambridge, 1932), VI, 150–1; Low, op. cit., II, 411–12.

8 Low, op. cit., II, 109–10.

9 Parry, Captain R. St. P., The Navy in the Persian Gulf, *Journ. R.U.S.I.*, 1930, LXXV, 323.

10 *Enclosures to Secret Letters from India*, Vol. 149. Minute by Canning, 21 March 1857.

11 Saldhana, *Précis on Naval Arrangements*, 12–15.

12 *Home Correspondence (Secret)*, Vol. 62. Alison to Stanley, 11 May 1868.

13 Saldhana, *Précis on Naval Arrangements*, 15.

14 *Secret Letters to India, etc., 1859–1869*. Northcote to Gov.-Gen. of India, 4 December 1868 and Argyll to Mayo, 30 July 1869; *Secret Miscellany Book*, Vol. 3, Merivale to Hammond, 21 September 1869.

15 Saldhana, J.A., *Précis of the Affairs of the Persian Coast and Islands, 1854–1905* (Calcutta, 1906), 27.

16 Ibid., 29.
17 Graham, *Naval Supremacy*, 57–8.
18 *Enclos. to Bombay Sec. Letters*, Vol. 147. Aitchison to Secy. to Govt. of Bombay, 23 July 1868.
19 *Enclos. to Bombay Sec. Letters*, Vol. 146. Enclos. to Sec. Letter No. 2. Kemball to Bulwer, 1 January 1862.
20 *Persian Gulf – Turkish Jurisdiction along the Arabian Coast, Part 1*. Pol. and Sec. Dept. Memo. Secret Letter from India No. 127 dated 22 May 1879, Aitchison to Mayo, 28 July 1871.
21 Ibid., Minute by Viceroy, 29 July 1871.
22 *Political and Secret Letters and Enclosures from India*, Vol. 22. Gov.-Gen. in Council to Secy. of State, 22 May 1879.
23 Lorimer, op. cit., I, 265–6.
24 Lorimer, op. cit., *passim* Low, op. cit., II, 411–12; *Precis on Commerce and Communications in the Persian Gulf, 1801–1905* (Calcutta, 1906), *passim*; Harris, C.P., The Persian Gulf Submarine Telegraph of 1864, *Geog. Journ.* 1969, CXXV, 169–90; *Wireless Telegraphic Stations in the Persian Gulf*. Pol. and Sec. Dept. Memo., August 1928.
25 Kelly, J.B., *Britain and the Persian Gulf, 1795–1880* (Oxford, 1968), 554.
26 Saldhana, *Persian Coast and Islands*, 57.
27 Aitchison, op. cit., XI, 256–7.
28 Ibid., 202, 238, 262, 310–18; Lorimer, op. cit., I, 299, 307.
29 Aitchison, op. cit., XI, 202; *Home Corresp. (Secret)* Vol. 180. Memorandum from Curzon, 26 November 1898.
30 Lorimer, op. cit., I, 317.
31 Lorimer, op. cit., I, 2556–86; Fraser, L., Gun-running in the Persian Gulf, *Proc. Cent. Asian Soc.*, 17 May 1911; *Persian Gulf Gazetteer, Part I.* Précis on Arms Trade in the Persian Gulf (Calcutta 1904); *Arms Traffic in the Persian Gulf, 1908–1928*. Pol. and Sec. Dept. Memo., 8 October 1928.
32 Bennett, T.J., The Past and Present Connection of England with the Persian Gulf, *Journ. Soc. Arts*, 1902, L, 646.
33 Saldhana, J.A., *Précis of Correspondence on International Rivalry and British Policy in the Persian Gulf, 1872–1905* (Calcutta, 1906), 33–6.
34 *Parliamentary Papers*, 1899, CIX, 124.
35 Busch, B.C., *Britain and the Persian Gulf, 1894–1914* (California, 1967), *passim*.
36 Graham, *Great Britain in the Indian Ocean*, 262.
37 Fraser, L., Some Problems of the Persian Gulf, *Proc. of Cent. Asian Soc.*, 8 January 1908.
38 Lorimer, op. cit., I, 325 ff.
39 Saldhana, *Precis on International Rivalry*, 47.
40 *The Times*, 6 May 1903.
41 Saldhana, *Précis re Trucial Chiefs*, 71.
42 Ibid, 51.
43 Viceroy's Speech to the Trucial Chiefs, 21 November 1903.

V Era of Indecision

*Upon the breaking and shivering of a great State and Empire you may
be sure to have wars.*

Bacon: Of Vicissitude of Things

In the preceding chapters the story of Britain's penetration into the
region of the Persian Gulf and her gradual assumption of control and
supremacy has been made evident from contemporary records.
Throughout the narrative three separate yet interwoven strands are
discernible in the cord which was fashioned steadily up to the time of
the dismemberment of the Indian Empire in 1947. The first concerns
itself with India, and viewed in that light the Persian Gulf is seen as
the westernmost bastion drawing Basra to the gates of Bombay. The
second comprehends the Persian Gulf as an essential part in Imperial
communications, linking the Eastern Mediterranean with the Indian
Ocean, and also as a pressure point whereby those powers whose
interests converged upon those of Britain in the region could be kept
in check. The last expresses the *raison d'être* for the original British
presence in the Gulf, reinforced by the treaties entered into with the
littoral shaikhdoms and the obligations emerging therefrom. Each
strand has had to bear its own part of the strain so that the cord might
not be sundered. The weaving of the cord was slow and painstaking
and not without cost, yet a remarkable element of consistency
prevailed, so it is now necessary to attempt to discover the relevance
of that effort in the context of our own times.

During the first two decades of the twentieth century a process of
co-ordination and consolidation was carried out whereby existing
relationships were reinforced and new engagements entered into. In
1900, consequent upon Curzon's recommendation of the previous
year, a Political Agent was appointed to Bahrain, that officer being
subordinate to the Chief Political Resident at Bushire, and in 1904,
despite Turkish opposition a Political Agent was appointed to Kuwait,
first in a temporary capacity in order to pacify the Porte but later to be
established on a permanent basis. In 1911 engagements were entered
into with Bahrain, Kuwait and the Trucial States to afford protection
to the pearling and sponge fisheries from both British and foreign
exploitation,[1] and importantly Qatar, whose earlier treaty of 1868
with Britain had lapsed on the death of the shaikh, Muhammad ibn

Thani, entered into fresh obligations in 1916 similar to those of the Trucial States and accordingly a breach in the continuity of British political influence along the entire extent of the Arabian shores was repaired.[2]

Anglo-Turkish relations within the Gulf region had long needed to be regulated since conflicting claims to oversight and protection had been established on both sides, especially concerning Kuwait, Bahrain and Qatar. In fact, during the nineteenth century Ottoman claims had been advanced or had receded, such fluctuations depending upon relative Turkish strength or the extent of her more pressing distractions elsewhere at the time; they had never been abandoned. This was an unsatisfactory state of affairs in British eyes since such presumed entitlements to sovereignty on the part of the Porte tended to conflict with engagements entered into between Britain and the coastal shaikhs. Accordingly, negotiations were instituted early in 1913, after Turkey had extricated herself from wars in the Balkans, and a convention between the two powers was signed in July of that year. In this, the independence of Kuwait and that shaikh's special relationship with Britain were recognized; a similar provision applied to Bahrain; Turkish claims to Qatar were renounced; the eastern boundaries of the Ottoman *sanjaq* of Najd were defined as a 'Blue Line' extending due south from the vicinity of 'Uqair; and finally, certain British rights concerning navigation and police duties in the Gulf were recognized.[3] This convention was due for ratification in October 1914 but by then war had broken out and since Britain and Turkey were on opposite sides it was therefore invalidated; it nevertheless possesses a form of validity in that it indicates the intentions and agreements reached between the two powers at that time.

Meanwhile, in May 1913 shaikh Abdul Aziz ibn Sa'ud had invaded Hasa and proceeded to annex that territory. Negotiations towards the Anglo-Ottoman Convention were proceeding at that time, and consequently in order to contain this campaign within reasonable proportions and also to avoid unnecessary embarrassment the Porte grudgingly conferred upon the triumphant ibn Sa'ud the title of *vali* of the *sanjaq* of Najd. Relations between the Sa'udi amirate and the British had, prior to this time, not reached the stage of entering into formal agreements, the status of that chief appearing to be equivocal, but the war of 1914–1918 found ibn Sa'ud in an indeterminate position between the British and Turks, who were at war with each other. In December 1915, however, relations between the Wahabi amir and Britain were established by the Treaty of Darin which, apart from imposing limitations upon the control of Sa'udi foreign affairs and providing for British assistance if ibn Sa'ud were attacked, contained a clause which significantly secured the Trucial States, Kuwait, Bahrain and Qatar from Sa'udi aggression.[4]

Prior to the outbreak of the First World War other events beyond the headwaters of the Gulf had conspired to present a threat to both the stability of the region and to British hegemony there. The most important development was that of a closer relationship between Germany and Turkey consequent upon the ascendancy of the Young Turks in 1908 whereby the extension of German influence by means of the *Drang nach Osten* policy was matched by the Turkish desire for military equipment and reinforcement. Without German support and ministrations the 'Sick Man of Europe' would probably have succumbed to his malaise, while the Young Turks would have found it difficult to continue an otherwise precarious existence. German ambitions, as already noted, had manifested themselves principally in the construction of the Berlin-Baghdad railway, which had reached Konya in 1896 and by 1914 it had been completed almost to Baghdad, but thereafter the reverses of the First World War caused Germany to retire from Asia in order to contemplate more immediate matters in Europe. Russian advances southward were viewed with continued apprehension and efforts accordingly had been made to check these, though a humiliating defeat in 1904 at the hands of the Japanese temporarily deprived Russia of further impetus in imperial expansion. The 1907 agreement between Russia and Britain had left the Persian shores within the Gulf as part of the Neutral Zone, a situation for which Kitchener has been held partly responsible. As Commander-in-Chief India, he had indicated to the British Government that the area subsequently identified as the British Zone of Persia was all that he could undertake to hold with the troops at his disposal.[5] Curzon, in a speech in the House of Lords in February 1908 was moved to say that he did not think that 'this treaty, in its Persian aspect, will conduce either to the security of India, to the independence of Persia, or to the peace of Asia',[6] but his anxieties were to be of short duration for the world war and its aftermath were to sweep away these zonal restrictions.

Yet unquestionably the most significant events during those early decades were those associated with the discovery of oil in the Middle East. In 1908 oil was struck at Masjid-i-Sulaiman in south-western Persia and the newly-formed Anglo-Persian Oil Company assumed the concession in 1909, later building its refinery at Abadan. In 1913 at the instigation of the First Lord of the Admiralty, Mr Winston Churchill, the British Government purchased a substantial interest in the Company and thereby the fuel supply of the Royal Navy was to be assured. In 1913, also, as an indication that the strategic significance of oil had now been recognized Kuwait undertook not to grant an oil concession 'to anyone except a person appointed from the British Government' and in the following year Bahrain entered into a similar agreement.[7] These manoeuvres were to bear implications carrying far beyond the waters and region of the Gulf, but the oil itself was an economic and strategic commodity the exploitation of which was to affect greatly the calm in which the Gulf states at that time had briefly become immersed. In those transitional days marking the change-over from coal to oil as a marine fuel, the technical and strategic aspects tended to obscure the nascent economic and nationalistic upsurges later to extend throughout the whole of the Middle East and which today pose problems as yet unresolved.

Without doubt, the close of the First World War stands as a watershed in the history of the Middle East in modern times. The Ottoman power was irretrievably broken, yielding place to a Turkey confined almost wholly to Asia Minor and incohesive Arab states under either mandatory control or the influence of Britain and France. Few voices have been raised to lament the dissolution of the Sublime Porte, yet upon reflection a rejuvenated and modified Turkish oversight of the lands of the Fertile Crescent might well have provided a unifying element binding the Near East into a coherent whole, one in which much blood and treasure need not have been squandered. In 1915 Sir Mark Sykes, whose name is associated with the Sykes-Picot Agreement made between Britain, France and Russia in 1916 respecting the dismemberment of Ottoman territories, had recommended to the Foreign Office that Britain's ultimate goal in the Arab lands of the Near East, consequent upon the exclusion of Turkish authority and jurisdiction from those regions, should be twofold: a declaration of an external protectorate over the Arabian littoral from Kuwait to Hodeidah, and of an internal and external protectorate in southern Syria and Mesopotamia, to be arranged with the concurrence of France and Russia.[8] In the event, Britain was indeed to exert either direct control or indirect influence over most of the areas mentioned by Sykes, though in a different outward manifestation, and to that extent Westminster was to become for a generation the implicit inheritor of most of the Asiatic dominions of the Porte.

On the opposite shores of the Gulf, Britain was not to be equally favoured. There is little doubt that the success with which Wassmuss, the 'German Lawrence', had rallied the tribes of south-west Persia against the British during the war, and the tacit support accorded to him by Tehran reflected the resentment felt against both Britain and Russia arising from the unpopular 1907 agreement.[9] A new Anglo-Persian treaty drawn up in 1919 would have abrogated the earlier agreement and yet would have conferred definite British advantages, especially in the appointment of British military and financial advisers to the Shah, as opposed to Bolshevik Russia. In effect, this would have placed Persia within a great British imperial crescent extending over the whole of western Asia, a concept long cherished by Curzon, at that time Foreign Secretary, and it would have represented the culmination of a lifetime devoted to consideration of Eastern problems and the consequent extension and fortification of imperial power and mission. A student of Curzon's later diplomacy has remarked:

> Always he had dreamt of creating a chain of vassal states stretching from the Mediterranean to the Pamirs and protecting, not the Indian frontiers merely, but our communications with our further Empire. It seemed in those early months of 1919 that this dream was about to be realised and that Providence had vouchsafed to him, in the evening of his life, the privilege of conferring one final benefit upon the India which he had served so lovingly, although with such unthankful recompense.[10]

That this treaty failed to become ratified by the Persian Majlis was due partly to Persian suspicions of Britain's motives, and partly to Britain's unwillingness or inability to withstand Russian advances in the regions of Transcaspia and Transcaucasia. Counter-diplomacy by Russia, together with open hostility to the plan by France and the United States, were directed against its success, but the death knell was sounded when Reza Khan at the head of his Cossack brigade seized the reins of Persian government in February 1921 and the treaty was soon denounced. Three years later Reza, now Prime Minister, arrested Khaz'al the shaikh of Mohammerah and thus removed a friend of Britain; in 1925 he deposed the last of the Qajars and ascended the Peacock Throne to institute the new Pahlavi dynasty.

The inter-war years witnessed further activities relating to agreements between powers. In 1919 the Bahrain Order in Council was brought into force and this emphasized Britain's role in the internal affairs of the island; later reference to international developments concerning Bahrain will be found in Chapter 7. It is sufficient here to observe that after the Trucial States the island of Bahrain had been the object of greatest solicitude within the Gulf by Britain, due partly to its insularity, to its quarrels with the mainland Arabs, to its importance in the pearling industry which has latterly given place to oil, and to the conflicting claims made upon it by Egyptians, Omanis, Turks and Persians. Here, more than elsewhere in the Gulf, lay the greatest possibilities to disturbance of maritime peace which it had been Britain's constant endeavour to preserve.

Disputes between the Sultans of Muscat and the Imams of Oman had presented opportunities for disorder throughout that part of the Arabian peninsula ever since the assumption of the sultanate by the Al Bu Sa'id dynasty. After dissensions commencing in 1898 when the Sultan's garrison at Sur had been forcibly expelled by adherents of the Imam, matters came to a head in 1920 when Britain considered it expedient to endeavour to establish a *modus vivendi* between the two parties. Tripartite negotiations resulted in the Treaty of Sib which was effected in September 1920 and in which the Sultan's rule was recognized as paramount while yet implying the existence of the people of Oman as a separate entity.[11] This treaty remained secret until 1957 when, as a result of renewed conflicts between Omanis and Muscatis, the provisions were published; the disputes, however, were to continue.

Relations with Iraq, as Mesopotamia was henceforward to be known, were established in 1921 when Faisal, son of Husain the Sharif of Mecca, was proclaimed king, and in 1922 a treaty between the new kingdom and Britain further regulated the relationships between the two countries, instituting Iraq as a British Mandate. This treaty was ratified in 1924 and thus the Arab headwaters of the Gulf and the deep channel of the Shatt-al-Arab came at long last under British supervision. The 1922 Treaty, however, was of short duration for in 1930 this was replaced by another which had been prepared in anticipation of Iraq being admitted to the League of Nations. This event occurred in 1932 and thereupon the independence of Iraq was recognized, the British High Commissioner being replaced by an ambassador and thereafter the two countries conducted their mutual affairs in accordance with the terms of the 1930 Treaty. Iraq, whilst continuing to be subject to British influence, ceased to be a British protectorate.

The railway line through Iraq was completed in 1939 so that the Gulf waters were linked by that means with the Bosphorus, and so the fears of the 1890s – later converted into the hopes of the 1930s – were at last realized.

Before the First World War the Sa'udi amirs had been regarded by the British as little more than desert princelings, but the 1915 agreement had imposed a formal basis of understanding between the two countries. Later, the Amir of Najd became King of the Hijaz by virtue of his invasion of that part of Arabia and the expulsion of Husain, Sharif of Mecca and Guardian of the Holy Places in 1926. The status of the new king, ibn Sa'ud, now required to be harmonized in law as well as in fact, therefore a fresh agreement known as the Treaty of Jeddah was signed in 1927, superseding the earlier agreement of 1916. This recognized the full sovereignty of the Sa'udi king but it also contained an important provision that the new Ruler 'undertakes to maintain friendly and peaceful relations with the territories of Kuwait and Bahrein . . . who are in special treaty relations with His Britannic Majesty's Government.'[12]

Bahrain at the same time had been achieving a form of strategic importance which had for long exercised British-Indian minds, and so in 1935 the British naval stations at Basidu and Henjam were transferred to Bahrain, a century after Hennell had somewhat diffidently proposed a formal acquisition of the island as a base in the Gulf.[13] In 1946, the Persian Gulf Lighting Service which had succeeded the British India Steam Navigation Company as the supervising authority for the safety of navigation, buoyage and the provision and maintenance of navigational aids throughout the Gulf[14] was likewise transferred to Bahrain, and on the removal of the Residency from Bushire to Bahrain soon afterwards the process of transfer and concentration of British seats of authority and administration within that island was completed.

The outbreak of war in 1939 did not, at first, present a set of circumstances in the Gulf identical with those which had prevailed a quarter of a century earlier. There was no hostile Ottoman power to be confronted since the new Turkish Republic remained neutral throughout this second war, the states of Arabia were bound to Britain by various agreements or treaties, whilst along the Persian shores no outward signs of discord could be discerned. Nevertheless this state of comparative calm was disturbed early due to two causes: the eastward drive of Germany and the corresponding need to support and supply Soviet Russia. A successful and not improbable German advance beyond the Volga could precede a Russian collapse and an over-running of the Middle East by Hitler's victorious troops who might succeed where Napoleon had failed. Already Syria was reported to be hostile to the Allied cause whilst Iraq was torn by opposing factions, the one favouring Britain and the other Germany. Meanwhile the Russians were placed logistically at a disadvantage since vital supplies were running dangerously low.

In Persia a new railway line had conveniently been completed in 1938 joining Tehran with Bandar Shapur at the northern extremity of the Gulf, and this presented an obvious supply route from seaward. Accordingly in August 1941 the British and Soviet governments informed Persia of their intention to occupy that country and to activate the supply route from the Persian Gulf. This was no sooner said than done, and in the following month Reza Shah was obliged to abdicate in favour of his son Muhammad Reza. This act demonstrated not only the removal of a king whose pro-German sympathies were suspect but also the strength of resistant forces within his own country, forces which resented his fierce autocracy, his rush towards modernization of institutions and attitudes, and his alienation of the *mullahs* and the faithful.

By 1942 the United States had entered the war and they were soon busy in augmenting the Gulf supply line. In fact, they were shortly afterwards to provide a preponderance of military equipment and installations in Persia, thereby freeing British supplies to meet increased and urgent demands on the Western front. The advent of the American military machine in the Middle Eastern theatre of war was to have profound significance for the future and by the end of hostilities one simple fact emerged: American commercial interests were dominant in that region, displacing the British who were by then reduced to a state of economic exhaustion. American oil interests were on the move and the whole history of the Gulf region in these post-war years has been mainly a narrative of immense developments in oil exploration and exploitation in which the expansionist attitude of the United States has been a major contributing factor. This point is relevant to the theme so far considered in that the economic equilibrium for so long maintained was now greatly disturbed and the resultant increased economic power had to a very large extent passed out of British hands. Britain was in danger of sustaining added burdens whilst simultaneously surrendering part of that power which should accompany responsibility.

The years immediately after the war therefore were notable for changes in physical disposition and political and emotional attitudes.

In 1945 the Arab League was formed and this swiftly lent itself to organizing the vociferous nationalism which has been a characteristic of the decades since then, and which has derived unending nourishment from the founding of an independent State of Israel in 1948 on the termination of the Palestine Mandate. In 1947 the Indian Empire ceased to exist but the creation of the successor states of India and Pakistan with their internal factions and external disputes tended to upset the centuries-old stability which British rule in the subcontinent had provided. Russian power in the north had visibly increased whilst Russian influences continued to penetrate into those parts of the Middle East where Britain was no longer the protecting state.

The events of the 1950s and 1960s within the Gulf were confined mainly to regional disputes. The nationalization of the Persian oil industry in 1951 provided a temporary dislocation in supply but the subsequent reorganization had no adverse effect upon long-term Western interests; Sa'udi Arabia's attack in 1952 upon the Buraimi oases in territory shared between Oman and Abu Dhabi was repelled by forces under British command though the Sa'udi claim has not since been abandoned; the Omanis under their newly elected Imam, Ghalib ibn 'Ali, rose once more against the Sultan of Muscat to denounce the Treaty of Sib but were quietened by the Sultan's troops, though a more serious revolt in 1957 under Talib ibn 'Ali, the Imam's brother, caused the sultan to seek British armed support in order to restore the situation; Iraq threatened Kuwait in 1961 but withdrew in the face of British armed opposition; and the Persian claim to Bahrain and certain smaller islands at the entrance to the Gulf was referred to the United Nations in 1970. Such was the state of affairs when Britain abandoned Aden in 1968 and such was the political climate when the Prime Minister, Mr Harold Wilson, declared to the House of Commons in January 1968 that

> We have accordingly decided to accelerate the withdrawal of our forces from their stations in the Far East . . . and to withdraw them by the end of 1971. We have also decided to withdraw our forces from the Persian Gulf by the same date.

Just as the Persian Gulf has long assumed, by virtue of its very position, a significance for both West and East, principally because of the means of communication it has afforded and also because of the corresponding means of maritime dominance open to any power able to establish itself there, so today the Gulf retains its essential importance within two inextricable interests: oil and political-military strategy.

With the British withdrawal in 1971 a power vacuum was created, and this has been detrimental to the peace of the world and the security of the inhabitants of the Gulf. Subsequent disturbances arising from rivalry between the states of the region, and especially the more recent despoliation of Kuwait by Iraq, bear witness to the fact that the great maritime artery of the Persian Gulf and the source region of vital oil supplies will continue to be vulnerable to unrest and turmoil until a more lasting form of political equilibrium has been achieved. In the nature of present dispositions, this will prove to be a slow process.

Notes

1 Saldhana, *Précis on International Rivalry*, 96–8; Aitchison, op. cit., XI, 196, 202, 203, 263.
2 Ritchie, R., *British Interests on the Coast of Arabia, etc.* Pol. and Sec. Dept. Memo. 30 January 1905; Aitchison, op. cit., XI, 258–60.
3 Hurewitz, J.C., *Diplomacy in the Near and Middle East* (Princeton, 1956), I, 269–72.
4 Aitchison, op. cit., XI, 206–8.
5 Fraser, L., *India under Curzon and After* (London, 1911), 130.
6 Nicolson, H., *Curzon: the Last Phase, 1919–1925* (London, 1934), 126.
7 Aitchison, op. cit., X, 264–5.
8 *Policy in the Middle East*: Memorandum by Sir Mark Sykes. Pol. and Sec. Dept. Memo. 15 November 1915.
9 Sykes, C., *Wassmuss* (London, 1936), *passim*.
10 Nicolson, op. cit., 121.
11 Al-Baharnah, H.M., *The Legal Status of the Arabian Gulf States* (Manchester, 1968), 241 ff, 315–6.
12 *Parliamentary Papers*, 1927. Treaty Series No. 25. Cmd. 2951, 73.
13 *Enclos. to Bombay Sec. Letters*, Vol. 19. Enclos. to Sec. Letter No. 5. Hennell to Willoughby, 10 November 1839.
14 Ferard, J.E., *Memorandum on the Lighting and Buoyage of the Persian Gulf*. Pol. and Sec. Dept. Memo. 28 December 1911.

SEVEN

Bahrain and the Persian Claim

*From Siraf we travelled to the town of Bahrayn, a fine large town with
orchards, trees and streams. Water is easy to get there; all one has to do
is to scoop the ground with one's hands.*

Ibn Battuta: The Travels

One of the many complex political issues in the Middle East was that
of the sovereignty of Bahrain, which for many centuries was, as
Curzon so aptly puts it, 'the object of much tender solicitude from all
parties'.[1] The independence of the island under the ruling Al Khalifah
family who have governed Bahrain since the end of the eighteenth
century was at intervals challenged by various powers, though the
main claimant was unquestionably Persia. But Britain formed the
protecting power whereby the Shaikh of Bahrain ruled the island in
his own right with British advice and restraint, as will be seen from
the preamble to the Bahrain Order of 1952: 'Whereas by treaty,
capitulation, grant, usage, sufferance, and other lawful means Her
Majesty the Queen has jurisdiction within the territories of the Ruler
of Bahrein . . .'[2] This Order, though since abrogated, springs from
earlier undertakings of the nineteenth century, and the purpose of this
chapter is to trace the British connexion and the Persian claim, for
although the shaikhdom is today fully independent and free of
external treaties binding it to another power, the situation needs to be
clearly appraised.

This appraisal may best be attempted by examining historical
records and treaties entered into, and for this purpose the turning
point of 1783 is taken, in which year the Persians were finally driven
from Bahrain and have never effectually returned. A short review of
events up to that date is therefore necessary in order to show how the

various conflicting claims to this insular sovereignty are not confined to the recent past.

During the first millenium of the Muhammadan era Bahrain was governed by chiefs who owed a shadowy allegiance first to one potentate and then to another impartially, irrespective of whether that power resided on the Arabian or Persian shores at the time. For a considerable period it was incorporated in the governorship of Othman ibn Abi al Asi and his successors, but by the tenth century A.D. it had been overrun by the followers of Hamdan Qarmat, an extremist Muslim sect, though when the traveller Idrisi visited Bahrain in the twelfth century he observed that 'the island is governed by an independent chief'.[3] In 1332 Ibn Battuta visited Bahrain and Qatif, which he described as being populated by Arabs of the Shi'ite persuasion,[4] and at about this time too Bahrain was made nominally subject to the King of Hormuz, who at one time was acknowledged tributary to Persia, and at another independent, according to the vicissitudes and trials of strength at the time. In the sixteenth century the Turks, Persians and Portuguese were contenders for the island, and in 1507 the King of Hormuz became a vassal of the Portuguese when he was subdued by Albuquerque. The Portuguese remained in possession of Bahrain until 1602 when they were forced to surrender the island to the Persians. During the ensuing 180 years the fortunes of Bahrain were chequered, the island passing successively from the Persian governors into the hands of Oman, then to the Huwala Arabs, back to the Persians and then in 1783 to the 'Utub Arabs from the mainland, and it is from that date that the history of Bahrain should be regarded in closer detail, for despite subsequent excursions and depredations by Omanis, Wahabis, Egyptians, Turks and Persians, the sovereignty of Bahrain has indisputably remained in the hands of the 'Utubis.

A summing up of this earlier period is made by Curzon: 'The history of Bahrein . . . has been one of constant vicissitudes, the result of covetous appetites of the surrounding nations. In all the conflicts for the supremacy of the Gulf waged by Arabs, Persians and Turks, each combatant has his eye fixed on Bahrein, and the victor has invariably sought to make it his first spoil.' It is in anticipation of what will unfold itself subsequently that he goes on to add, 'These selfish ambitions have only been controlled at the instance and by the interference of Great Britain, who, having entered into treaty engagements with Bahrein analogous to those concluded with the trucial chiefs, has always insisted on their due observance, and has in turn vindicated the independence of the island against the pretensions of whatever foreign power.'[5]

Like many of the Arab tribes, the 'Utubi were migrants from the Arabian hinterland and it was one of their principal branches, the Al Khalifah, which finally subdued the Persian garrison, compelling the Persians to retire, from which time Persia ceased to exercise effective occupation or jurisdiction in Bahrain, though despite a *fait accompli* of more than two centuries ago Persia continued to maintain a pretence of sovereignty over the island and other territories on the western shores of the Persian Gulf. The Imperial Court was not alone, however, in advancing this title, for the Sultan of Muscat likewise claimed the island, making an equally valid appeal to history and prior occupation, and these rival claims, to which at a later stage may be added those of Egypt and Turkey, form an important part of the island's history. Indeed in 1800 the forces of Muscat did occupy Bahrain which subsequently remained in dispute among the Omanis, the 'Utubis and the Wahabis until 1811 when the al Khalifah succeeded in reasserting their authority. Their rule was often precarious and for expediency's sake they tended to play lip service to such powers as offered an immediate threat or proffered protection; nevertheless their rule was (sometimes tenuously) maintained and has continued without serious interruption since they assumed power.

At this time Britain was active in the Gulf since the interests of the East India Company had been steadily developing in that direction, and as the Company's primary concern was the furtherance of trade it had no territorial ambitions. The British Political Residents appointed in the Gulf were engaged in diplomatic activities to ensure the peace in that part of the world and to overcome the depredation of the pirates who were ravaging the coasts from their bases within the Gulf.

Captain William Bruce was Resident at Bushire when the al Khalifah returned, and he was to play a fateful part in subsequent Anglo-Persian relations. He had travelled extensively in the Gulf and in the Province of Fars, and in 1817 he sent a long despatch to Bombay in which he reviewed British interests in the Gulf and especially in relation to Bahrain. He was disposed to disparage the Shah's claim to Bahrain by observing that

Little more . . . need here be advanced to prove how vain and futile are His Majesty's pretensions than to state that nearly two

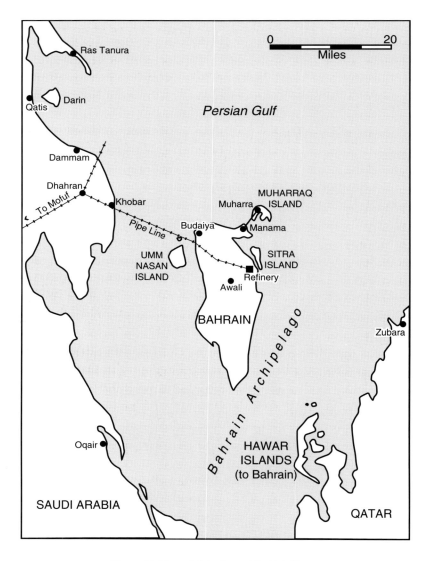

Figure 11 Map of Bahrain and its Neighbours

successive reigns of a second dynasty of Persian kings have succeeded to the lapse of a former line, since the object of his pretensions has owned the sway of foreign lords and that the monarch, who with such empty pride asserts his supremacy over the island, is not in possession of the slightest ship on which he could convey his Viceroy across a few leagues of unsighted sea to the sail of his own ambition.[6]

Though quaintly expressed, this opinion is of importance and should be taken in conjunction with an earlier report when, after visiting Bahrain, he found the Al Khalifah to be sole and undisputed rulers of the island,[7] for the Persian claim had since rested heavily on a contrary statement briefly assented to by Bruce in the so-called Treaty of Shiraz in 1822.

Protracted negotiations were also being conducted between Saiyid Sa'id and the Prince Governor of Fars who, from his seat at Shiraz, was viceroy for the Shah. Sa'id was desirous of acquiring Bahrain whose revenues were considerable and whose pearling industry had for so long aroused the cupidity of her neighbours; he had long and seemingly in vain endeavoured to enlist Persian support for his plan of conquest of the island. Notwithstanding this, in 1819 the Turks established their influence over the Shaikhs of Bahrain much to Sa'id's chagrin, and Henry Willock, Chargé d'affaires at Tehran, referring to this matter noted that 'The Imam supposes that the proud spirit of the Shah will not permit such a valuable possession, which has for ages acknowledged the sovereignty of Persia, to pass under the Turkish Government without a remonstrance or without an attempt to recover it.'[8] Such a dubious appeal to history was nevertheless invoked in vain, for the Shah, besides being impotent at sea, wished to steer a middle course and to avoid provoking the Turks whom he was powerless to dislodge.

Sa'id had been angered by Bruce's recent dealings at Bahrain in 1816 when an agreement was proposed between Shaikh 'Abdullah and the British Government[9] and this had caused Muscat to protest against a high-handed attitude by the British Resident.[10] A disavowal of Bruce's actions had, however, been made by the Government of Bombay who informed the Governor-General that 'the agreement entered into . . . has never received the confirmation of this Government'.[11] Saiyid Sa'id continued assiduous in his intrigues to secure possession of Bahrain, and his activities did not pass unnoticed. Sir Evan Nepean, Governor of Bombay, in referring these to Lord

Hastings, the Governor-General, stated that 'an arrangement was some time since concerted between His Majesty the King of Persia and the Imam of Muscat, by which the former agreed to relinquish all claims to the island of Bahrein, under the condition of receiving a portion of its revenues . . .'[12] Bruce, on the other hand, had expressed his opinion that this arrangement would not be carried into effect since the Prince of Shiraz had been instructed to demand the Imam's brother as surety for his good-will, and this the Imam would not concede.[13] Sa'id then began conducting direct negotiations with the Shaikh of Bahrain for payment of an annual tribute of 30,000 dollars provided that the British Government consented to provide security for its payment[14] but this underwriting was not forthcoming.

The British position, in the midst of all these tergiversations, was in need of clarification and definition; the desire was to avoid becoming embroiled in intrigues then afoot and to keep a resolute eye on trade and peaceful expansion. Sir William Grant Keir who from 1819 was in command of an expeditionary force in the Gulf against the pirates was thereupon instructed by the Bombay Government that

> In regard to the view which the Imaum of Muscat and the Prince of Sheraz meditate against the island of Bahrein, however much the Governor-in-Council has to regret the prosecution of those hostile operations, it is our obvious policy to maintain a strict neutrality, and in particular to impress the Uttoobee Arabs with a conviction that so far from being a party to those proceedings we view them with regret, and that the British Government would have cordially seized any opportunity that presented itself to promote the general tranquillity of the Persian Gulf.[15]

During this time the British authorities had resolved to put fully into effect that policy which they had so frequently protested and accordingly the General Treaty with the Arab Tribes in the Persian Gulf had been signed by the Shaikhs of Bahrain at Keir's instigation on 5 February 1820. This condemned plunder and piracy by land and sea. An important step forward towards the Company's avowed aims had been achieved and it was undesirable that this should be nullified by vexatious disputes and internecine strife in the region. Saiyid Sa'id was accordingly informed that in the spirit of this general agreement all intentions of attacking Bahrain should be abandoned. 'The Shaikh of Bahrain', it was added, 'having made himself a party to the treaty which has been negotiated, it is the determination of the British Government to observe a strict neutrality in any operation that may be contemplated against that Island, so long as those operations do not lead to piratical aggression.'[16]

In furtherance of that object, Keir was prosecuting a vigorous campaign against the Qawasim pirates whose principal stronghold was Ras al Khaimah. He not only had to step warily between the Shah and the Imam in order to avoid a semblance of partisanship, but it appeared necessary also to dispel the impression that Britain was seeking territorial expansion in the Gulf. Mountstuart Elphinstone, Governor of Bombay, had earlier expressed his appreciation of this difficulty in a letter addressed to Hastings when, after disavowing all interference in the affairs of Bahrain, subject of course to a cessation of piracy on the part of the Shaikh, he turned towards an earlier suggestion of forming a British establishment in the Gulf. 'We anticipate, however,' he added, 'some opposition on the part of the Persian Government to that measure since it would be difficult, we apprehend, to satisfy that Power that our views were limited to the professional object of our policy, the more especially as the Persian Government has manifested some degree of alarm at our contemplating the occupation of the Island of Bahrain.'[17]

Elphinstone's hesitancy towards involvement was understandable, but the Company's servants were more realistic in their appreciation and especially in assessing the difficulty in the Shaikhs maintaining their independence without assistance from outside. Francis Warden, Secretary to the Bombay Government, who had applied himself to mastering the intricacies of tribal histories and rivalries in the Gulf, wrote an extensive Minute on the status of Bahrain in which he expressed his views clearly on both the island's status and the Shaikhs' motives in soliciting external aid, and he informed Elphinstone that

> My opinion in respect of Bahrein remains unchanged . . . we are informed that the present rulers of Bahrein have enjoyed an independent power for some years, that policy and necessity obliged them to bend to the Wahabee yoke . . . they wish however to be on the most friendly terms with the British being determined to throw off the power of the Wahabee Chief and to decline all communications with the Joasmees at as early a period as possible. They gained the Island (we are told) by force and retain it solely by the same right.
>
> Now I cannot imagine on what stronger grounds the right of any other sovereign to a possession can be established than those

on which it is admitted that the rulers of Bahrein have acquired
and retain the island . . .

Having thrown off their allegiance to Persia and being
constantly threatened by the Imam of Muscat and experiencing
no encouragement from the British Government to confirm the
engagement they were desirous of contracting, it is not
surprizing that they should seek the protection of the Wahabees,
'necessity' compelled them to that alternative. The same course
influences them in seeking the protection of Ibrahim Pacha.[18]

Warden counselled the Government to pursue a policy of conciliation
and encouragement towards the Shaikhs of Bahrain but Elphinstone
preferred one of mediation. Whilst conceding a general concurrence
to Warden's views he nevertheless wrote to Willock that there was
reason to believe that the Shaikh would pay a tribute to Persia in
return for undisturbed possession of Bahrain, 'and for this purpose the
mediation of the British Government would be gladly afforded,
provided it can be employed in such a manner as to avoid anything
that might in any shape involve us in the transactions of the parties.'[19]
He went on to express his entire repugnance of involving the British
Government in the policies of the Gulf and desired to maintain a
benevolent neutrality; there he hoped the matter would rest. However,
despite this temporizing approach, the turn of events was to be in a
different direction and the Company found itself becoming drawn
more deeply into a situation from which it could not extricate itself.

In 1822 Bruce wrote to the Bombay Government advising that he
had received a *firman* from the Prince Governor of Fars in which
Bruce was requested to visit Shiraz in order to discuss certain
outstanding issues between the two governments, and he intimated
that it was his intention to proceed accordingly.[20] Instructions in reply
were forthwith sent to Bruce from Bombay informing him that the
Governor-in-Council 'entirely disapproves of your journey to Shiraz
and positively directs your immediate return to your station.'[21] Bruce,
without awaiting receipt of instructions, met the Prince and from that
meeting emerged an agreement between the two men sometimes
referred to as the Treaty of Shiraz.[22] This agreement covered a number
of points for settlement between Britain and Persia, the first article of
which included a statement that 'the Island of Bahrain has always
been subordinate to the Province of Fars', a further paragraph
rescinds the Persian Government's earlier application for Bruce's
removal from his post at Bushire and recommends his renomination

to his former duties, whilst a later clause states a request from the Prince for the loan of some cruisers from the East India Company 'when an expedition is in contemplation against Bahrain, to reduce it to obedience.'[23]

The reasons for this extraordinary action are not difficult to seek. Bruce had been under a cloud both at Tehran and Bombay, and more than once his arbitrary and unilateral actions had caused offence at the Persian Court. His actions of that nature had not passed unnoticed in Bombay where his previous unauthorized agreement with the Shaikhs of Bahrain had been disavowed, so Bruce's concern was to re-establish himself in both British and Persian eyes. To state that Bahrain had always been subordinate to Fars (despite Bruce's earlier opinions noted above) was undoubtedly an easy concession in exchange for Persian felicitations for his future employment, and possibly the recommendation for naval support should also be seen in that light. The Prince too, had motives of his own which are set forth in Bruce's letter to Bombay covering the agreement, the opening paragraph of which is illuminating. Referring to the projected expedition to Bahrain, Bruce writes,

> The ostensible reason of the Prince being more urgent for the Expedition taking place so soon, is to avoid being called up to the Court this winter, which he certainly will be unless he can occupy himself on some Expedition of the kind that will require his personal attention with the principal officers of his Court, while at the same time the charges attending an armament necessary for a service of this kind will be a State charge and afford reasons sufficient for any default that may arise in the regular remittance to the Royal Treasury, whereas if he should proceed to Court expences and the necessary presents required would amount to something very considerable and be entirely out of his own privy Purse.[24]

In expressing the surprise of the Governor-in-Council that these negotiations should have been undertaken at Shiraz, the Secretary wrote to Bruce in uncompromising terms. Referring to the agreement Farish replied that 'it acknowledges the King of Persia's title to Bahrain, of which there is not the least proof, and which the British Government cannot assert . . .' Having condemned the impropriety of the negotiations Farish concluded that as a mark of disapprobation of the whole proceeding Bruce was to be removed from his appointment at Bushire and was directed to return to Bombay.[25] A prompt repudiation was at the same time sent to the Prince at Shiraz in which Elphinstone stated that 'the Treaty which he had concluded was his own act and not that of this Government. I accordingly disavow it, and it to be considered exactly as if it had never been written.'[26] To the Shaikh of Bahrain Elphinstone also wrote to express his assurance that relations between Britain and Bahrain remained as hitherto and undiminished.[27]

Nor was the agreement acceptable at the Persian Court, for Willock records that the Prince's envoy who had been despatched to Tehran to obtain ratification of the agreement did not meet with a favourable reception and that the Shah, whilst refusing his accordance to the stipulations, expressed his displeasure that the Prince should have entered into any engagements with the British Government without his knowledge and injunctions.[28]

It is necessary to dwell upon this episode, not for its implications at the time since disclaimers were made by both the governments involved so that the so-called Treaty was never called into existence, but for the emphasis which was unwarrantably laid upon it in later Persian official representations and in a more recent advocacy of the Persian case.[29]

During the following two decades the Shaikhs of Bahrain courted the favours of rival claimants to the sovereignty of the island and dexterously contrived to play off one against the other. In 1820, as already noted, the Shaikhs had negotiated to pay an annual tribute of 30,000 crowns to Saiyid Sa'id conditional upon the British Government providing surety which however was not forthcoming. The tribute was later reduced to 18,000 crowns but ceased entirely when Saiyid Sa'id attempted an attack upon the islands. In 1830 the Wahabis demanded a tribute and this was agreed upon, amounting to 4,000 crowns annually. This sum was reduced in 1833 to 2,000 crowns after Shaikh 'Abdullah of Bahrain had stirred up the neighbouring tribes to resist the Wahabi claims, and in return for this new tribute the Wahabis undertook to support Bahrain against Sa'id or any other aggressor.[30] Shaikh 'Abdullah became sole ruler of Bahrain in 1834 on the death of his associate and nephew Khalifah ibn Sulaiman. In 1839 the island was threatened by Egyptian forces under Khurshid Pasha on the grounds that it had always been tributary to the Viceroys of Egypt,[31] whereupon the British Government was provoked into warning Egypt that this attempt would not be tolerated. In a despatch to the Bombay Government the Government of India made quite clear its views that if Khurshid

Pasha were to attempt an invasion of the island the British naval commander-in-chief should be authorized to use the utmost influence to deter him in his meditated aggression, but if the Egyptian general were to persist in his designs then the Shaikh of Bahrain should be afforded every encouragement to resistance and all support.[32] Meanwhile Shaikh 'Abdullah continued his tactics by inviting support elsewhere and made application to the Persian Government for permission to place himself and his island under its protection in the event of an expedition against his territory being considered by the Egyptian forces.[33] This provoked the Prince of Fars into sending an emissary from Bushire bearing not only a dress of honour for the Shaikh but also a demand for payment of an annual tribute in return for countenance and protection thus afforded by Persia.[34] 'Abdullah however felt little disposed to comply with this demand and declined to pay tribute.

Samuel Hennell, the Political Resident in the Gulf, made a shrewd appraisal of the Persian motives which closely accorded with that made by Bruce seventeen years before. 'The Prince of Shiraz and his Ministers,' Hennell reported to Bombay, 'finding their influence on the decline at Court, and under the fear of supersession by the Shah, may have set on foot this project of invading Bahrain solely for the purpose of avoiding compliance with a summons to Tehran, but without any real intention of carrying it into effect. Indeed, when I call to mind the almost insuperable obstacles opposed to the Persian Government undertaking any maritime operation, I can hardly believe that the Project of attacking ... Bahrain can be seriously entertained.'[35] The Egyptians had meanwhile continued to harry 'Abdullah whose offer of payment of 13,000 dollars had been refused as inadequate; on the Shaikh protesting that he had hitherto paid a yearly tribute to the Persians he was invited to produce receipts for these, but they were not forthcoming.[36] In a letter to Hennell, Khurshid Pasha had summarily rejected the Persian pretensions to sovereignty over Bahrain since any title which Persia may have possessed had been wrested from them long ago by the sword, and rather sourly he added, 'Their place of residence therefore became fixed in that part of Asia now called Persia, and even this they are not able to rule over properly.'[37] A compromise was eventually reached, though subsequently disclaimed, whereby the Shaikh of Bahrain promised to pay the Egyptians an annual *zakat* or tithe of 3,000 crowns in return for the Shaikh's retention of power in Bahrain.[38] A remonstrance from Hennell caused 'Abdullah to observe that he had entered into these negotiations because he had given up all hopes of either support or assistance from the British, but if they would offer him protection he would be willing to drop all connection with the Pasha and would avow himself a dependent of the British Government.[39]

Throughout this rather tangled skein of circumstances it becomes apparent that declarations of allegiance and promises of tribute were exacted from the Shaikhs of Bahrain by the ruler of Muscat, the Wahabi chiefs, the Egyptian general and the Persian governor, and each demand was in turn conceded by the Shaikh as expediency required, all to be dismissed by a final offer of submission to the British Government, an offer which was indeed considered but finally rejected.[40] The principle of neutrality in the affairs of Bahrain was still the declared objective of the British authorities as it had been expressed twenty years before when Keir had been instructed to work for 'the complete pacification which we are desirous to introduce amongst all the States in the Gulph of Persia',[41] whilst decrying any attempt at a British occupation of Bahrain if that state of maritime peace could be assured.[42]

Overtures by Persia were renewed in 1842 and in August of that year Colonel Sheil, the British chargé d'affaires at Tehran, reported to the Foreign Secretary, Lord Aberdeen, that an attack was impending by Persia upon Bahrain and other ports in the Persian Gulf. He added that Mirza Abul Hassan Khan, the Foreign Minister, had assured him that 'the inhabitants of Bahrain had solicited the protection of Persia, but that no steps had been taken with regard to that Island'.[43] The Government of India were equally cognisant of the matter for Ellenborough, the Governor-General, had communicated to the Bombay Government that 'In the event, however, of the Persian Government sending out any force of armed vessels, or vessels carrying armed men, such vessels should be watched and any actual attempt to possess themselves of territory belonging to Arab chiefs in friendly alliance with the British Government should first be remonstrated against; and then, if persevered in, resisted.'[44]

In the following year, 1843, 'Abdullah's nephew Muhammad ibn Khalifah seized power, expelling his uncle from the island, whereupon 'Abdullah placed himself under the protection of the Prince of Shiraz with whom he entered into an agreement to acknowledge Persian suzerainty in return for Persian support in recapturing the island. Aberdeen was fully aware of the implication of such a manoeuvre and expressed himself unequivocally to Sheil. 'The question of the right of

Persia to interfere and of the Indian Government to prevent interference necessarily depends upon the validity of the pretensions put forward by Persia to the sovereignty of Bahrain.' Aberdeen then expressed the view that the British Government were unaware of any such validity and therefore considered that such claims should be contested by Britain. He went on to add the following uncompromising statement:

> Unless Persia can show that she has a clear and indisputable right to the sovereignty of Bahrain, that she has exercised it without interruption under the dynasty of the Kajar family, and that consequently her present policy is directed to the maintenance of her lawful claims, and not to the assertion of a pretension not founded in law, Persia must be prepared to encounter in any scheme of this kind the active opposition of the British Government in India.[45]

Sheil's representations to the Persian Court were not without effect; Hajji Mirza Aghasi, the Prime Minister, wrote to Sheil reaffirming Persia's claims to Bahrain, and to substantiate this the Hajji reintroduced the agreement entered into by Bruce in 1822 and at the same time he denied the necessity for establishing proof that Bahrain was a dependency of Persia.[46] In reply, Sheil drew the Hajji's attention once more to the fact that the agreement was a wholly unauthorized document and disavowed by both Britain and Persia,[47] and this, in return, drew from the Persian Minister a lengthy memorandum on the subject. Several points were enumerated and these, briefly, resolve themselves into two general contentions: a rather tendentious appeal to history in its broadest and most effusive terms, and a reaffirmation of the validity of the 1822 agreement.[48] The main point of interest in this argument is that it is repetitive, establishing the precedent for all succeeding presentations of the Persian case, whilst the British rejections of the argument invariably followed the same pattern. The whole affair appearing unprofitable, Sheil pursued it no further, and this had Aberdeen's concurrence.[49]

On 8 May 1847 the treaty with the Arab tribes in the Gulf was renewed with Bahrain, but shortly after this had taken effect the Turkish authorities at Basra commenced negotiations with Sheikh Muhammad in the endeavour to obtain his recognition of the supremacy of the Porte. Palmerston, who was now Foreign Secretary, urged upon the Government of India the view that 'if the Bahrain chief is really an independent Ruler the best course would be to make a Treaty of Alliance which would secure his independence and his friendly connection with England'.[50] This direct course of action was, however, not acceptable in Calcutta, despite the fact that there was no treaty engagement with Persia precluding such an act,[51] for the Government of India still adhered to earlier views of not being directly involved in undertakings of this nature. In consequence, both Persia and Turkey resumed activities towards the subjecting of the island to their own suzerainty. Nevertheless, with regard to the Persian threat which at that time appeared the more potent of the two, Palmerston was moved in December to order the Admiralty and the East India Company to direct their naval forces in the Gulf to the protection of Bahrain.[52] When, a year later, a Turkish assumption of sovereignty of the island appeared imminent Palmerston instructed Stratford Canning at Constantinople 'that H.M. Government could not acknowledge nor acquiesce in any such arrangement seeing that the Government of Britain has had relations with Bahrain as an independent State and has concluded with it certain treaties . . . and the British Government must object to any arrangement which would transfer Bahrain to the dominion or protectorship of any other Power.'[53]

Britain had occasion to make further remonstrations in Tehran in 1848 when Farrant, the British Minister, complained of the activities of certain Bahrainis who had sought refuge on Persian soil and from there were threatening to attack the island, taking the opportunity to repeat to Hajji Mirza Aghasi the instructions which Sheil had earlier received from Aberdeen.[54] In his reply the Hajji expressed his astonishment at this view and there quite inconclusively the matter rested once more.[55] However, barely a year had passed by when in February 1849 Shaikh Muhammad renewed his offer to place himself under the British Government, stating that this proposal had also received the concurrence of the principal members of his family and leading notables,[56] but again this offer was not taken up since British policy in the Persian Gulf remained unchanged.

Persia's maritime weakness was apparent throughout the whole of the nineteenth century and after, and this was a principal reason for Britain assuming responsibility for peace and order in the Gulf since this state of affairs could only be ensured by the power commanding the sea. Towards the end of 1850, therefore, the Persian Government renewed its approach to Britain for assistance in the formation of a small naval establishment and for the provision of two sloops-of-war of 25 guns each. Sheil passed this request on to Palmerston with the observation that 'the only evil I am able to foresee is the probability of the Persian Government making an attempt to reduce Bahrain; an announcement of the light in which such a proceeding would be viewed by the English Government would . . . suffice to deter the Shah from interfering with the independence of that island.'[57] Palmerston was inclined to agree in this latter conclusion and so the matter was allowed quietly to drop.

The General Treaty was renewed between Britain and Bahrain in 1856 without reference to any outside power, for by that time the Shaikh's status was recognized as being sole arbiter of the island's affairs, with or without the payment of protection money to those who appeared to threaten his security. It had, indeed, only recently been noticed that 'the Chief of Bahrain is independent but pays *zakat*, or religious tithe, to the Wahabee ruler at the rate of 4,000 crowns per annum.'[58]

The ominous calm of these few years was interrupted at the end of 1859 when Shaikh Muhammad began to levy imposts on Wahabi vessels and to carry off their property in defiance of the treaties signed and reinforced over the previous thirty years. The outcome of the Shaikh's action was bizarre:

> On being remonstrated with he made simultaneous application for protection to the Persian Governor of Fars and the Turkish Wali of Baghdad. The Persian flag was hoisted on the arrival of an Agent of the former (Mirza Mehdi), only to be immediately pulled down and replaced by the Turkish flag on the arrival of an Agent of the latter. Both agents disappeared from Bahrein after a short interval . . .[59]

Sir Henry Rawlinson, then at Tehran, delivered a forceful admonition to the Persian Court, pointing out that 'under no possible circumstances can the British Government be expected to concur in the proposed transfer of sovereignty of Bahrain to the Persian Crown'[60] whilst to Lord John Russell he reported the consequence of this rebuke. 'The immediate result of my appeal to the Shah has been that orders have been sent . . . to the Prince Governor of Fars to take no steps in confirmation or prosecution of Mirza Mehdi's proceedings but in the event of further solicitation on the part of the Arab Chief to await instructions from Tehran.'[61] In extension, explicit assurances were given by the Shah that before proceeding further in the affairs of Bahrain the Shah's Government would consult Britain and ascertain whether the Shah's suzerainty over Bahrain were recognized, and if so, whether it would conform with British policy that Persia should assert her authority.[62]

Winding up the episode, Rawlinson expressed his views in a forthright manner on a situation which appeared to be as unnecessary as it was unjustified. Reviewing the rival claims to Bahrain by the Ruks, Wahabis and Persians, Rawlinson gave his opinion that 'hostilities against Bahrain from any quarter are to be repelled by us by force of arms. Persia has put forward a claim to sovereignty over Bahrain for many years past, and in spite of our direct refusal to recognise the validity of such a claim, has never withdrawn it. It is a standing order indeed at Shiraz to advance and realize that claim whenever an opportunity may offer . . .'[63] In these perplexing circumstances it was hardly surprising that the Bombay Government should seek guidance, which they did in a despatch of September 1860 to the Secretary of State for India, observing that it should be the declared policy that the Shaikhdom of Bahrain should be regarded as subject neither to the Sublime Porte nor to Persia, but its independence be recognized.[64] In his reply the following February the Secretary of State expressed the Government's concurrence in this view.[65]

It is difficult to establish a sense of proportion in relation to the events of the preceding years, with claims and counter claims being advanced, rebuffed and then renewed with undiminished vigour, regardless of cogency or consequences. At times a degree of naïvety is rather surprising, for not long after Rawlinson and Palmerston had fired their broadsides the Persian Court approached the British Government to afford protection from insult and attack for the Persian Flag, which had been hoisted for such a short spell at Bahrain, and moreover it was represented in all seriousness that 'Britain should maintain as heretofore the maritime police force of the Persian Gulf pending a settlement of Persia's claim to the suzerainty of Bahrain'. Colonel Pelly, who had relieved Rawlinson, had occasion to remonstrate with Mirza Sa'id Khan, the Persian Foreign Minister, in terms no less forthright than his predecessor's. 'Here was Persia', he stated coldly, 'placing an apparently independent Territory under the protection of her Flag and then, within a few days, craving, first, that England would forbear from herself interfering to disgrace that Flag and, secondly, that she would, if occasion should require, actively interfere to protect that Flag.'[66]

In accordance with his complete disregard for principle and in violation of his treaty engagements, Shaikh Muhammad early in 1861 resumed his blockade of the Wahabi ports and was constrained to abandon these activities at the insistence of the Resident, Captain Felix Jones; at the same time he was obliged to sign a perpetual treaty of peace and friendship.[67] It is interesting to note that in anticipation of the later events of 1869 both the Turkish and Persian Governments were informed of these proceedings in order to allay any fears they might have entertained of Britain's motives,[68] but this elicited from Persia the response that this action of Captain Jones was considered very strange, having regard to the fact that the island and its shaikh were deemed to be subject to the Persian Crown.[69]

This year of 1861 marks a turning point in British relations in the politics of the Persian Gulf. Hitherto Britain had been pursuing a frequently asserted policy of peaceful neutrality whereby Bahrain was considered to be independent of her neighbouring states, irrespective of demands for tribute occasionally conceded, but now it was becoming apparent that this policy could not be maintained if the Shaikhs of that island were to maintain that elusive and devious attitude epitomised by Muhammad ibn Khalifah, of whom it was written that 'no form of words . . . or signature could bind that crafty old fox'.[70] Clearly a greater measure of supervision in the affairs of all the independent Arab tribes in the Gulf was imperative unless anarchy was once more to reign over those waters. The new treaty with Bahrain provided that the Shaikh, described as an independent ruler, should not only abstain from maritime aggressions of every description but would in return receive the support of the British Government in the maintenance of the security of his own possessions. By this step Britain was forced into assuming the role of protecting power. How uneasily this perpetual peace was imposed will presently be noticed.

The next move towards disorder in the Gulf occurred in October 1867 when the Shaikhs of Bahrain and Abu Dhabi set about attacking and destroying a large number of Qatar boats and then with the utmost ferocity sacking and plundering the Qatar towns of Waqra and Bida for good measure. As both these shaikhs were bound by treaty with Britain to abstain from such activities and to acknowledge Britain as arbiter in all disputes, action was taken to effect a remedy and Pelly, who was now Resident at Bushire, invested Bahrain with naval forces. Muhammad ibn Khalifah fled the island and his brother 'Ali became ruler in his stead with the full and written concurrence of the other shaikhs of the territory. An agreement to this effect was signed in September 1868.[71] This was no less than a straightforward police action carried out in support of existing engagements and treaties and was fully in accordance with the policy Britain had repeatedly declared for at least half a century: to maintain peace and order in the Gulf. Nevertheless Persia lodged a protest on the ground that Bahrain had menaced a dependency of Persia, and without prior notice of such action having been communicated to Tehran.[72] The Under Secretary at the India Office was thereupon constrained to remark almost plaintively that 'for the thousandth time Persia asserts her sovereignty over Bahrain – but we have never acknowledged it. The Bahrain Chief seems to have called down on himself, by his own violations of the Peace of the Gulf, the punishment which he has received, and the Government of India has approved of what Captain Pelly has done.'[73]

On considering these reports Lord Clarendon, the Foreign Secretary, felt that it might be politic and less conducive to Persian exacerbation of feeling if that Government were informed in advance should action of that sort have to be carried out in the future, and he communicated this view to the Duke of Argyll at the India Office.[74] The expected protest followed, nevertheless, for a few days later Hajji Mohsin Khan, the Persian chargé d'affaires in London, complained that Pelly's grievances against the Shaikh, whom he styled as Persian governor of the island, should have been represented to the Persian Government who would have afforded redress.[75] Argyll was not greatly moved by this representation of the Shaikh's vassalage nor by the notion of prior appeal to Tehran and he made the observation to Clarendon that 'either proposition involves the admission of quasi-sovereignty on the part of Persia over Bahrain – a point which the British Government has never conceded'. He went on to add that he was fully of the opinion that Persia's attitude assumed in this instance was quite unwarranted. 'The Shaikh of Bahrain', he told Clarendon, 'is an independent Chief, whose independence we have recognized by entering into treaty engagements with him. We have not only never recognized but on the other hand have always denied the right of Persia to assert her sovereignty to that territory . . .' He made a further observation that it would perhaps be advisable to abstain so far as possible from discussing the question with the Persian authorities other than to stipulate the independence of Bahrain.[76] Accordingly, in March 1869 Clarendon addressed a short note to Mohsin Khan in which he reasserted the independent status of the Shaikh of Bahrain with whom the British Government had treaty arrangements.[77]

There the matter should have rested but Mohsin Khan was unwilling to pass on to Tehran such an abrupt communication; he therefore sought interviews with both Clarendon and Argyll in order to secure some modification of these uncompromising views, though without success. He accordingly wrote to Argyll pointing out that he had understood that both Argyll and Clarendon had expressed their firm conviction that they were treating with the Shaikh as an independent chief but, he added, '*Permettez moi de protester, au nom de mon Gouvernement, contre une telle supposition que rien n'autorise.*'[78] For good measure, he also enclosed a supposed declaration of the wily Shaikh Muhammad dated nine years earlier in which he expressed his fealty to the Shah.

Neither Argyll nor Clarendon saw much point in carrying the argument further, and after supplementary exchanges of views between the two Secretaries of State a letter was sent on 29 April 1869 by Clarendon amplifying the statement expressed in his shorter communication of the previous month.[79] Mohsin Khan again demurred, for he regarded the sense of this letter as remaining identical with that of its predecessor, whereupon he submitted a long memorandum containing fresh points which he would like to see inserted in Clarendon's reply before this was transmitted to Tehran.[80] When these two fresh proposals were referred to Argyll for comment he replied that he saw

> . . . no objection to an admission on the part of the British Government that the Shah has protested against the Persian rights of sovereignty over Bahrein being ignored by the British authorities and that that protest has received due consideration, but His Grace cannot consent to debar the officers of the British Government, to whom the superintendence of the police of the Persian Gulf is entrusted, from the exercise of the right of punishing, by prompt measures, any violations of Treaty engagements by the Shaikh of Bahrein, when a reference to the Court of Tehran would be attended with embarrassing delays which might jeopardise the general peace of the Gulf.[81]

Upon receipt of the Minute Clarendon sent a revised reply to Mohsin Khan in which his original draft of 29 April was ameliorated, yet still embracing the terms and sense of his earlier communication.[82]

The events of 1869 were rounded off in September by an engagement between Shaikh 'Ali and the Beni Hajar tribe who were supported by Muhammad ibn Khalifah. In this action 'Ali and several other shaikhs were killed and the island pillaged, whereupon Pelly proceeded once more to afford redress and, with the complete concurrence of the Government of India, instituted a blockade of Bahrein. In November, a *buglah* attempting to run the blockade was boarded and found to carry a man accompanied by a dress of honour for the principal marauder and a letter promising Persian countenance and support. There was some confusion concerning the instigation of this action, though Mirza Medhi Khan, the agent of the Prince of Fars, was implicated, but the Shah's Government was not directly involved by the issue of a firman for this enterprise. In an exchange of telegrams between the Resident and Bombay, the former's action was approved and Pelly, observing the due proprieties, allowed the intercepted letter to reach its intended destination.[83] Isa, a son of 'Ali, was in due course installed as Shaikh. Thomson at Tehran was meanwhile instructed to take an early opportunity of expressing to the Shah the regret of the British Government that, notwithstanding the assurances which had been given, Persia seemed unable to prevent piracy in those waters. In speaking on the subject to Thomson, the Persian Foreign Minister admitted that his Government had not acquired sufficient power or authority in that part of the Gulf to enable them to repress acts of piracy and to maintain order.[84] This provoked the Government of India to address a despatch to the India Office observing that 'the Persian Government . . . are at the present moment powerless to stop disturbances by sea. They have no navy, and even if they were in a position to purchase vessels of war we could not surrender to them the protectorate of the Gulf without the certainty of hostilities . . .'[85] In a subsequent despatch Lord Mayo pointed out that these actions and the impotency of Persia at sea had the effect of reviving equally obsolete claims on the part of Turkey who had declared that Bahrain was a portion of Ottoman territory.[86] Indeed, Turkish pretensions were to be advanced on various occasions subsequent to that time but they may now be disregarded as irrelevant to the narrative since Turkey finally renounced all claims to Bahrain in a convention signed in July 1913 between the Turkish and British Governments.

Calm descended upon the scene. In 1880 an agreement was signed by Shaikh 'Isa, described as independent Ruler of Bahrain, whereby he undertook to abstain from entering into negotiations or treaties with any power other than the British and in effect to place all his foreign relations in British hands. This agreement was followed by a similar undertaking in 1892 and it is remarkable that on neither occasion does any response from the Persian Government appear to have been forthcoming.

It was without any forewarning, however, that in September 1886 the Shah asked Nicolson, British Minister at Tehran, to communicate to London his wishes to establish his authority effectually over Bahrain, and in anticipation of British support he quoted Clarendon's letter to 29 April 1869 as recognizing his authority over the island. In addition, he also desired that the maritime police in the Gulf should continue in the hands of the British naval forces, for clearly the Shah was quite unable to assume this responsibility. The reason for this approach was puzzling since nothing had led up to it or provoked the move, but Nicolson expressed the opinion from private information received that it had been prompted by the Russians to create a division between Persia and Britain. The proposal was disclaimed in London and the matter then lapsed.[87]

Twenty years were to elapse before the issue was once more raised. In 1906 a difference of opinion arose between Britain and Persia concerning the status of Bahrainis on Persian soil. The Shah's representation that all Bahraini citizens were Persian nationals was denied by the British Government as being entirely inadmissible, but in September the question was again revived by the Persian Court in a letter in which reference was made to Captain Bruce's unauthorized negotiation of 1822. The British reply pointed out, and not for the first or last time, that this agreement had been repudiated by both governments and the two negotiators had received censure for their proceedings.[88]

The Bahrain Order-in-Council was brought into force in February 1919 and this more clearly defined Britain's role in the island's internal affairs, having as its principal object the introduction of British civil and criminal laws. This in turn elicited no response from Persia though some inspired demonstrations were staged in both Bahrain and in the Persian Majlis.

The next interesting development occurred in 1927 when an agreement was concluded between Great Britain and ibn Sa'ud in which the special treaty relations existing between Britain and Bahrain were acknowledged. This drew a protest from the Persian Government; in a letter to Sir Robert Clive, British Minister at Tehran, it was stated that this agreement infringed the territorial integrity of Persia since Bahrain was incontestably in Persian possession, and that that fact was understood in Clarendon's letter of 29 April 1869.[89] Sir Austen Chamberlain, Foreign Secretary, in reply denied Britain's acceptance of the validity of the Persian claim on either historical or geographical grounds. He then turned to the alleged British recognition of Persia's suzerainty and directed his attention to the letter of Clarendon's referred to. 'I desire, however, to point out that your Government are under a complete misunderstanding in inferring from the terms of the communication made by the late Earl of Clarendon to the Persian Minister on April 29th, 1869, that any recognition of the validity of the Persian claims to sovereignty in Bahrain was at that time intended.' Far from admitting the Persian right, Chamberlain argued that the British Government had regarded the Shaikhs of Bahrain as independent rulers and had negotiated with them accordingly. This Clarendon letter, as the Persian Government had been informed in December 1871, had contained nothing more than an acknowledgment that the Persian claim to suzerainty had previously been made.[90]

The Persian reply was made to Chamberlain in August 1928 and the opening argument proceeded as follows:

A territory belonging to a sovereign State cannot be lawfully detached so long as the right of ownership has not been transferred by this State to another State in virtue of an official act, in this case a treaty, or so long as its annexation by another State or its independence have not been officially recognized by the lawful owner of the territory. As a matter of historical truth, it is beyond question that the Bahrein islands belong to Persia. No independent State known as Bahrein has ever existed. Persia has never renounced her sovereignty over these islands, nor has she ever ceded it to another State, nor ever recognized any of the Shaikhs of these islands as independent chiefs.[91]

Nor was the Persian Minister to be rebuffed by denial of British recognition of Persia's right. He once more invoked Clarendon's 1869 letter as proof of British admission and argued again that Persia's sovereignty over Bahrain had been confirmed in the Shiraz agreement of 1822 for, he continued ingenuously, 'though disavowed, it continued to be an historical document of inestimable value'.[92]

Chamberlain's reply in February of the following year was a lengthy document subjecting the whole matter of the status of Bahrain to a thorough and searching review. 'His Majesty's Government have examined with the greatest care the views set forth in the Persian Government's note . . . and have endeavoured to extract from the many unsupported declarations that Bahrein forms an integral part of Persia . . . the essential arguments on which the claim is based.' He found that the claim was based on three main arguments: on uninterrupted possession except for the period of Portuguese occupation; on a contention that since Persia had not recognized the status of Bahrain which had existed for 150 years then that status was invalid; and on certain documentary evidence that during this latter period the shaikhs of the island had made their submission to the Shah and had paid tribute to him. A full examination of these arguments, however, had not convinced the British Government that they were substantiated.

After reviewing the early history of Bahrain and surveying its chequered fortunes under first this power and then the other, Chamberlain observed that 'in 1783 . . . the troops of His Majesty the Shah were finally driven out by the Utubi Arabs, and the authority of Persia ceased, never to be re-established.' Having regard to the fact that no Persian dominion over the island had been exercised since that date, the British Government 'cannot but regard the claim of Bahrein to independence from Persia as abundantly established.'

Turning to the second main argument, Chamberlain considered that the contention that acquiescence of a former power must be obtained before a change in status is internationally recognized could not be sustained. But, he continued, 'Even if the contention could be accepted as valid, it would still be necessary for Persia to prove that she is, or ever has been, the lawful owner of Bahrein, and that such rights as she may have acquired in former ages by conquest and the exercise of force outweigh those not only of the Portuguese but of the Arab inhabitants themselves.'

Giving his consideration to the documents which purport to acknowledge the shaikhs' submission to Persia, although no specific details had been given in the Persian note, the British Government were perfectly prepared to admit the possibility that such documents might exist. However, their existence should not be considered as establishing the Persian claim, for the British Government

> . . . have always been well aware that the unfortunate rulers of the islands, surrounded by warlike and more powerful States which menaced their independence, professed on various occasions . . . an unwilling allegiance to Muscat, to Persia, to Turkey, to the rulers of mainland Arabia, even to Egypt – to any Power, in short, who would agree to offer them protection and seemed at the time in a strong enough position to do so . . . Any argument based on the payment of tribute would therefore be available in support of a claim to sovereignty over Bahrein by any of the States to which tribute was in fact paid . . .

Even so, he concluded on this point, such a timid and vacillating policy by his predecessors could not be held to affect the position of the present Shaikh, whose position was regularized by international law.

The Foreign Secretary next considered the references to British recognition in the past having been given to Persian claims, and he turned to the only two extant documents. Bruce's agreement of 1822 was disavowed at that time since it acknowledged the Shah's title to Bahrain, of which there was not the least proof, and since that time the British Government had never seen any reason to alter their opinion. Of Clarendon's letter of 1869 Chamberlain said that it meant exactly what it stated: the advancement of the Persian claim was admitted, but its validity was not, and on the contrary it affirmed the British intention to maintain unimpaired the treaty relations with the independent ruler.[93]

These detailed exchanges are the last of any significance to have passed between the two countries and they adequately summarize the respective positions adopted. Further notes were exchanged in 1929 on the subject of passports for Persians visiting Bahrain[94] and in 1930 on the matter of oil concessions in the islands,[95] whilst in 1934 a complaint was addressed to the U.S. Minister on the same subject.[96] In each case the protest was confined to the brief contention that these matters infringed Persia's sovereignty in Bahrain. Since 1934 no further exchanges are recorded, though declarations of Persian sovereignty over the islands were made in 1948 by the Majlis and again by the Shah ten years later. The Shah was also reported to have stated that he would gladly accept the allegiance of the Ruler of Bahrain as Governor of the island on Persia's behalf, though this statement was interpreted as a concession to nationalistic feeling and as an indication that Persia was by no means subservient to the West.[97]

Had the matter remained there, a stalemate would have resulted without particular advantage to any party in the dispute. Fortunately, the situation did not remain static, for in 1970 the Shah announced his agreement to a plebiscite being held in Bahrain to determine the wishes of the people in the matter of the island's sovereignty. The results of this plebiscite, in which the majority of the people voted for independence as a sovereign state, were accepted in Tehran and thus Persia's long-standing claims extending over two centuries were withdrawn and accordingly this prolonged chapter in the history of the Gulf was brought to a close.

Power on accession demands a continuance of that power to maintain possession. In reviewing the rival claims of Muscat and Persia in 1821 the British Resident at Bushire observed that

> It is, I believe, the universal law of nations to claim as a right that which they have obtained by the sword. Persia, with equal presumption, claimed the island of Bahrein, because it was once tributary to it, tho' it has thrown off that yoke and paid no tribute these thirty years. Persia may, with equal justice, lay claim to Delhi, at the present day, because Nadir Shah once conquered and plundered it.[98]

From this tangle of circumstances two facts relevant to the main theme stand out. First, Persia in common with Muscat lost her early footing in Bahrain because she was unable to defend and support the island by sea. Second, the protection of that shaikhdom by Britain was due to the presence of a naval force superior to that of any rival power, despite its many vicissitudes during three centuries. Britain persevered in the defence of Bahrain's independence simply because of its insularity and therefore because of its strategic significance as an element in the preservation of the maritime peace of the Gulf. Present-day events in no way invalidate those of yesterday, whilst the lesson learned will still be instructive tomorrow.

Notes

1 Curzon, G.N., *Persia and the Persian Question* (London, 1892), II, 455.
2 *Statutory Instruments 1952 No. 2108* – Foreign Jurisdiction, Bahrain.
3 cited Wilson, A.T., *The Persian Gulf* (London, 1928), 90.
4 Ibn Battuta, *Travels in Asia and Africa, 1325–1354*, trans. H.A.R. Gibb, (London, 1929), 122.
5 Curzon, op. cit., II, 457–8.
6 *Bombay Secret Proceedings, Vol. 41.* Consultation 29 of 21 July 1819. Bruce to Chief Secretary, Bombay, 26 January 1817.
7 *Bombay Sec. Proc., Vol. 41.* Cons. 29 of 21 July 1819. Bruce to Chief Secy. Bombay, 31 July 1816.
8 *Bombay Sec. Proc., Vol. 41.* Cons. 29 of 21 July 1819. Bruce to Chief Secy. Bombay, 31 July 1816.
9 *Bombay Sec. Proc., Vol. 41.* Cons. 29 of 21 July 1819. Bruce to Chief Secy. Bombay, 31 July 1816.
10 *Bombay Sec. Proc., Vol. 41.* Cons. 29 of 21 July 1819. Imam of Muscat to Adam, 27 July 1816.
11 *Bombay Sec. Proc., Vol. 41.* Cons. 29 of 21 July 1819. Chief Secy. Bombay to Secy. to Supreme Government, 21 July 1819.

12 *Bombay Sec. Proc., Vol. 41.* Cons. 29 of 21 July 1819. Nepean to Secy. Supreme Govt., 21 July 1819.

13 *Bombay Sec. Proc., Vol. 46.* Cons. 10 of 5 April 1820. Bruce to Warden, 7 March 1820.

14 *Bombay Sec. Proc., Vol. 46.* Cons. 10 of 5 April 1820. Keir to Warden, 1 April 1820, enclos. trans. of proposals to Imam of Muscat by Syed Abdul Jalil.

15 *Bombay Sec. Proc., Vol. 46* Cons. 10 of 5 April 1820. Warden to Keir, 1 April 1820.

16 *Bombay Sec. Proc., Vol. 46.* Cons. 10 of 5 April 1820. Simon to Keir, 1 April 1820, enclos. draft letter to Imam of Muscat.

17 *Factory Records (Persia & Persian Gulf) Vol. 34.* Elphinstone to Hastings, 15 December 1819.

18 *Bombay Sec. Proc., Vol. 40.* Cons. 17 of 14 April 1819. Minute by Warden, 11 April 1819.

19 *Factory Recs. (Persia) Vol. 34).* Elphinstone to Willock, 15 December 1819.

20 *Enclosures to Bombay Secret Letters Received, Vol. 7.* Enclos. to Sec. Letter No. 1. Bruce to Warden, 28 June 1822.

21 *Enclos. to Bombay Sec. Letters Rec., Vol. 7.* Enclos. to Sec. Letter No. 2. Farish to Bruce, 8 August 1822.

22 Adamiyat, F., *Bahrein Islands* (New York, 1955), 107 ff, 253–5.

23 *Enclos. to Bombay Sec. Letters Rec., Vol. 7.* Enclos. to Sec. Letter No. 3. Bruce to Elphinstone, 3 September 1822.

24 Ibid.

25 *Enclos. to Bombay Sec. Letters Rec., Vol. 7.* Enclos. to Sec. Letter No. 4. Farish to Bruce, 1 November 1822.

26 *Enclos. to Bombay Sec. Letters Rec., Vol. 7.* Enclos. to Sec. Letter No. 4. Warden to Farish, 27 October 1822, enclos. Gov. of Bombay to Prince Regent of Fars.

27 *Enclos. to Bombay Sec. Letters Rec., Vol. 7.* Enclos. to Sec. Letter No. 4. Warden to Farish, 27 October 1822, enclos. Gov. of Bombay to Sheikh of Bahrein, 27 October 1822.

28 *Factory Recs. (Persia) Vol. 35.* Willock to Secret Committee of Bombay Govt., 25 January 1823.

29 Adamiyat, op. cit.

30 Aitchison, C.U., *A Collection of Treaties, Engagements and other Sanads relating to India and Neighbouring Countries* (Delhi, 1933), XI, 191.

31 *Factory Recs. (Persia) Vol. 64.* Hennell to Sec. Committee, 28 February 1839, enclos. trans. of letter from Khurshid Pasha.

32 *Enclos. Bombay Sec. Letters Rec., Vol. 12.* Enclos. to Sec. Letter No. 41. Maddock to Willoughby, 13 March 1839.

33 *Factory Recs. (Persia) Vol. 64.* Hennell to Sec. Committee, 24 January 1839.

34 *Factory Recs. (Persia) Vol. 64.* Hennell to Sec. Committee, 15 March 1839.

35 *Factory Recs. (Persia) Vol. 64.* Hennell to Willoughby, 19 January 1839.

36 *Factory Recs. (Persia) Vol. 64.* Taylor to Sec. Committee, 21 March 1839.

37 *Factory Recs. (Persia) Vol. 65.* Hennell to Willoughby, 30 May 1839, enclos. trans. of letter Khurshid Pasha to Hennell, 4 April 1839.

38 *Factory Recs. (Persia) Vol. 65*. Hennell to Willoughby, 30 May 1839, enclos. trans. of Agreement between Shaikh 'Abdulla and an envoy of Khurshid Pasha, 7 May 1839.

39 *Factory Recs. (Persia) Vol. 65*. Hennell to Willoughby, 4 July 1839.

40 *Enclos. to Bombay Sec. Letters Rec., Vol. 12*. Enclos to Sec. Letter No. 41. Willoughby to Hennell, 1 April 1839.

41 *Bombay Sec. Proc., Vol. 46*. Cons. 10 of 5 April 1820. Warden to Keir, 1 April 1820.

42 *Factory Recs. (Persia) Vol. 34*. Elphinstone to Hastings, 15 December 1819.

43 *Factory Recs. (Persia) Vol. 76*. Sheil to Aberdeen, 12 August 1842.

44 *Bombay Sec. Proc., Vol. 192*. Cons. 39 of 7 September 1842. Maddock to Red, 13 August 1842.

45 *Board's Drafts of Secret Letters to India, Vol. 18*. Aberdeen to Sheil, 1 May 1843.

46 *Enclos. to Bombay Sec. Letters Rec., Vol. 76*. Enclos. to Sec. Letter No. 42. Sheil to Aberdeen, 25 February 1845, enclos. trans. of letter Haji Mirza Aghasi to Sheil, 4 February 1845.

47 Ibid.

48 *Enclos. to Bombay Sec. Letters Rec., Vol. 76*. Enclos. to Sec. Letter No. 42. Sheil to Aberdeen, 18 March 1845, enclos. trans. of letter Haji Mirza Aghasi to Sheil, 15 March 1845.

49 Ibid.

50 *Board's Drafts Sec. Letters to India, Vol. 19*. Addington to Enfield, 11 October 1847.

51 *Factory Recs. (Persia) Vol. 34*. Warden to Keir, 10 February 1820.

52 *Board's Drafts Sec. Letters to India, Vol. 19*. Stanley to Wyse, 2 December 1847.

53 *Board's Drafts Sec. Letters to India, Vol. 20*. Palmerston to Canning, 12 February 1851.

54 *Factory Recs. (Persia) Vol. 89*. Farrant to Palmerston, 17 February 1848, enclos. letter Farrant to Haji Mirza Aghasi, 7 February 1848 and letter Haji Mirza Aghasi to Farrant, 8 February 1848.

55 Ibid.

56 *Factory Recs. (Persia) Vol. 91*. Hennell to Chief Secy. Bombay, 28 February 1849, enclos. trans. of letter Shaikh Mohammad bin Khalifah to Hennell, 9 February 1849.

57 *Factory Recs. (Persia) Vol. 95*. Sheil to Palmerston, 19 December 1850.

58 *Selections from the Records of the Bombay Government* (Bombay, 1856), XXIV, 291.

59 Aitchison, op. cit., 192.

60 *Persian Gulf Gazetteer, Part 1*. Historical and Political Materials. Precis of Bahrein Affairs, 1854–1904 (Secret), 8.

61 *Factory Recs. (Persia) Vol. 115*. Rawlinson to Russell, 10 May 1860, enclos. letters Jones to Rawlinson, 15 March 1860 and 17 April 1860.

62 *Persian Gulf Gazetteer*, 8.

63 *Factory Recs. (Persia) Vol. 115*. Rawlinson to Jones, 4 May 1860.

64 *Persian Gulf Gazetteer*, 9.

65 *Sec. Letters to India etc. 1859–69, Vol. 1*. Secy. of State India to Gov.-in-Council Bombay, 18 February 1861.

66 *Factory Recs. (Persia) Vol. 115.* Pelly to Russell, 9 June 1860.

67 *Factory Recs. (Persia) Vol. 116.* Alison to Russell, 6 July 1861, enclos. copy of Agreement with Shaikh Mohammed of Bahrain, 31 May 1861.

68 *Memorandum on the Separate Claims of Turkey and Persia to Sovereignty over the Island of Bahrein* (Foreign Office, 1874), 11.

69 *Factory Recs. (Persia) Vol. 116.* Alison to Russell, 28 August 1861, enclos. trans. of letters Mirza Sa'id Khan to Alison, 25 August 1861; Alison to Mirza Sa'id Khan, 28 August 1861; Mirza Sa'id Khan to Alison, 29 August 1861.

70 Curzon, op. cit., II, 458.

71 Aitchison, op. cit., 192

72 *Enclos. Bombay Sec. Letters Rec., Vol. 147.* No. 275 Political Dept. Alison to Viceroy of India, 28 October 1868, enclos. trans. of letters Mirza Sa'id Khan to Alison, 24 October 1868 and Seton-Karr to Alison 31 December 1868.

73 *Home Correspondence (Secret) Vol. 62.* 1868. Merivale to Hammond, 31 December 1868.

74 *Home Corresp. (Secret) Vol. 63.* 1869. Hammond to Merivale, 1 February 1869.

75 *Home Corresp. (Secret) Vol. 63.* Hammond to Merivale, 15 February 1869, enclos. Mohsin Khan to Clarendon, 11 February 1869.

76 *Home Corresp. (Secret) Vol. 63.* Merivale to Hammond, 27 February 1869.

77 *Home Corresp. (Secret) Vol. 63.* Hammond to Merivale, 3 March 1869.

78 *Home Corresp. (Secret) Vol. 63.* Hammond to Merivale, 16 April 1869, enclos. Mohsin Khan to Argyll, 15 April 1869.

79 *Home Corresp. (Secret) Vol. 63.* Hammond to Merivale, 26 April 1869, enclos. Clarendon to Mohsin Khan, 29 April 1869.

80 *Home Corresp. (Secret) Vol. 63.* Hammond to Merivale, 11 May 1869, enclos. memorandum from Mohsin Khan, 8 May 1869.

81 *Home Corresp. (Secret) Vol. 63.* Melvill to Hammond, 19 May 1869.

82 *Home Corresp. (Secret) Vol. 63.* Hammond to Melvill, 24 May 1869, enclos. Clarendon to Mohsin Khan, 29 April 1869.

83 *Persian Gulf Gazetteer*, 25.

84 *Memorandum of the Separate Claims etc.*, 17.

85 *Persian Gulf Gazetteer*, 27.

86 Ibid, 28.

87 *Home Corresp. (Secret) Vol. 89.* Telegrams Nicolson to Iddesleigh, 27 September 1886 and Iddesleigh to Nicolson, 8 October 1886.

88 *Bahrein: Chief's Relations with British Government and other Powers, 1903–1912, Vol. 1.* Grant Duff to Cox, 1 February 1906, enclos. trans. of letter Mushir ed Dowleh to Grant Duff, 9 January 1906; Grant Duff to Grey, 27 February 1906, enclos. Grant Duff to Mushir ed Dowleh, 19 February 1906; Grant Duff to Grey, 26 September 1906, enclos. trans. of letter Grand Vizier to Grant Duff, 13 September 1906.

89 *League of Nations Official Journal*, May 1829, 605.

90 *League of Nations Official Journal*, May 1928, 606–7.

91 *League of Nations Official Journal*, September 1928, 1360.

92 *League of Nations Official Journal*, September 1928, 1361–2.

93 *League of Nations Official Journal*, May 1929, 790–2.
94 *League of Nations Official Journal*, March 1929, 351.
95 *League of Nations Official Journal*, September 1930, 1083.
96 *League of Nations Official Journal*, August 1934, 968.
97 Avery, P., *Modern Iran* (London, 1965), 480.
98 *Factory Recs. (Persia) Vol. 35.* Jukes to Warden, 14 August 1821.

EIGHT

The Persian War of 1856–7

The battle being thus won seemed to put an end to the Persian Empire.

Plutarch: Life of Alexander the Great

In making a brief military appreciation of this Persian campaign Colonel Wylly stated that with much truth it had been said that it arose out of circumstances so complicated that it was difficult to bear in mind the relations of one to another. The existence of intrigues among contending parties in the State of Herat; the frequent strife between the Afghans of Kabul and Kandahar and those of Herat; the well-remembered and never-abandoned claims of Persia upon the last-named State; the open desire of Russia to obtain a hold over the Persian Court; the tendency of Persia to disregard those courtesies to Western nations which 'oriental potentates' have never willingly conceded – all were current causes, he stated, in bringing about the British expedition to the Persian Gulf in 1856.[1] This is an admirably succinct appraisal of the varied and manifold motives which led to an obscure war owing its formal inception to the Persian assault upon Herat whereby, as Sir Henry Rawlinson observed, 'the object was accomplished at which Persia had laboured for twenty years and which we had as persistently opposed'.[2]

This short war, occasioned by the besieging and capture of the city of Herat in present-day Afghanistan, was resolved nearly a thousand miles away in the Persian Gulf; and thus, by repeating itself, history shows that so often that Gulf had been an Achilles' heel of Persia. Nor was this episode an isolated affair, for it stemmed from events which had preceded it for a generation or more. Its roots are found to have their depth in earlier times, since the Qajar Shahs had long cherished the illusion that they were the heirs to the Safavid kings whose realm extended into Afghan territories, whilst those roots were watered assiduously by Russian intrigue in the desire for expansion into Central Asia. Fortune determined that conflicts among the Afghan khans and diplomatic affronts at the Persian Court should make their contribution to the explosion which occurred in 1856, the reverberations of which were, however, muffled by the clamour of greater events both to the west and the east in which Britain, as a principal participant, was so profoundly involved.

The Treaty of Turkmanchai in 1828, concluded with a victorious Russia which had wrested from Persia the provinces of Erivan and Nakshivan, had ended Persia's hopes for aggrandisement or even containment in the west, since she was not strong enough to contest the ground there with her other formidable neighbour, the Ottoman Empire. Eastward the frontier was less clearly defined and her Afghan neighbours disunited. As a means, therefore, of offsetting his territorial losses to Russia, as a way of re-establishing the sway of the Safavids and as an occasion for imperial expansion towards the east, Muhammad Shah had laid seige to Herat in 1837, and though this took place twenty years before our event and ended in a withdrawal, it nevertheless forms a prelude to the later campaign of a more decisive character. The immediate cause of that advance against Herat was the refusal of Shah Kamran, the Ruler of Herat, to acknowledge the sovereignty of Persia and in this affair the Persian Muhammad was supported in intrigue and overtly by Russia whilst the Afghan Kamran received British backing. Significantly, John M'Neill, at that time British Minister at Tehran, advised Palmerston that 'he regarded it of the utmost importance to our security in India that Herat should not become available to any Power which might obtain control over the councils of the Shah',[3] though Auckland, the Governor-General, was reluctant to come to a decision and grasp this particular nettle. Nevertheless the issue was settled early in 1838 by the landing of British troops on the island of Kharg in the Persian Gulf, and thus ended the inconclusive ten-months' hostilities against Herat, to be renewed more fiercely in the next generation.

Shah Kamran was deposed and murdered in 1842 by his *vazir* Yar Muhammad who died in 1851, to be succeeded by his son Saiyid Muhammad Khan. This potentate's rule was precarious, for he faced threats from Kohandil Khan at Wandahar and from Dost Muhammad Kham Shah. This was ostensibly for the purpose of subduing rebellious Turkman tribes, though its real object was to conquer

Herat. This action was alarming to the British Government and Lord Malmesbury at the Foreign Office expressed the disquiet felt by the Government towards Persia's aggression and the subsequent Persian declaration that Herat province formed part of the Persian domains. Such was the extent of this disquiet that the Persian Minister in London was declared *persona non grata* and further, no other representative of the Persian Government would be recognized until the independence of Herat had been restored. Malmesbury told Colonel Sheil at Tehran, with a reference to the events of 1838:

> The Persian Government must be aware from what took place some years back, that the British Government can easily cause its displeasure to be felt by Persia in a manner which may sensibly affect the material interests of that country. It is far from the wish of Her Majesty's Government to enter upon a course which would be as painful to their own feelings as it would be prejudicial to Persia. But Her Majesty's Government must distinctly declare that they will not allow any systematic attempt on the part of Persia to effect a change in the state of possession in the countries lying between the Persian frontier and British Territories in India.[4]

Malmesbury thereupon directed that an accurate translation of this instruction be forwarded to the Persian Court and the result of this firm declaration was that Nasr-ud-Din signed an agreement in January 1853 in which the Persian Government undertook to refrain from sending troops to the territory of Herat unless that city were threatened from eastward; furthermore the Shah agreed not to interfere in the internal affairs of Herat, nor to coin money there bearing the Shah's inscription, nor to cause the *khutba* to be recited in the mosques.[5] *Khutba* is a sermon or oration delivered at divine service on Fridays in which the preacher, *inter alia*, blesses the Prophet, his successors and the reigning sovereign, and this was effectively an acknowledgment of submission by preacher and people.[6] This agreement was signed with great reluctance by Nasr-ud-Din and by his Sadr Azam, Mirza Agha Khan, and thus was laid the foundation for the hostility shown towards Charles Murray, the incoming British Minister at Tehran, which manifested itself later from a state of personal antipathy to a diplomatic rupture of far-reaching consequence.

At the same time copies of this agreement and the Shah's accompanying *firman* were delivered to the Ruler of Herat together with assurances that 'these documents sufficiently explain the views of Great Britain, which, briefly stated, are a determination that Herat shall remain in Afghan hands and in independence.'[7]

In March 1854 the Crimean War broke out and great anxiety was felt in both Britain and India concerning its possible implications in Persia where Russian influence was enhanced by the contiguity of frontiers. Indeed, in the autumn of 1853 Prince Dolgoruki made secret proposals to the Shah that Persia, in the event of war, should threaten Turkey with the prospect of territorial gain at the expense of the Porte, whereupon Clarendon, the Foreign Secretary, advised the British Chargé d'affaires at Tehran on the course which should be pursued by Persia, namely one of strict neutrality.[8] This counsel, when transmitted to the Persian Court, aroused great displeasure, predisposing the Court to regard Britain with disfavour since neutrality would afford no opportunity for advantage. Dalhousie, the Governor-General, was informed of the views of the home Government concerning the north-western frontiers of India. 'We also feel', the Secret Committee wrote to him, 'that in Afghanistan is to be found the most effectual barrier against Russian encroachment in whatever direction the Russians might attempt to advance on India; and that it cannot but be important for our interest in India that the barrier against any attempt at aggression on the part of Russia should be as far as possible from our frontier.' To secure this end, the Secret Committee went on to recommend that relations of amity should be re-established with Dost Muhammad, though such relations should be of a purely defensive character, concluding with a final guarded utterance: 'And we must not make conditions or use language, which would occasion just cause of umbrage to Persia.'[9] The desire to have the best of both worlds in that troubled region of quarrelling amirates, since coalesced into a unitary kingdom, was to prove unattainable and showed that a divided objective can rarely be realized.

Persia at this time was putting out feelers in Afghanistan, having sent an emissary to Dost Muhammad with the intention of endeavouring to contain him in the eastern half. In discussing this in a private letter to Herbert Edwardes, Commissioner for Peshawar, Dalhousie expressed the view that despite these overtures it was his opinion that matters still looked promising and progressive. 'Herat Persia can never have,' he wrote, 'nor can Dost Muhammed have it . . . We are more than a match for Persia, and Persia, unopposed by us, is more than a match for the Dost. So Herat is safe from these two.'[10] Events were to confound this optimistic utterance, though in relation to Dost Muhammad a treaty was subsequently entered into during March 1855 pledging perpetual peace and friendship between the two countries, and thereby the Dost protected his exposed western flank whilst Britain secured his neutrality in the war which followed.

Sheil's health gave out in Tehran and the ill-starred Charles Murray was appointed to relieve him. This gave Clarendon the occasion for laying down British policy in Persia and Afghanistan, and after reiterating the necessity for Persia to maintain neutrality in relation to Britain and Russia he continued in his letter to Murray,

> You will not fail to caution the Shah not to be persuaded by any prospects which Russia may hold out to Persia of furthering her ambitious aspirations after sovereignty in Afghanistan. On this point it is essential that the Persian Government should be clearly informed of the determination of the British Government not to tolerate any attempt by Persia to extend her influence over the Afghan races, in such a way as to interfere with their independence. . . . the British Government could not witness with indifference the continuance of Persian intrigues among the Afghan States, the tendency of which would be to weaken still more the barrier which those States, either united or single, might unquestionably oppose to any schemes which Russia might entertain of assailing the British Empire in India.[11]

The unfortunate Murray, however, was to be bedevilled with other considerations of apparently a more minor nature. A Persian subject, Mirza Hashim Khan, who had previously been in the Shah's employ, was appointed as Agent in Shiraz for the British Mission. This incensed both the Shah and the Sadr Azam, and the Mirza was threatened with imprisonment if he took up his post; as an earnest of their intentions the Persian Government seized and imprisoned his wife. Murray endeavoured, but in vain, to obtain redress, for the Court was obdurate being no doubt mindful of British insistence that Persia should stand clear of the Crimean dispute, so Murray struck his flag in Tehran in December 1855, withdrawing towards the Turkish frontier. The Sadr Azam lost no time in issuing an official notification to justify the Court's attitude in these proceedings, at the same time adding certain insinuations against the character of the British Minister. In retrospect it was a sorry affair and Murray was perhaps conscious of this when he addressed a letter to Clarendon from Baghdad, whence he had later withdrawn himself, in which he stated that his regrets that a peremptory demand for reparation for insults tendered had not been made by the British Government 'are the more deep in consequence of my profound conviction, that if it had been followed, the Mission would have returned to Tehran with increased weight and influence and the expedition to Herat would never have been attempted.'[12] Thus do great affairs depend upon lesser events.

The foregoing is preparatory to the main theme of this narrative and forms the groundwork on which the subsequent Persian assault upon Herat and the consequent war with Britain were based.

The first step towards precipitating the crisis occurred in 1855 when Muhammad Yusuf, one of the Sadozai chiefs, who had up to that time been a refugee at Meshed and a client of the Shah, put Saiyid Muhammad to death and usurped his place as Ruler; then feeling himself insecure applied to the Shah for assistance. Despite the engagement entered into in 1853 and the strained relations with the British Government, the Persian forces were ordered to march towards Herat in December. From the other end of Afghanistan, at Kabul, Dost Muhammad watched the situation with growing interest, making his calculations when he, rather than the Shan, would be master of Herat, and accordingly as a first step in January 1856 he annexed Kandahar to his amirate.

The Persians sought to justify their action by publishing a manifesto in the official *Tehran Gazette*. This interesting document is as verbose as it is bellicose and it may be reduced to comprehensible proportions by quoting one final paragraph. Evincing apprehension that Dost Muhammad, whom the Persians seemed to consider subordinate to the Shah, was about to march upon Herat and even beyond into Khorassan, the manifesto proclaimed that the Government could not 'calmly contemplate so violent a convulsion in its internal affairs, but it behoves it to counteract the evil, and by sending an equipped army to Herat preserve intact its own institutions, maintain its own territorial integrity, rescue that Kingdom from the grasp of Dost Muhammed and never allow that Government to fall into the hands of a stranger.'[13] An inference from this statement was that the Persians were marching to the aid of Muhammad Yusuf and to assist him in maintaining his domain inviolate, but that wily potentate knew better; indeed he quickly perceived the danger of being crushed between the Shah and the Amir.[14] Accordingly he requested the Persian general to delay sending the army beyond Meshed as he hoped to be able to arrange matters amicably with Dost Muhammad, but Sultan Murad Mirza in command of the Persian force was instructed from Tehran to push forward with all speed.[15]

Britain at this time was placed at a diplomatic disadvantage since her Minister, having withdrawn from the capital, had consequently lost contact with the Shah's Court; but there remained in Tehran the consul, Mr R.W. Stevens, who formed the only link by which intelligence could be transmitted to London and Calcutta, and despite the limitations imposed upon him he discharged that duty singularly well. Murray was also being further denigrated by the Sadr Azam who accused the British Minister of intriguing with Dost Muhammad contrary to the 1853 agreement, and in this accusation the French Minister had sided with the Persian Court. Denying this charge, Murray declared roundly that 'the whole story has been fabricated by the Persian Government in order to vilify and calumniate the British Mission and to endeavour to produce a misunderstanding between it and the French Mission.'[16] Quite undeterred by this denial, the Court repeated the charges and also its jurisdiction for marching upon Herat in a circular letter to all diplomatic envoys in Tehran, thereby giving the impression that the British Mission was to blame for the current turn of events across the Afghan frontier.[17] Murray wrote almost in despair that 'it is evident that the insults offered to myself and this mission in the affair of Meerza Hashem Khan are only part and parcel of a general determination to quarrel with Great Britain and to put the Indian Government to a great cost of money and exertion by throwing Afghanistan into tumult and disorder.'[18] There is indeed all the evidence available to substantiate this accusation, yet one is left with some lingering doubt whether the events of these two fateful years would have transpired had the hostility between the two men not manifested itself. It is easy, from this distance, to express astonishment that personal antipathies could lead to such disastrous consequences, yet those were still the days when relationships between men of standing could largely determine peace or war.

Towards the end of March 1856 Sultan Murad approached Herat from Turbat-i-Jam and sent a demand to Muhammad Yusuf that he should receive Persian troops within the citadel, that a coin should be struck in the Shah's name and that the *khutba* should be read for Nasr-ud-Din. This was, in short, nothing less than a demand for total submission, to which the Herati chief replied that whereas he himself was devoted to the person of the Shah, he could compel neither his people nor his clergy to allow the Qajars to hold Herat; accordingly he was obliged to decline the request.[19] No doubt the resistance of Muhammad Yusuf was stiffened by the seizure of the Mufti of Herat who, on setting out on a peace-making mission to the Shah was imprisoned at Meshed and subjected to insults and indignities.[20] Such was the fate of a Sunni fallen amongst Shi'a.

In London meanwhile, these events and Murray's despatches had not been regarded with indifference. During 1855 Clarendon had been priming Murray to dissuade Persia from embarking on adventures which might bring Russia in on her side, for the Crimean War was still being waged, and he reiterated the necessity for securing Persian neutrality during that war. 'The best security the Shah can have for Persia obtaining the protection of England', Clarendon counselled, 'will be first, his own honourable conduct towards England so long as she is at war with Russia, and secondly, that it is the policy of England to maintain the integrity and independence of Persia, and thirdly, that England will never look with indifference upon the encroachments of Russia, which encroachments the Shah knows by experience he has every reason to apprehend.'[21] The measure of the Shah's possible apprehension was no doubt enhanced by a subsequent letter in which Murray was informed that British policy would require the despatch of an expedition to the Persian Gulf and effective occupation there if Persia broke her neutrality to side with Russia.[22]

In Afghanistan the situation was becoming further confused by fresh overtures from the Shah to Dost Muhammad of a nature hostile to the British Government, though Stevens correctly deduced that 'it is probably more in the belief that this will delay the Afghan Chief's march upon Herat and thus give the Persians time to reach the place, than from any real hope of drawing him into an alliance against British India.'[23] In almost the same breath the India Board gave its rather equivocal views to the Government of India that Dost Muhammad must not be supported in his assaults upon other States but that if he captured Kandahar he must be recognized as *de facto* ruler; that Herat should remain independent but that no objection should be raised if a Persian force marched on Herat to protect it against Dost Muhammad.[24] Such contradictory and vacillating counsel did nothing to clarify the issue in the eyes of Calcutta, and the confusion of the Government of India remained apparent until many months had passed.

Dalhousie expressed his hesitations in his correspondence with the Bombay Government, for the latter would become directly and immediately involved in the event of hostilities outbreaking. To Lord Elphinstone, Governor of Bombay, he confessed his perplexity in determining the course to be pursued in the event of any requisition being made by Murray for the despatch of an armed force to the Persian Gulf. It was admitted that London might not be fully acquainted with developments and that Murray, then at Tabriz, was hardly any better placed than the Government of India itself in receiving current intelligence concerning Herat, and there was no evidence yet forthcoming concerning the fall of Herat since it might be the Shah's intention merely to make a show of force against Dost Muhammad.[25] In a further letter he observed that since the opinions of the Government of India were of no greater authority than the orders of the Secret Committee, which prescribed compliance with the demand that Murray might make, the Bombay Government was left free to act as it deemed fit.[26] This was hardly masterly counsel, and it reflected the difficulties prevailing where distances were great, communications tediously slow, reliable intelligence from Tehran or Herat absent, and authority between Britain and India divided.

In Herat the situation had deteriorated. Under threat from both east and west Muhammad Yusuf in desperation declared himself a vassal of the Queen and thereupon hoisted the British colours. This however availed him nothing. Canning, who had now succeeded Dalhousie, instructed Stevens at Tehran 'that Muhammad Yusuf is without any authority for his audacious act of presumption in placing himself under the British flag',[27] though even this remonstrance was of no effect for Muhammad Yusuf found himself shortly afterwards a prisoner in the hands of his *vazir* 'Isa Khan, who delivered him to the Persians, remarking cynically that 'the Shahzadeh being of no utility in Herat, he was sent to the Persian camp where perhaps he might be turned to account.'[28]

Stevens summarized the confused situation in a letter to Clarendon during June:

> In considering the Herat question, it may perhaps be requisite to bear in mind that the Persian expedition, according to the Government declaration, was undertaken at the urgent request of the Shahzadeh Mohammed Youssuf and of the Heratees, in view of an expected attack from the Ameer Dost Mohammed Khan. The actual state of things shows that the Persians were actuated by far different motives. The Shahzadeh himself is a prisoner in their camp, the Heratees are gallantly and so far successfully opposing the Persians, and the Ameer who was represented as being in full march upon Herat in December last, is quietly occupied in consolidating his position at Candahar.

The question therefore occurs, why do the Persians persist in their schemes of conquest? There can be but one answer: their determination to show the people of Central Asia that they dare brave the British Government, and the hope already alluded to, of alarming the British Government into an easy settlement of the other differences existing with the Persian Government.[29]

Two other points are also made by Stevens: a report from Constantinople that if, in the event of war between Persia and Britain, Turkey sided with the latter, then Russia would support Persia, from which information Persia had derived satisfaction,[30] but this was however tempered by another despatch referring to Russian troop movements along the shores of the Caspian carried out with the connivance of the Persians which had come to naught by the cessation of hostilities in the Crimea, to the Shah's undisguised disappointment.[31]

'Isa Khan, meanwhile, was confined in Herat and looking around for a way out of his impasse. Correspondence between Herat and Tehran had been intercepted by the British, and Murray at Baghdad exclaimed that 'both parties, in truly Oriental fashion, are endeavouring to blind and deceive each other, the Persian giving assurances of grace, favour and protection, whilst besieging the Town of Herat and devastating its neighbourhood, and the Heratee humbly representing his loyalty and obedience to the Shah, while openly and energetically opposing the advance of the Persian Army . . .',[32] and as if to prove himself as astute as his predecessor, 'Isa Khan went through the ceremony of hoisting the British flag in Herat and claimed to have received an envoy of the British Government, this again invoking Canning's contumely.[33] The Herati chief at this time sent a message to Murray offering to place Herat unreservedly under the British Crown in return for aid, whereupon the British Minister was moved, and not for the first time, to counsel Clarendon on the obvious course of despatching a force to the Persian Gulf in order to paralyse the south of Persia and thereby bring the matter to a conclusion.[34] The news from Herat placed Canning in a quandary. If he were to support 'Isa Khan with troops he would without doubt alienate Dost Muhammad, yet if he reinforced the Dost's claim to Herat he must expect strong resistance from 'Isa Khan, a sworn enemy of the Amir. Further, there was the great difficulty in maintaining lines of communication with any British troops in Herat, separated from British India by 500 miles of difficult and dangerous country. Finally, a totally ineffective expedient was reached and 'Isa Khan was sent two *lakhs* of rupees as a bounty.[35]

The Persian assault upon Herat had now been under way for several months and despite the supersession of one Chief of Herat by another, the attacking force of 20,000 troops was making no headway against the besieged. Ineptitude and unwillingness were the two main factors contributing to this slow progress; Persian ammunition depots were accidentally blown up thus depriving them of both arms and men, and false information led them on to disastrous enterprises, whereupon

> by way of stimulating the Prince [Sultan Murad] to increased exertion the King has . . . threatened him with the fate of a State Criminal if Herat be not occupied within a certain number of days, and holding him responsible in case of such failure for the reimbursement to the Crown of the amount of coin which he has from time to time received from Tehran. The Royal Autograph concluded with some rather indelicate allusions to the female members of His Royal Highnesses' family, which of course will not bear repetition in a European despatch.[36]

Notwithstanding such encouragement and exhortation, the city was to hold out for almost a year after the Persian host had commenced to move in that direction.

Russia and France had not at that time been standing idly by. The conclusion of the Crimean War in April 1856 had permitted resumption of direct diplomatic relations between England and Russia and it had also freed Russia from a distraction in the west so that her eyes might once more turn eastward where her covetous ambitions were, within the next two decades, to be amply realized. France, at the termination of the war, was no longer the ally of Britain, but was drifting into apathy if not rivalry, and the attitudes of both countries towards Britain's interests in the East were epitomized by Sir Henry Willock who, formerly British Minister at Tehran, addressed this review to the Chairman of the East India Company of which Willock was now Vice-Chairman.

> The interests of England and France may be identical as connected with Europe, but when the Western hemisphere is passed, all sympathy ceases. France is indifferent to the progress of Russia towards India, and in future times she may not object to see our possessions in Asia molested and injured by Russia.

[Asians] see and hear of the close union between Russia and Persia, that the latter Power, uninfluenced by any inducements England may have offered to separate her from the Russian alliance, faithfully adheres to her in the time of need, and sends an Embassy to St. Petersburgh to render unquestionable her feelings and policy . . . and the occupation of Herat by Persia speaks rather of glorious conquest to Russia and her ally, than of defeat . . .

and at this point Willock is referring to the Russian defeat in Europe as passing unnoticed in the Eastern world, whilst Russia in possessing her Eastern territories inviolate impresses Asians as a symbol of continued and undiminished power.[37]

Cautious advances were continued towards Dost Muhammad by the Government of India. Dalhousie had earlier recorded that it was desirable to strengthen intimacy with Afghanistan and that 'For the attainment of this advantage it would be well worth while to run the risk of giving dissatisfaction to Persia, whose displeasure could not extend to hostility without bringing her within the reach of our power in a degree which she dare not venture.' Having said so much, he next recalled the 1853 agreement and relapsed into an equivocal attitude for, he added, 'while the engagement . . . shall exist, such a policy is of course impracticable in its full extent.'[38] Herbert Edwardes at Peshawar had already recommended closer relations with Dost Muhammad and had observed that 'It seems far preferable that Herat should be annexed by Cabul than by Tehran. The former lies under our hand. The latter has a large Russian Army within call.'[39] But this practical and sensible advice had been rejected by Dalhousie, despite his almost identical views of the year before, in declaring that Edwardes had gone beyond his province in this matter.[40] Sir John Lawrence, Chief Commissioner of the Punjab, next had occasion to press similar advice upon the Governor-General who reviewed the matter afresh in the light of more recent intelligence – the suspension of relations between Britain and Persia on the withdrawal of Murray, the march of Persian troops on Herat, and the offensive imputations publicly made by the Persian Court against the British Government – and weighing all these considerations he reached the masterly conclusion that the Government of India should play for time and remain non-committal the meanwhile,[41] so the Amir was left in a state of dangerous expectancy which might well have lead to disastrous disappointment.

This undesirable state of affairs was resolved by a Persian affray in Kalat and by Canning's supersession of Dalhousie. The Khanate of Kalat, later incorporated into Baluchistan, had borders contiguous with Persia, Afghanistan and Sind and the Khan was in treaty relationship with Britain. Canning considered reports of Persian troop movements and their levying of revenue in that friendly territory, and deemed this to be a menacing move, for, he said,

> If it is a fact that whilst one Persian army is before Herat, another, 400 miles to the South, is threatening Kelat, it seems pretty clear that a 'systematic attempt' is being made by Persia to effect a change in the state of possession in the countries lying between the Persian frontier and the British territories in India. Such an attempt it was distinctly declared to the Shah in 1852 that Her Majesty's Government would not allow.[42]

Concurrently with this event, Canning was authorized by the Secret Committee to enter into communication with Dost Muhammad and to offer him arms as a protection against Persia whose troops had penetrated as far as Farrah, between Herat and Kandahar, and the despatch closed with a declaration that this was to be the open and only object of the assistance from the Indian Government which might be given to any power strong enough to offer co-operation and entertaining an identical interest against Persian aggression. Canning rejoiced in this decision, concluding that the earlier policy adopted towards Dost Muhammad must be altered and that from that time he should be afforded all support.[43]

By now the British Government realized that the Persian aims were not the liberation but the subjection not only of the province of Herat but of the Afghan territories beyond. Clarendon thereupon addressed the Sadr Azam, recapitulating previous undertakings by Persia to Britain not to invade Herat and stating that the current reports of Persian aggression, if substantiated, would constitute an act of open hostility against Great Britain and that unless hostilities ceased and troops were withdrawn the British Government would act as it saw fit.[44] Orders were also given that an expedition should be prepared at Bombay sufficiently powerful to occupy the island of Kharg in the Persian Gulf and the district of Bushire on the mainland, though the expedition was not to sail until further orders were received from London.[45] The response at Tehran was, however, not reassuring, for Stevens reported that after delivering Clarendon's letter to the Sadr Azam a fresh mobilization was proclaimed for service in the south.

'From this measure,' Stevens concluded, 'it may be inferred that the Sadr's answer to your Lordship's communication will not be a satisfactory one.'[46]

In August the British Mission Agent was expelled by the Persians from Asterabad and in September an advance body of Persian troops captured Farrah, whilst in October the *Tehran Gazette* carried 'a sort of manifesto preparing the Nation for the arrival of British forces in the Persian Gulf, and concluding with an appeal to the religious feeling of the people'.[47] It was evident that the Persian Court was far from being in a conciliatory mood, though a gesture was made by Tahmasp Mirza, Prince Governor of Fars, who expressed his desire 'that the British Government employ me as the organ of effecting a reconciliation between the two kingdoms.'[48] Whether this was a diplomatic feeler put out from Tehran, opportunism on the part of the Prince, or simply a move to keep the impending war away from his doorstep, is open to conjecture. Perhaps the Prince was cognisant of the dismay felt amongst the mercantile community at the imminent outbreak of hostilities in the Gulf, for Felix Jones, the Political Resident, reported that 'the appearance of a superior force will be a signal for plunder by the [Persian] troops . . . Nor can I be indifferent to the license practised by an Asiatic soldiery, or to the ficle [*sic*] temper of a fanatical mob in times of public excitement.'[49] Having despatched that message Commander Jones prudently withdrew from the Residency at Bushire to transfer his flag to a vessel anchored near the shore.

Herat fell to the Persians on 26 October 1856, owing to the utter exhaustion of its defenders, and 'Isa Khan was forced to submit to the Shah. In anticipation, the British consuls at Tehran and Tabriz had been instructed in September to withdraw from Persian territory, and the expedition mounted at Bombay was ordered to proceed to its destination in the Persian Gulf.[50] Simultaneously, the Sadr Azam was informed of these movements 'intended to compel the Shah to make for Great Britain the complete reparation for the disregard of his engagements and the insults offered to the Queen of England'.[51] These formalities having been effected, and the rights and safety of Persian nationals in British India having been assured, Britain declared war on Persia on 1 November 1856.

Few wars have resembled that which followed. The usual question is how to injure an enemy most effectively, but on this occasion the efforts of our statesmen were directed to securing

the evacuation of Herat without inflicting a heavy blow upon
Persia. Alternative schemes presented themselves to the British
military authorities. The Indian Army might march direct on
Herat with a friendly and allied Afghan army. Another plan,
more difficult to execute, was to march on Herat from Bandar
Abbas. Both would have involved immense effort and cost. It
was finally decided to operate in the Persian Gulf . . .[52]

The military operations in the Gulf and in the south of Persia were
swift and decisive, and can briefly be told. The expedition under the
command of General Stalker effected an unresisted occupation of
Kharg on 4 December 1856 and Bushire surrendered six days later.
Stalker was, however, only temporarily in command since General Sir
James Outram, on leave in England from India, had been appointed
commander-in-chief, for the Secret Committee had 'deemed it
advisable that the Expedition to Persia should be commanded by an
officer who can also be implicitly trusted with the important duty of
conducting negotiations which, it is hoped, will speedily follow the
Military demonstration.' In dwelling upon the implication Canning
expressed his disquiet that Outram should serve in two capacities:
Diplomatic, receiving his orders from the Foreign Office; and
Military, under orders from the Government of India. He properly
deprecated one man serving two masters, observing that 'I cannot
disguise from myself that the unquestionable advantage of uniting the
Military and Diplomatic functions in one head runs some risk of being
neutralized by placing that head under two directing authorities.'[53]
That Canning's fears were not realized reflects upon the stature of
Outram rather than the wisdom of the policy employed.

Outram quickly made his appreciation of the difficulties which
then appeared to lie ahead when he wrote to Elphinstone that 'I
cannot myself see much hope that we shall get out of our Persian
embarrassments so easily as the public appear to expect; for France as
well as Russia are too deeply interested in undermining our influence
at Tehran to give any disinterested advice to the Shah, and not
underhandly to encourage him to persevere in hostility to us, however
they may profess to advocate an amicable course.' He went on to say
that if the Shah was to be impressed by British determination then the
small force already despatched to Bushire would need to be reinforced
and the Shah made aware of it.[54] This call for reinforcements was met,
though not without difficulty and with due regard to Colonel Jacob's
remonstrance at denuding the Bombay Presidency and especially the

North-West Frontier of all its troops for Persia,[55] for the Bombay Government had been instructed that 'we are no longer restricted to the occupation of Bushire and Karrack. We are to take possession of Shuster and Mahommura and to threaten from those parts Shiraz and Ispahan.'[56] Clearly both the Government of India and Outram expected, not without reason, that the war would last much longer than in fact it did.

Outram's arrival at Bushire gave a fresh impetus to military action, Borazjan being attacked and captured on 5 February, the Persians fleeing from their encampment almost without striking a blow; three days later the engagement at Khusab took place in which the Persian army was decisively routed. Mohammerah, which had been heavily fortified notwithstanding the Turks' objections, was assaulted on 6 March and captured in just over an hour's fighting, with 13,000 Persian troops quickly dispersed, and 'to prove how utterly they were disorganized, it may suffice to mention that Captain Malcolm Green pursued them with only forty-five sabres, and yet they did not dare to make a stand'.[57] Ahwaz was captured on 1 April whereupon hostilities virtually ceased, for news of the peace between England and Persia was received the following day. It may not be irrelevant to add that this campaign must be unique in that the two service commanders both committed suicide during the early stages of hostilities, General Stalker being harassed by pecuniary matters and Commodore Ethersey experiencing a sense of personal inadequacy.

In Herat the Persians had for some months been masters of the city and 'Isa Khan did not long survive to experience their clemency, for he was summarily executed and his relatives seized and cast into prison.[58] Not long after a similar fate awaited Muhammad Yusuf. The way was clear, therefore, at the end of the war, for a Persian *protégé* and disaffected nephew of Dost Muhammad to be installed as Ruler of Herat and this position, almost in vassalage to the Persian Crown, he was able to maintain until overthrown by his uncle in 1863. Acquiescence in this appointment would appear to have been a blunder on the part of the British negotiator and a signal success for the Persian Government, which was able both to adhere to the terms of the Treaty of Paris and yet rule Herat effectively through Sultan Ahmed Khan.

The Persian Court had sued for peace directly after the capture of Bushire and the conclusion of hostilities was sealed by the Treaty of Paris on 4 March 1857 which was formally ratified two months later; this treaty obliged Persia to relinquish all claims to the sovereignty of

Herat and to abstain from further interference in the internal affairs of Afghanistan. Provision was made for Britain's role as arbiter in any disputes which might arise between Persia and the Afghan States and an *amende* was exacted from the Court for the contumely and dignities heaped upon Charles Murray. A further important article provided for the establishment and recognition of British consular authorities freely in Persia on a 'most favoured nation' basis, likewise the treatment of subjects, commerce and trade.[59]

From this tangled web of circumstances certain facts and factors can be extracted in order to resolve two questions: what were the forces which gave cause to this unnecessary and futile war, and what were its consequences?

Attempting to appreciate the Persian view, there was an apparent desire to make good earlier losses to Russia in 1828 by expansion eastward. Here geography and certain natural affinities encouraged a movement in that direction, since no great mountain barriers interpose themselves between north-eastern Persia and western Afghanistan; the Heratis were of similar stock and language to the Persians, even if they were acknowledged Sunnis; whilst history recalled that not long since Herat and beyond had formed part of Nadir Shah's Persian domains. Further, by absorbing that province the natural frontiers of Persia would tend to assert themselves and so contribute to the greater security of that State.

The chiefs of Herat, on the other hand, evinced little desire to become absorbed into a Greater Persia, because they could see that they would be reduced to client status at best, because their dynastic affiliations caused them to look to their compatriots to the east and because of their antipathy towards the Persian Shi'a. In September 1856, when treachery by the Shi'a minority of Herat was suspected, those unfortunate people were massacred. Reporting this incident, Stevens wrote that 'A slight consideration of these events may afford some idea of what would inevitably follow the occupation of Herat by an exasperated and undisciplined Persian Army . . . and the longer its resistance the more terrible will be the closing scene of a drama which public opinion in Central Asia will not fail to ascribe to weakness or to indifference on the part of Her Majesty's Government, whose policy . . . encouraged the Heratees in the belief that the subjugation of the country by Persia would not be tolerated by Great Britain.'[60] That this was not an exaggeration may be seen from a short narrative of events.

British policy since 1838 had openly been avowed to be the preservation of the Afghan amirates in their independence and this was specifically taken into account in the later engagement of 1853. Britain was justifiably apprehensive of the potent threat from Russia to India and this apprehension was reinforced by Sir George Clerk, a member of the Secret Committee in October 1857, for in answering Murray's inquiry for instructions respecting the recognition of Sultan Ahmed Khan as Ruler of Herat, Sir George noted that 'We uphold the independence of Herat, not because we should dread the strength of Persia, even if Herat were added to her dominions, but because we fear the claims which a mightier Power might put forth . . . if Herat were considered as part of the Persian territory . . .'[61] Where Britain failed was in her resolution to apply her policy, as she had done twenty years before in identical circumstances, in a determined and timely manner. It is true that she was at some disadvantage because communications were still slow, her Minister had withdrawn from Tehran on a different issue, and divided counsels arose between Her Majesty's Government and the Government of India, in that policy was largely determined in London whilst military enterprise and resources were afforded by India. Nor was this situation ameliorated by the fact that the British Minister at Tehran was responsible to the Foreign Office whilst the Political Resident in the Persian Gulf who in certain Persian affairs had to defer to the British Minister was himself under the orders of the Government of India who transmitted their general requirements through the Bombay Government.

Russian influence was evident during the whole period under review, although this did not manifest itself as any form of direct intervention, most probably as a result of the exhaustion of resources during the Crimean War. Lord Wodehouse, Ambassador at St Petersburg, noted that Prince Gortchakoff, the Imperial Chancellor, had raised continual objections to the British ultimatum to Persia, but especially to the appointment of consuls in the north of the country as being inimical to Russian interests.[62] From Costantinople Lord Stratford de Redcliffe advised Clarendon in more general terms that Anitchkoff, the Russian Minister at Tehran, 'plays his cards so dexterously that it appears as if Russia deplored the present attitude of Persia, whilst it is she who secretly guides her in the false path she has taken'.[63] In 1837 Persia was openly supported against Herat by Russian officers and engineers as well as by Russian money, whilst in 1854 and 1855 the Tsar Nicholas was presented with plans for a practicable line of advance to India through Astrabad, Meshed and Herat.[64] Constant influential pressure on the Persian Court was paramount and 'it was evident that . . . Russia, without throwing any strain on her resources, would secure her influence in Afghanistan, whereas a serious strain would be placed on Great Britain to meet the demands of a new situation.'[65] Herat has often been called 'the key of India', fully deserving its reputation as the most important military position in Central Asia, the unchallenged occupation of which by Russia would have placed the whole military resources of Persia and Afghanistan at her disposal.[66]

France remained seemingly indifferent to the issue, though she provided Persia with an engineer officer, Captain Buhler, to mine the stout walls of Herat, whilst Turkey declared her neutrality contingent upon neutrality also being observed by Russia[67] – though this declaration did not deter her from demanding that Persian fortifications at Mohammerah should be dismantled on pain of Turkish troops being despatched for that purpose.[68]

Britain possessed two inactive allies: the Sultan of Muscat and the Amir of Kabul. The former claimed Bandar Abbas under a convention with the Shah and was willing to allow British troops to land there;[69] also he had further committed himself to stating that in the event of hostilities in the Persian Gulf he would unhesitantly side with Britain,[70] though this advantage was neither sought nor required. Of Dost Muhammad and of British relations with Afghanistan during this time, Curzon blisteringly stated that these were 'successively those of blundering interference and of unmasterly inactivity. The first period . . . culminated with the restoration of Dost Muhammed, the sovereign whom he had forcibly deposed and defeated, but who ended by forcing his recognition on us.'[71] In January 1857, to secure the Amir's friendship, a treaty was signed whereby mutual assurances were given in respect to the frontiers of India and Afghanistan and to strengthen these assurances the Amir was granted a subsidy.[72] Nevertheless, beyond this agreement and the deputation of British officers to Kandahar during the campaign, no positive move was made by Dost Muhammad towards Herat until six years later when, in 1863, it fell to his arms.

The Crimean War ended in April 1856 and the Indian Mutiny began in May 1857. During those intervening months the contest with Persia began and ended, and towards the end of 1856 the Governor of Hong Kong was also appealing to India for reinforcements in his war with China, though these could not be spared.[73] Therefore, as the Duke of Wellington observed after Waterloo, the Persian campaign was indeed a 'damned close-run thing'.

The treaty of peace signed in 1857 between Britain and Persia ended that country's hopes of eastward expansion and guaranteed the existence of an effective buffer state between Russia and India. Its terms were sufficiently generous to arouse the astonishment of the Persian Court in that no indemnity was exacted, no concessions demanded, and the Sadr Azam's dismissal was not insisted upon, to his immense relief and gratification. Amity was quickly established and indeed the Sadr Azam paid Murray a visit, after having previously tendered his apologies for insults offered, declaring that though, during the course of hostilities, he had been in correspondence with Muslim chiefs in India inciting them to insurrection, now as an earnest of goodwill he offered to place a Persian army to fight the mutineers under the British flag in India.[74] To what extent the Mutiny owed its support or inception to the Persian war is not evident, though it was known early in 1857 that a prince had arrived from Delhi and had promised a large sum of money if the Persians would march in India during a meditated insurrection there.[75]

The year 1857 marks a watershed in Anglo-Persian relations which, after the war, underwent a great improvement together with an absence of bitterness. Prior to that time the conditions and attitudes encountered by English diplomats from the time of Sir Dodmore Cotton had largely prevailed. Traffic in the Gulf had been desultory and the main point of entry was still Bushire. But now a change was discerned, as the percipient Stevens observed. 'The war with Russia', he noted, 'has shown that steam navigation, and its immense development has rendered the conveyance of troops to distances however great, a work of comparative ease.'[76] Outram's expeditionary force had relied upon steam for its transport, marking the final stage of transition from sail in those waters. The way was now opened for the extension of the overland telegraph so that India at last was linked with England by a line extending the length of the Shah's dominions. This need for direct telegraphic communication between the two countries had become apparent and imperative during the Mutiny, and it was finally effected by negotiations commenced in 1861 and terminating in the convention of 1868,[77] marking a revolutionary change from Murray's *chapar* galloping across the desolate wastes on horseback. As a result, therefore, of this campaign and the realignment of forces subsequent to it 'the first considerable breach was effected in that crust of exclusiveness which had hitherto isolated Persia from all contact with European civilization, the pioneer of progress in this instance being the electric telegraph, for which Persia was mainly indebted to the enterprise and encouragement of England'.[78] Other important and consequential developments were the adjustments of territorial differences between the Shah and his eastern neighbours effectively carried out by the British Boundary Commission under General Goldsmid, a British arbitration in Seistan resolving an ancient dispute between Persians and Afghans, the Reuter concession, the opening of the Karun River to navigation and commerce by the Lynch Brothers, and the unprecedented visit by the Shah to Europe. These all contributed to drawing Persia within the orbit of the Western world and away from its age-old self-imposed isolation.

In a private letter to John Jacob who accompanied Outram, Bartle Frere observed,

> As regards this Persian Expedition, I look on it as a necessary consequence of sending such a man as Mr Murray, good for Europe but ignorant of the East, to Tehran, and of our weak and wicked policy towards Persia for the past 30 years. As a momentary expedient to obtain redress for evils brought on by our own folly I consider it the best thing Ministers could have done – but like all such expedients it is in itself an evil and only more tolerable because we can more easily retract our steps than [in] an occupation of Afghanistan.[79]

This seems rather hard on poor Murray though most probably the situation in which he found himself could have been resolved with more patient diplomacy and a little less regard for an offended *amour-propre*.

That the treaty which concluded the whole affair brought no immediate gain to Britain, and was not otherwise sought by her, has already been indicated, and there was indeed a high level of disinterest which in part redeemed the fumbling attitude of the preceding years and which inaugurated a fresh chapter of amicable relations, which long endured. A final word may be said in appraisal of the treaty and of its significant portent:

> But what did people think of Persia and what did they expect us to get by the war? No doubt, the expedition of Alexander the Great was attended with more tangible and remarkable results. But his object was conquest, and ours was to keep Persia and its neighbours in a state of independence and mutual respect. Our object is founded on the *status quo*, and the abandonment of mere traditional claims and visionary prospects. It is, then, the greatest praise of a treaty which professes to carry out this

policy, that it seems at first sight to do nothing, to create nothing, to give nothing, and to take away nothing . . . We could not have gained anything from Persia but to her irreparable loss and disgrace. This is the very thing most opposed to our interests in the East. It is our interest that all the various races between us and Russia should remain as they are, only growing stronger, more practicable, more settled, and more consolidated in natural combinations . . . But the weakness of Persia, which compels it to recede on the North-West, makes it listen to schemes of aggression on its Eastern frontier. It is pushed against us by a stronger hand. We show it, then, as much kindness as to ourselves when we ascertain its position, decide its frontiers, and disabuse it of pretensions which may make it a prey to foreign intrigue. This is the work of the treaty before us. It is not a very showy work. It does not read like the life of Alexander, or even of Philip. We are neither conquering Persia nor plotting for a supremacy over it. We are only teaching it to let others alone, and be itself independent of others.[80]

Notes

1 Wylly, C.H., Our War with Persia in 1856–57 (*United Service Magazine*, March 1912), 642.

2 Rawlinson, H., *England and Russia in the East* (London, 1875), 89.

3 *Correspondence relating to Persia and Afghanistan* (London, 1839). McNeill to Palmerston, 30 June 1837.

4 *Board's Drafts of Secret Letters to India, Vol. 21*. India Board to Governor-General of India, 7 July 1854 enclos. Malmesbury to Sheil, 27 October 1852.

5 Aitchison, C.U., *A Collection of Treaties, Engagements and other Sanads relating to India and Neighbouring Countris (Delhi, 1933)*, XIII, 77–8.

6 *Enclosures to Secret Letters from India, Vol. 145*. No. 4 of 22 January 1856. Enclos. No. 3. Temple to Edmonstone, 31 December 1856 enclos. letter Dost Muhammed Khan to Lawrence, 28 November 1855. See also *The Shorter Encyclopaedia of Islam* ed. Gibb and Kramers (Leiden and London, 1953), 259.

7 *Board's Drafts, Vol. 21*. India Board to Gov.-General, 7 July 1854 enclos. Sheil to Saiyid Muhammed Khan, 29 January 1853.

8 *Board's Drafts, Vol. 21*. Clarendon to Thomson, 18 May 1854.

9 *Board's Drafts, Vol. 21*. India Board to Gov.-General, 9 August 1854.

10 *Relations with Afghanistan* – Sir Herbert Edwardes' Private Correspondence with Dalhousie, Lawrence and Canning. Dalhousie to Edwardes, 23 August 1854.

11 *Board's Drafts, Vol. 21.* Clarendon to Murray, 20 November 1854.

12 *Factory Records (Persia & Persian Gulf) Vol. III.* Murray to Clarendon, 20 June 1856.

13 *Fac. Records (Persia) Vol. III.* Murray to Clarendon, 4 January 1856 enclos. extracts from the *Tehran Gazette* of 20 December 1855.

14 *Fac. Records (Persia) Vol. III.* Murray to Clarendon, 16 January 1856 enclos. copy of despatch Murray to Secy. to Govt. of India, 9 January 1856.

15 *Fac. Records (Persia) Vol. III.* Murray to Clarendon, 8 January 1856.

16 *Fac. Records (Persia) Vol. III.* Murray to Clarendon, 8 January 1856 enclos. copy of despatch Murray to Stevens, 31 December 1855.

17 *Fac. Records (Persia) Vol. III.* Murray to Clarendon, 7 March 1856 enclos. copy of circular from Sadr Azam to the Foreign Missions in Tehran, 27 February 1856.

18 *Fac. Records (Persia) Vol. III.* Murray to Clarendon, 7 March 1856 enclos. Stevens to Murray, 25 and 29 February 1856.

19 *Fac. Records (Persia) Vol. III.* Murray to Clarendon, 31 March 1856 enclos. report from Mission Native Agent at Meshed.

20 *Fac. Records (Persia) Vol. III.* Stevens to Clarendon, 9 April 1856.

21 *Board's Drafts, Vol. 21.* Clarendon to Murray, 18 June 1855.

22 *Board's Drafts, Vol. 21.* Clarendon to Murray, 22 October 1855.

23 *Board's Drafts, Vol. 21.* India Board to Gov.-General, 6 March 1856. enclos. Stevens to Clarendon 8 January 1856.

24 *Board's Drafts, Vol. 21.* India Board to Gov.-General, 22 March 1856.

25 *Bombay Secret Proceedings, Vol. 300.* Sec. Consultation No. 8 of 23 April 1856. Edmonstone to Anderson, 24 March 1856.

26 *Bombay Sec. Proc., Vol. 301.* Sec. Cons. No. 10 of 21 May 1856.Edmonstone to Anderson, 29 April 1856.

27 *Bombay Sec. Proc., Vol. 301.* Sec. Cons. No. 11 of 11 June 1856. Edmonstone to Anderson, 10 May 1856.

28 *Fac. Records (Persia) Vol. III.* Stevens to Clarendon, 19 May 1856.

29 *Fac. Records (Persia) Vol. III.* Stevens to Clarendon, 22 June 1856.

30 *Fac. Records (Persia) Vol. III.* Stevens to Clarendon, 22 June 1856.

31 *Fac. Records (Persia) Vol. III.* Stevens to Clarendon, 19 May 1856.

32 *Fac. Records (Persia) Vol. III.* Murray to Clarendon, 22 July 1856.

33 *Fac. Records (Persia) Vol. III.* Stevens to Clarendon, 20 June 1856.

34 *Fac. Records (Persia) Vol. III.* Murray to Clarendon, 8 August 1856 enclos. Isa Khan to Murray, 16 June 1856.

35 *Enclos. Sec. Letters from India, Vol. 147.* No. 43 of 22 September 1856. Enclos. No. 6. Minute by Canning, 10 September 1856.

36 *Fac. Records (Persia) Vol. III.* Stevens to Clarendon, 22 September 1856.

37 *Secret Home Correspondence (Persia) Vol. 40.* Willock to MacNaghten, 3 January 1856.

38 *Enclos. Sec. Letters from India, Vol. 145.* No. 4 of 22 January 1856. Enclos. No. 5. Minute by Dalhousie, 14 January 1856.

39 *Enclos. Sec. Letters from India, Vol. 145.* No. 11 of 8 March 1856. Enclos. No. 3. Edwardes to Temple, 9 November 1855.

40 *Enclos. Sec. Letters from India, Vol. 145.* No. 11 of 8 March 1856. Enclos. No. 4. Minute by Dalhousie, 7 December 1855.

41 *Enclos. Sec. Letters from India, Vol. 145.* No. 11 of 8 March 1856. Enclos. No. 7. Minute by Dalhousie, 23 February 1856.

42 *Enclos. Sec. Letters from India, Vol. 147.* No. 31 of 30 July 1856. Enclos. No. 5. Minute by Canning, 22 July 1856.

43 *Enclos. Sec. Letters from India, Vol. 147.* No. 33 of 21 August 1856. Enclos. No. 17. Minute by Canning, 18 August 1856.

44 *Board's Drafts, Vol. 21.* India Board to Gov.-General, 16 July 1856 enclos. Clarendon to Sadr Azam, 11 July 1856.

45 *Board's Drafts, Vol. 21.* India Board to Gov.-General, 22 July 1856.

46 *Fac. Records (Persia) Vol. III.* Stevens to Clarendon, 15 August 1856.

47 *Fac. Records (Persia) Vol. III.* Stevens to Secret Committee, 23 October 1856 enclos. trans. of *Tehran Gazette* of 16 October 1856.

48 *Fac. Records (Persia) Vol. III.* Jones to Sec. Committee, 12 November 1856 enclos. trans. of letter from British Agent at Shiraz, 7 November 1856.

49 *Fac. Records (Persia) Vol. III.* Jones to Sec. Committee, 17 November 1856.

50 *Board's Drafts, Vol. 21.* India Board to Gov.-General, 26 September 1856.

51 *Board's Drafts, Vol. 21.* India Board to Gov.-General, 10 October 1856 enclos. Clarendon to Sadir Azam, 10 October 1856.

52 Sykes, Sir Percy, *A History of Persia* (London, 1921), II, 349.

53 *Enclos. Sec. Letters from India, Vol. 149.* No. 5 of 9 January 1857. Enclos. No. 3. Minute by Canning, 7 January 1857.

54 *Enclos. Sec. Letters from India, Vol. 149.* No. 5 of 9 January 1857. Enclos. No. 4. Outram to Edmonstone, 7 December 1856.

55 *Bombay Sec. Proc., Vol. 306.* Sec. Cons. No. 2 of 4 February 1857. Anderson to Edmonstone, 19 January 1857.

56 *Bombay Sec. Proc., Vol. 303.* Sec. Cons. No. 23 of 31 December 1856. Minute by Elphinstone, 24 October 1856.

57 *Sir James Outram's Persian Campaign in 1857* (London, 1860), v, vi.

58 *Fac. Records (Persia) Vol. 112.* Outram to Canning, 14 February 1857 enclos. précis of intelligence received from Tehran.

59 Aitchison, op. cit., XIII, 82.

60 *Fac. Records (Persia) Vol. III.* Stevens to Clarendon, 2 October 1856.

61 *Board's Drafts, Vol. 22.* India Board to Gov.-General, 15 October 1857, enclos. Hammond to Clerk, 9 October 1857 and 15 October 1857.

62 *Board's Drafts, Vol. 22.* India Board to Gov.-General, 9 January 1857 enclos. Wodehouse to Clarendon, 19 December 1856; also *Boad's Drafts, Vol. 22.* India Board to Gov.-General, 27 March 1857 enclos. Wodehouse to Clarendon, 13 March 1857 and Clarendon to Wodehouse, 25 March 1857.

63 *Board's Drafts, Vol. 22.* India Board to Gov.-General, 14 April 1857 enclos. Stratford de Redcliffe to Clarendon, 30 March 1857 and Colonel Materrazza to Stratford de Redcliffe, 13 February 1857.

64 Edwards, H. Sutherland, *Russian Projects against India* (London, 1885), 260 ff.

65 Sykes, Sir Percy, *A History of Afghanistan* (London, 1940), I, 400.

66 Rawlinson, H., op. cit., 286, 287.

67 *Board's Drafts, Vol. 22.* India Board to Gov.-General, 22 January 1857 enclos. despatch from Sir H. Seymour, Vienna, 6 January 1857.

68 *Fac. Records (Persia), Vol. III.* Stevens to Clarendon, 15 October 1856.
69 *Bombay Sec. Proc., Vol. 303.* Sec. Cons. No. 19 of 15 November 1856. Murray to Elphinstone, 15 September 1856.
70 *Fac. Records (Persia) Vol. III.* Murray to Clarendon, 29 September 1856 enclos. trans. of letter Imam of Muscat to Murray, 2 July 1856.
71 Curzon, G.N., *Russia in Central Asia* (London, 1889), 356.
72 Aitchison, op. cit., XIII, 238, 239.
73 *Enclos. Sec. Letters from India, Vol. 148.* No. 63 of 22 December 1856. Enclos. No. 5. Bowring to Canning, 24 November 1856; also Enclos. No. 6. Edmonstone to Bowring, 11 December 1856.
74 *Fac. Records (Persia) Vol. 112.* Murray to Canning, 1 October 1857.
75 *Fac. Records (Persia) Vol. 112.* Outram to Canning, 14 February 1857 enclos. précis of intelligence received from Tehran.
76 *Enclos. Sec. Letters from India, Vol. 146.* No. 14 of 8 April 1856. Enclos. No. 12. Stevens to Secy. to Govt. of India, 27 December 1855.
77 Aitchison, op. cit., XIII, 179–85.
78 Rawlinson, op. cit., 105.
79 *Correspondence and Papers of Brig. General John Jacob, 1840–1858.* Frere to Jacob, 4 March 1857.
80 *The Times,* 12 June 1857.

Dynastic Table

For lo, the kings of the earth are gathered, and gone by together.
They marvelled to see such things; they were astonished; and suddenly
cast down.

Psalm 48, iii-iv.

In the following table are listed only those rulers who have received individual mention in the text.

Achaemenids
(c. 650–330BC)

Acheaemenes	c. 650
Cyrus I	c. 600
Cambyses I	c. 575
Cyrus II (the Great)	559–530
Darius I (the Great)	522–485
Xerxes I	485–465
Artaxerxes I	465–424
Cyrus (the Younger)	d. 401
Darius III	336–330

Macedonian

Alexander (the Great)	334–323

Seleucids
(323–140BC)

Seleucus I	312–281

Arsacids or Parthians
(247BC–AD226)

Arsaces	c. 247
Tiridates I	c. 210
Mithridates I	171–138
Artabanus V	213–226(AD)

Sassanids
(AD226–651)

Ardashir	226–240
Shapur I	240–272
Shapur II	309–379
Yazdigird I	399–421
Khusrau II Parviz	591–628
Yazdigird III	632–651

Omayyid Caliphate
(661–750)

Abbasid Caliphate
(750–1258)

Samanids
(874–999)

Buwayhids
(932–1055)

Seljuks
(1055–1220)

Tughril Beg	1055–1063
Malik Shah	1072–1092

Mongols
(1220–1316)

Jenghiz Khan	1220–1227
Hulugu Khan	1251–1265
Arghun Khan	1284–1294
Ghazan Khan	1295–1304
Oljaitu	1304–1316

Timurids
(1380–1506)

Timur	1380–1405
Shah Rukh	1408–1446

Safavids
(1500–1722)

Isma'il I	1500–1524
Tahmasp I	1524–1576
Isma'il II	1576–1577
Khudabandeh	1588–1586
Abbas I (the Great)	1586–1629
Safi	1629–1642
Abbas II	1642–1666
Husain	1694–1722

Afghans and Zends
(1722–1779)

Mahmud	1722–1725
Nadir Quli	1736–1747
Karim Khan	1750–1779

Qajars
(1787–1925)

Agha Muhammad	1787–1797
Fath Ali Shah	1798–1834
Muhammad	1834–1848
Nasir ud-Din	1848–1896
Muzaffar ud-Din	1896–1907
Muhammad II	1907–1909
Ahmad	1909–1925

Pahlavis
(1925–1979)

Reza Shah	1925–1941
Muhammad Reza	1941–1979

Index